# PARMIGIANINO

## THE VISION OF SAINT JEROME

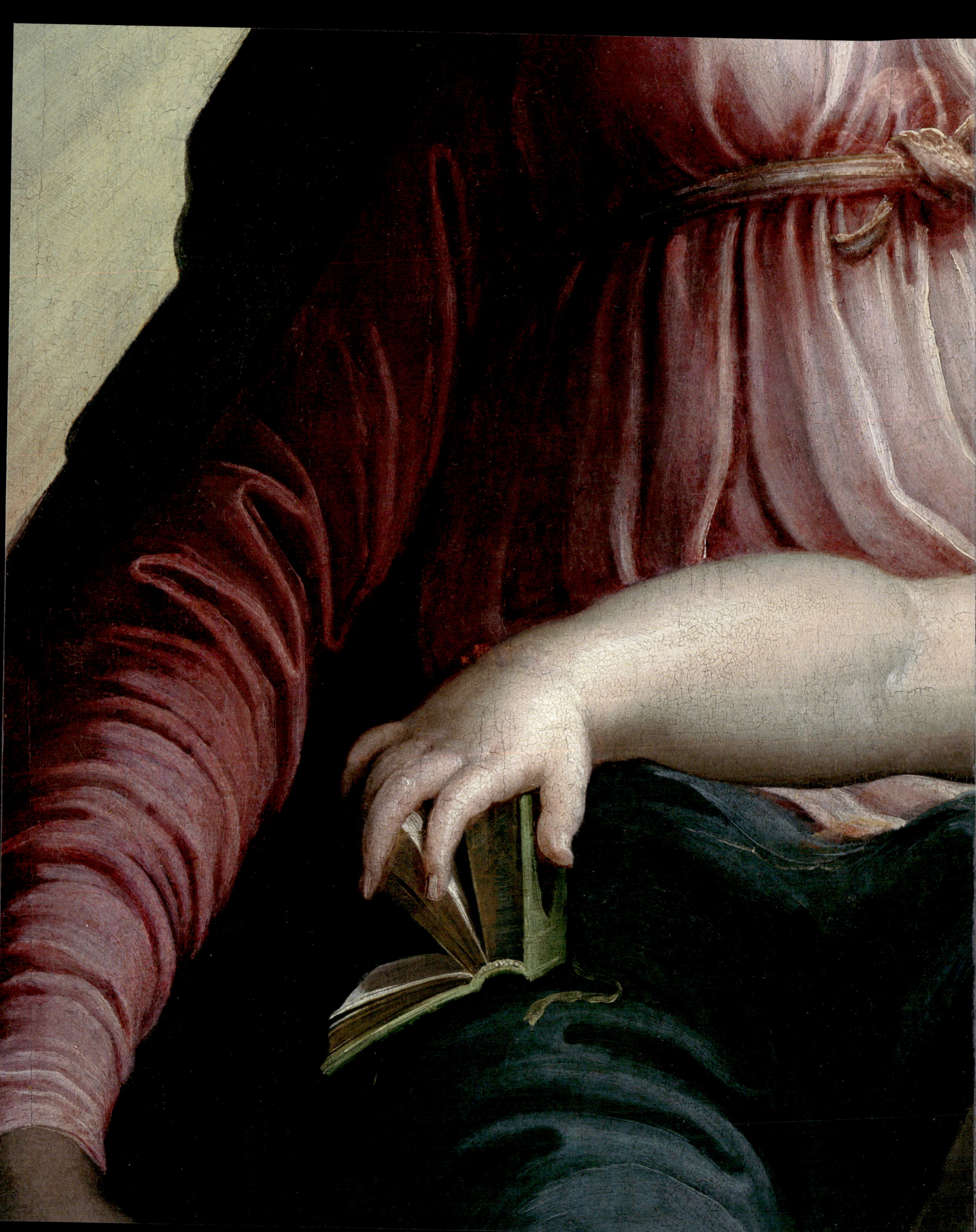

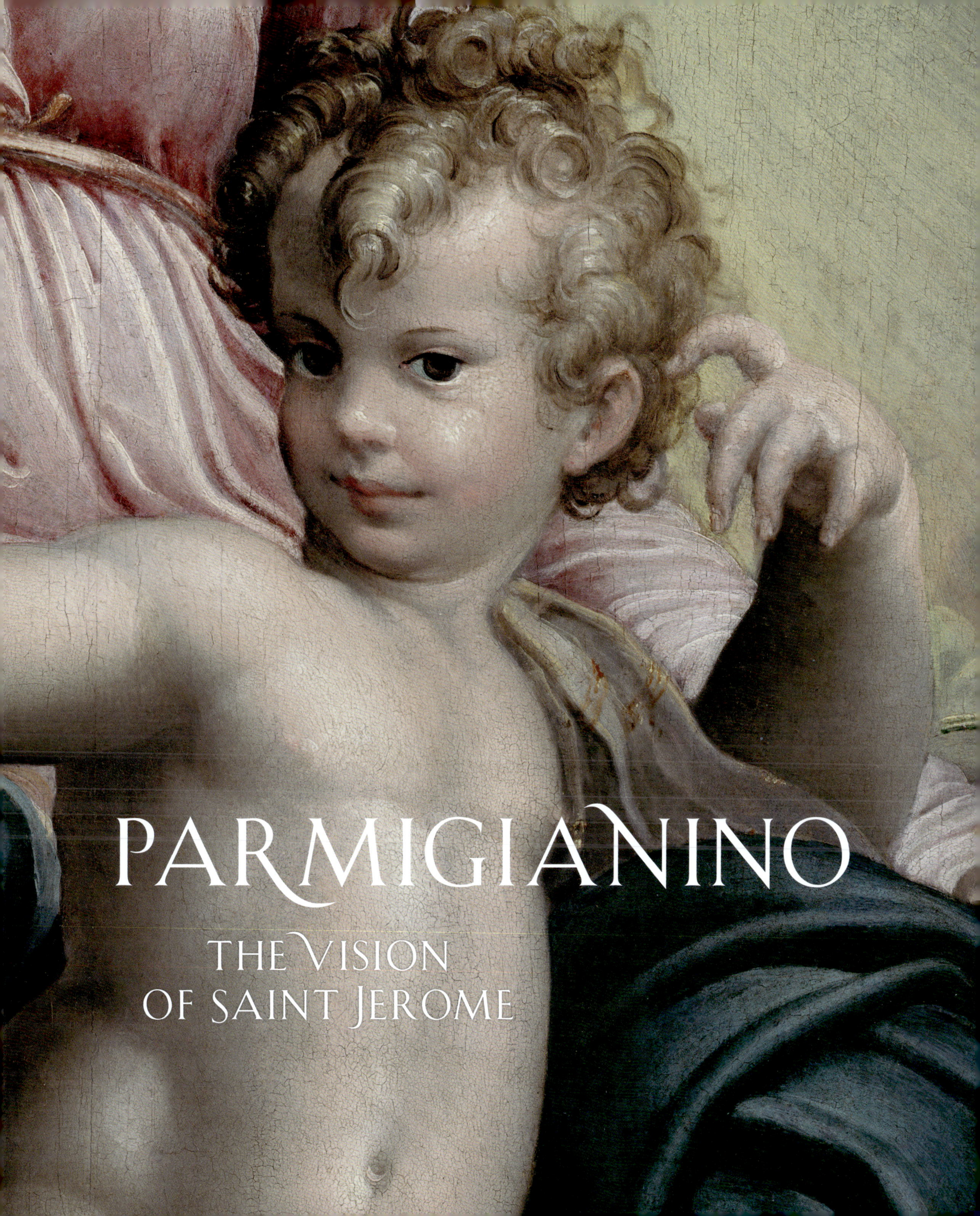

# PARMIGIANINO

## THE VISION OF SAINT JEROME

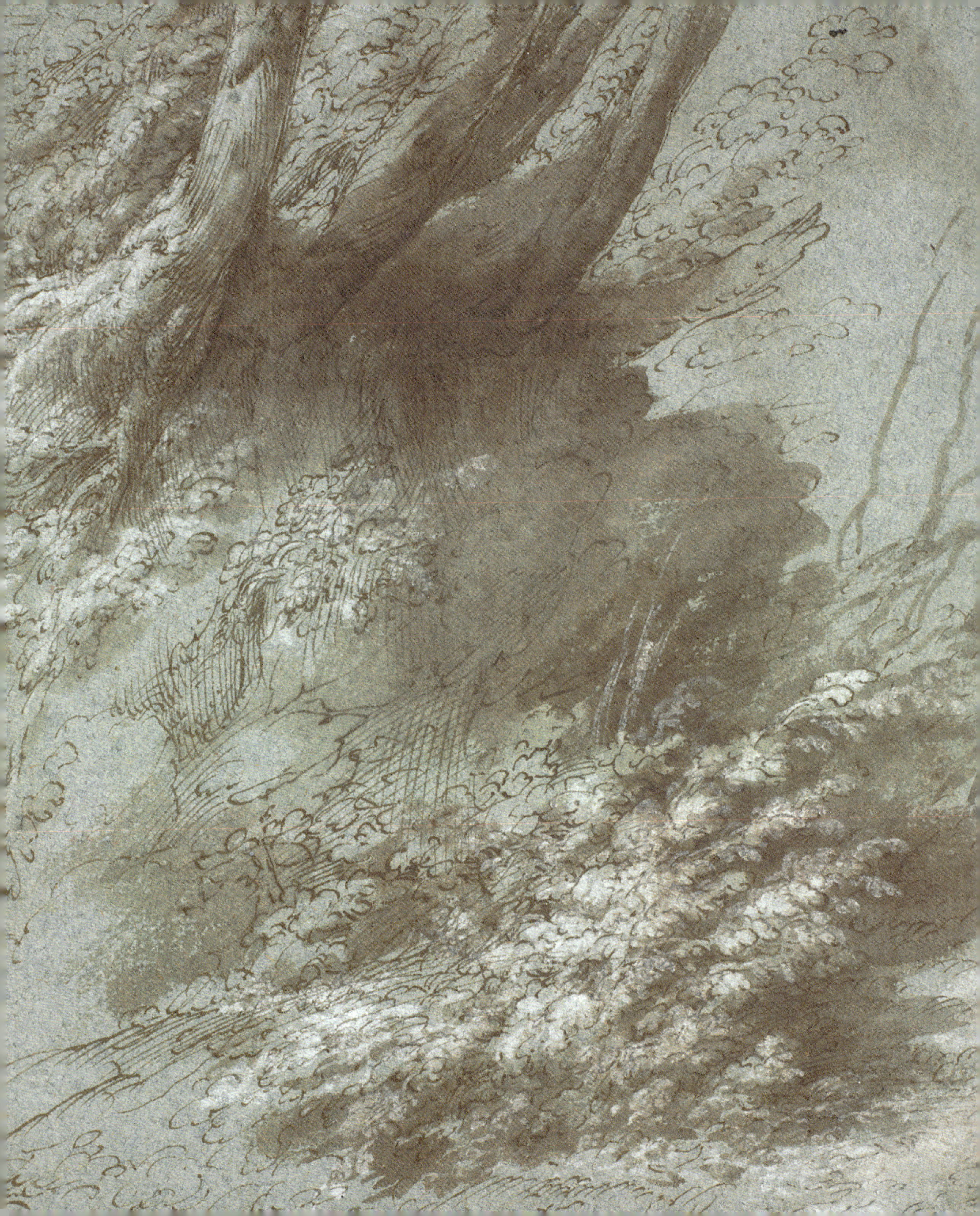

# CONTENTS

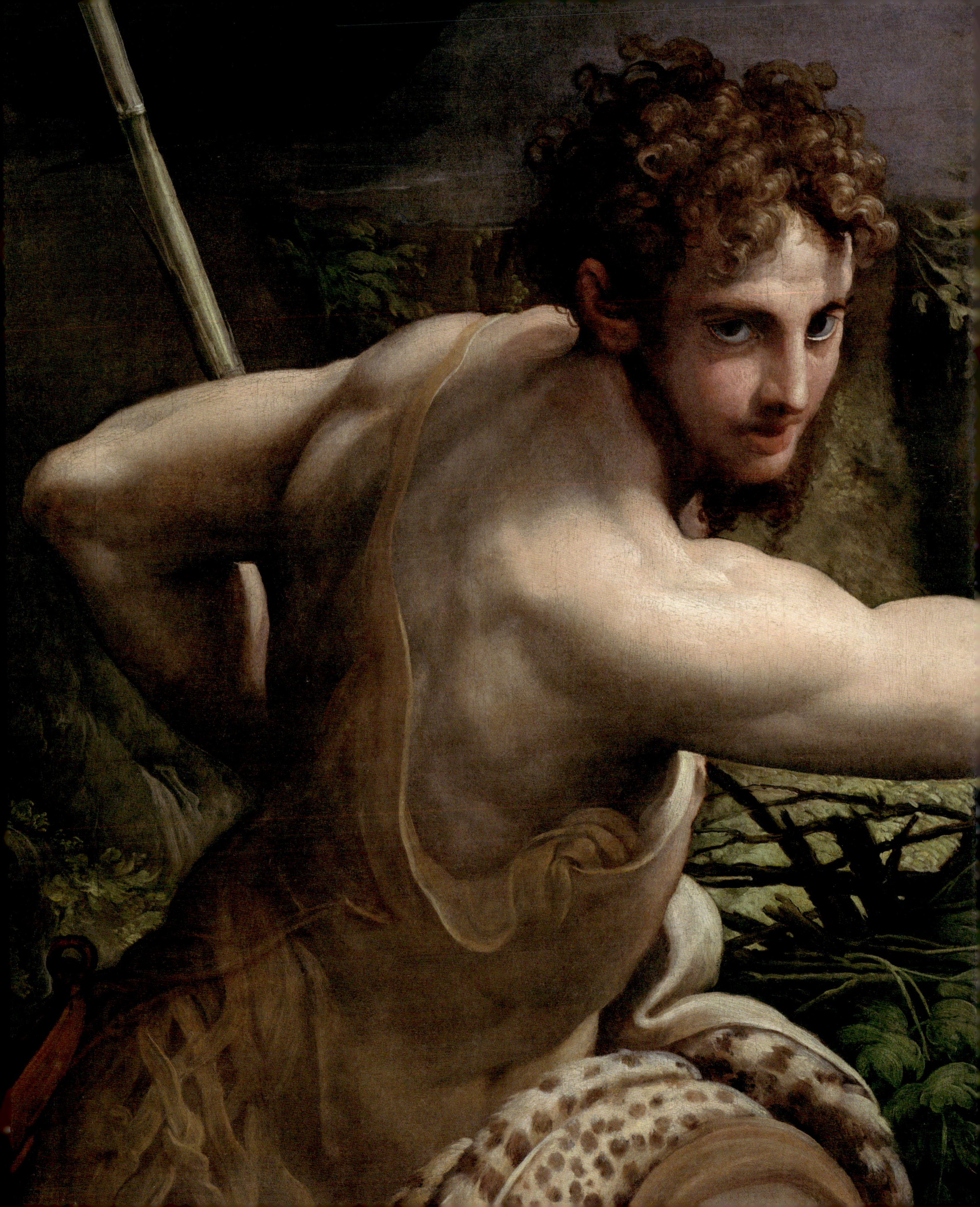

# DIRECTOR'S FOREWORD

It is astonishing to think that Parmigianino was only 22 years old when he received the commission for *The Madonna and Child with Saints John the Baptist and Jerome*, better known as *The Vision of Saint Jerome*, and only 23 when he painted it. Nearly 3.5 metres tall, this monumental altarpiece is astoundingly bold in its conception, richly allusive to the achievements of Michelangelo, Leonardo, Raphael and Correggio yet intensely personal and distinctive in its style. Painted with a stunning virtuosity by this young artist hailing from Parma in northern Italy, it announced the arrival of a new star in the artistic firmament of Rome. In the event, it was never placed on the altar in the church of San Salvatore in Lauro for which it was intended. In fact, it is all but miraculous that it survived at all. The Italian biographer Giorgio Vasari recounts that the mercenaries who sacked Rome in 1527 were so impressed by the painting when they broke into Parmigianino's studio that they allowed him to carry on working on it. Transferred to the refectory of Santa Maria della Pace for safekeeping during the looting of the city, the panel therefore escaped the fire that ravaged San Salvatore in Lauro in 1591. And in the eighteenth century, Parmigianino's altarpiece narrowly missed being destroyed by an earthquake in Città di Castello, the town in Umbria to which it had been taken by the descendants of Maria Bufalini, the original patron.

*The Vision of Saint Jerome* has formed part of the collection of the National Gallery practically from its establishment. After being brought to England, in 1823 it became the property of the British Institution, a society established to exhibit the works of living and dead artists, and three years later it was donated to the fledgling National Gallery. As we continue to celebrate the Gallery's Bicentenary – this catalogue accompanies the sixth exhibition of 2024 to mark the anniversary – we considered it appropriate to focus on this foundational acquisition and to celebrate the lengthy conservation of the painting that has recently been brought to completion.

Parmigianino prepared very thoroughly to paint the altarpiece and more than two dozen sheets of drawings have survived, reflecting the intense and fertile process undertaken by the artist. They are all reproduced in this publication and a selection has been lent to the exhibition. We are grateful to His Majesty the King and to colleagues at the Ashmolean Museum, the British Museum, the Royal Collection, the Gallerie degli Uffizi and the J. Paul Getty Museum for their generosity, and to the Stephen Kohl Art Foundation, which has loaned a rarely exhibited study for the figure of Saint Jerome (see p. 75). The exhibition has been conceived and curated by Matthias Wivel, the Gallery's former Curator of Sixteenth-Century Italian Paintings who recently left us to take up a new position at the Ny Carlsberg Glyptotek in Copenhagen, and Maria Alambritis, Project Curator: Parmigianino at the National Gallery. To them, and to Aimee Ng, curator at The Frick Collection in New York, who has contributed a fascinating essay to the catalogue, we are most grateful.

Larry Keith, the National Gallery's Head of Conservation and Keeper, led the restoration project of *The Vision of Saint Jerome*, a particularly complex and delicate one. I would like to express my gratitude and appreciation for his work in this regard and for leading the Gallery's conservation initiatives with great skill and sensitivity for nearly two decades now. The new frame has been designed and made by our Head of Framing, Peter Schade.

Finally, I would like to express my gratitude to the sponsors and supporters who have made the exhibition possible, the Capricorn Foundation, the Rick Mather David Scrase Foundation, and to our Deputy Chair of Trustees, Katrin Henkel, and to Marco Voena. I extend our grateful thanks to the Wolfgang Ratjen Stiftung for their support of this catalogue.

Gabriele Finaldi
**Director, The National Gallery**

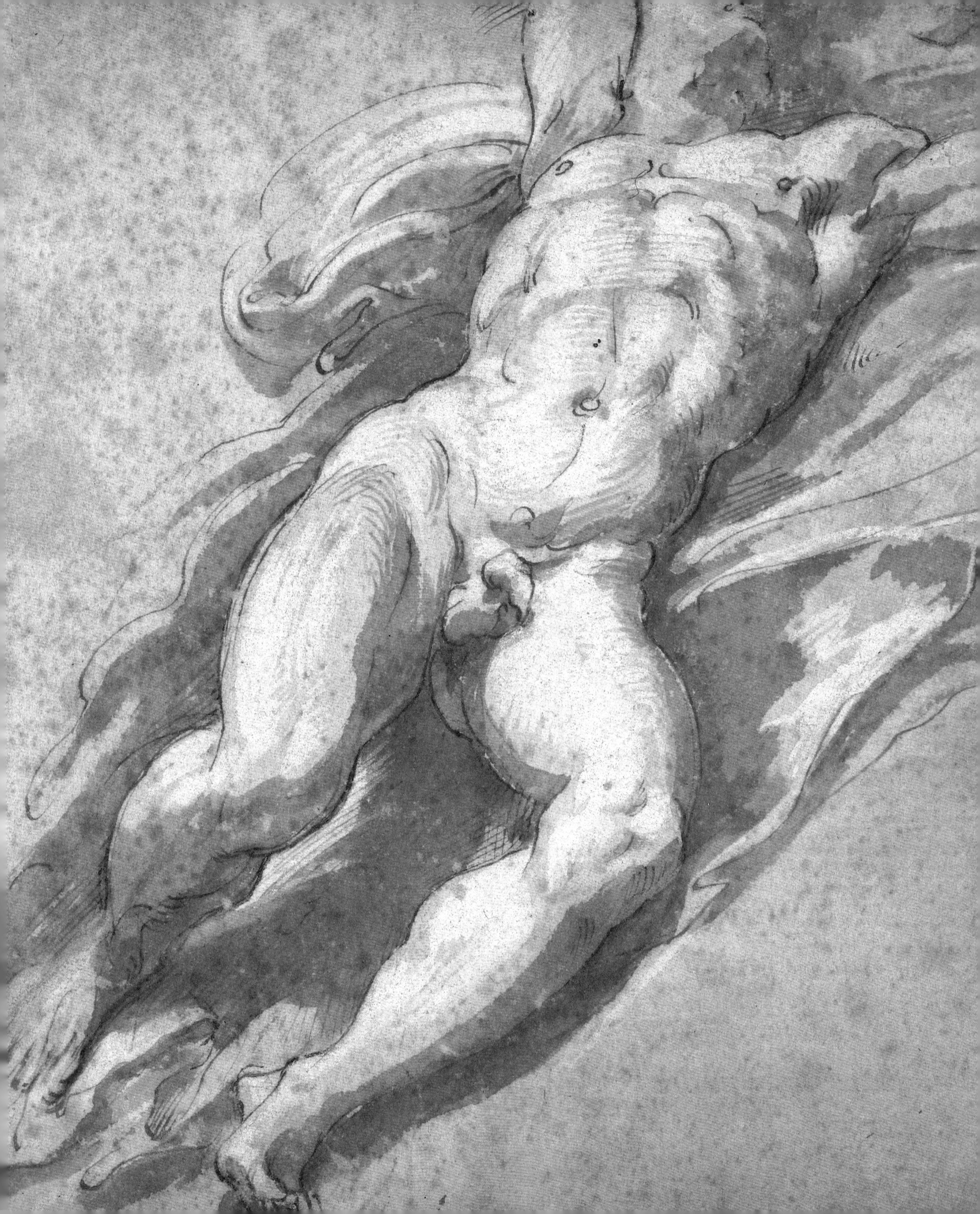

# WHEN IN ROME: PARMIGIANINO IN THE ETERNAL CITY, 1524–7

**AIMEE NG**

Like many Renaissance artists, Girolamo Francesco Maria Mazzola (1503–1540) came to be named after his birthplace, the northern Italian city of Parma. Parmigianino carries the diminutive form '-ino', i.e. 'the little one from Parma'. This is appropriate for a precocious youth from a family of artists, of whom he is by far the most famous today. Leonardo da Vinci (1452–1519), Michelangelo (1475–1564) and Raphael (1483–1520) were already icons in his time and supreme models for him and his peers. He would have been immensely proud to know that his contemporaries would later refer to him as 'Raphael reborn', comparing him to one of the greatest artists of the age, though he might not have appreciated the coincidence that, like Raphael, he too would die at age 37.

An accomplished painter, prolific draughtsman and pioneering printmaker, Parmigianino is one of the principal artists often referred to as Mannerists. This much-debated label was invented by modern scholars to describe the 'mannered' or 'styled' artistic language they observed in art by the generation after Raphael, including a complex (and at times oppositional) relationship to ideals of classicism; it was derived from the term *maniera* ('manner' or 'style'), as discussed by the artist and writer Giorgio Vasari (1511–1574) in his *Lives of the Artists* (two editions, 1550 and 1568).[1] In Vasari's characterisation of what he calls the *maniera moderna*, or modern style of his time, he emphasises the personal style of his contemporaries as a privileged aspect of their practice, pointing to the variation and diversity among them. Imperfect though the term remains – as is any generalising category imposed on a group of artists centuries later – today, 'Mannerism' can be useful to refer broadly to those European artists active after about 1520 whose work tends towards (but not always, and to varying degrees) pronounced elegance, elongated figures and the artifice of *sprezzatura* – a sense of nonchalance in pose and expression. In contrast to the 'perfect' geometric and anatomical proportions that anchor defining High Renaissance images such as Leonardo's *Vitruvian Man* (about 1490), Parmigianino's most famous painting, the *Madonna of the*

*Long Neck* (fig. 1), is popularly known for his exaggeration of the neck of the Virgin Mary, her refinement and aloof disposition in tension with the robust toddler about to slip from her lap.[2]

Wit and innovation characterise Parmigianino's paintings. Among them *The Madonna and Child with Saints John the Baptist and Jerome* (1526–7; see fig. 9), known since the nineteenth century as *The Vision of Saint Jerome*, stands out for its conceptual inventiveness. Created in Rome during a time of crisis in the Catholic Church when Protestant ideas challenged the role, value and possibilities of sacred images, Parmigianino's altarpiece offers a novel experience of devotional art. It pictures the radiant Madonna and Child above Saint John the Baptist, who points towards them, and the receding Saint Jerome, who lies supine on the ground with eyes closed. The unusual composition suggests that viewers witness Saint Jerome seemingly overcome by his miraculous vision of the Madonna and Child, seen perhaps in his mind's eye – and at the same time that viewers have the miraculous vision themselves, with urging from the Baptist.

The painting is also associated with human tragedy. As the most important professional opportunity of Parmigianino's promising career in Rome, the painting he hoped would be a triumph became a catastrophic failure. According to Vasari, whose *Lives of the Artists* is the main source for Parmigianino's biography, just as he was finishing it, the imperial troops sacked Rome in 1527, and devastated the papal city. The artist fled for his life, never returning to Rome and never again seeing the painting, which was hidden in a monastery for safekeeping. A seismic event in the history of the papacy, Rome and the Italian peninsula, the Sack has been seen as having catalysed the spread throughout Europe of the 'Mannerist' style – or rather, aspects of the style associated with artists in Rome at this time, as they were among the thousands who fled the city. Parmigianino's *Vision of Saint Jerome* offers a crucial reminder of the human experience of this history, of the people and the lives behind centuries-old works of art.

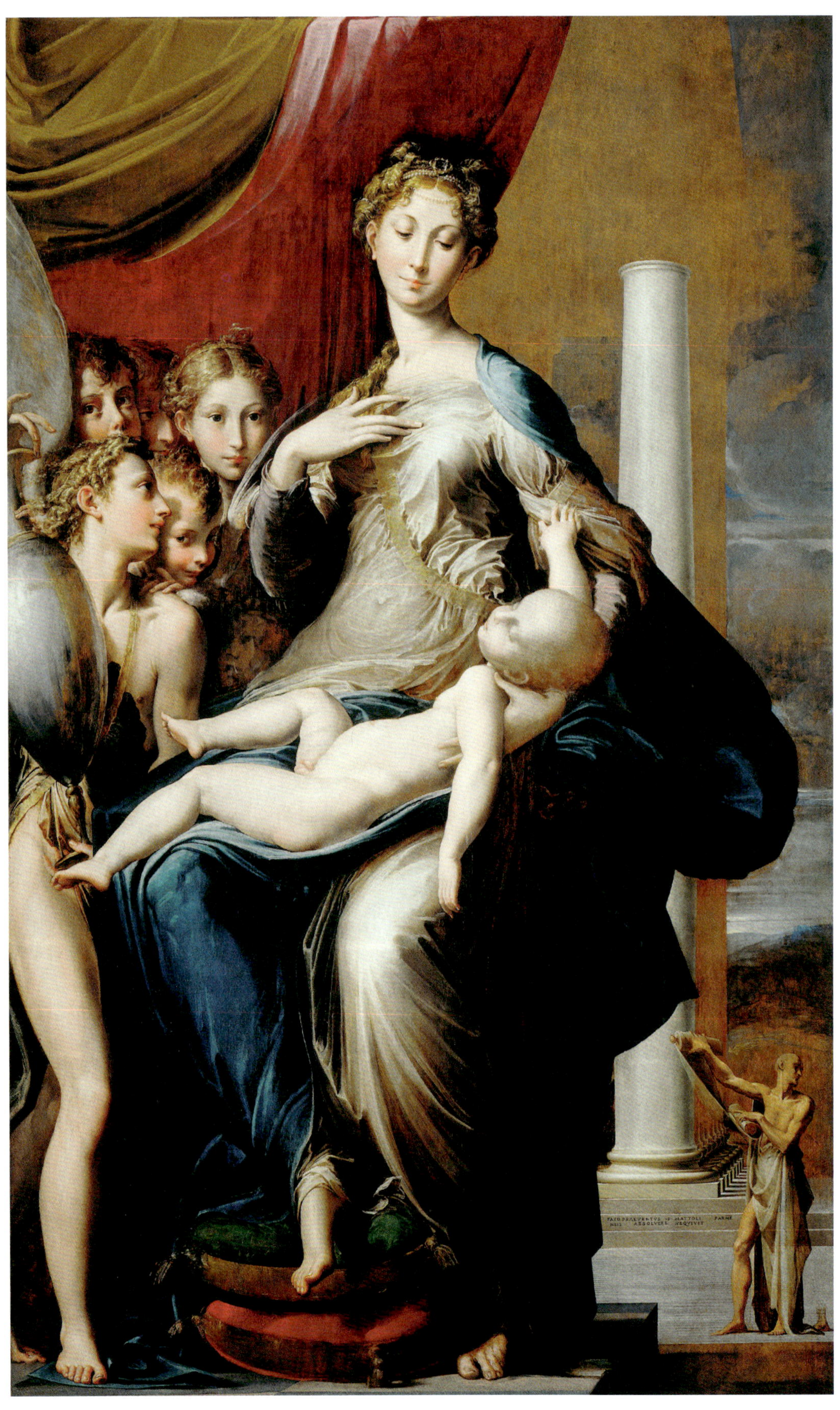

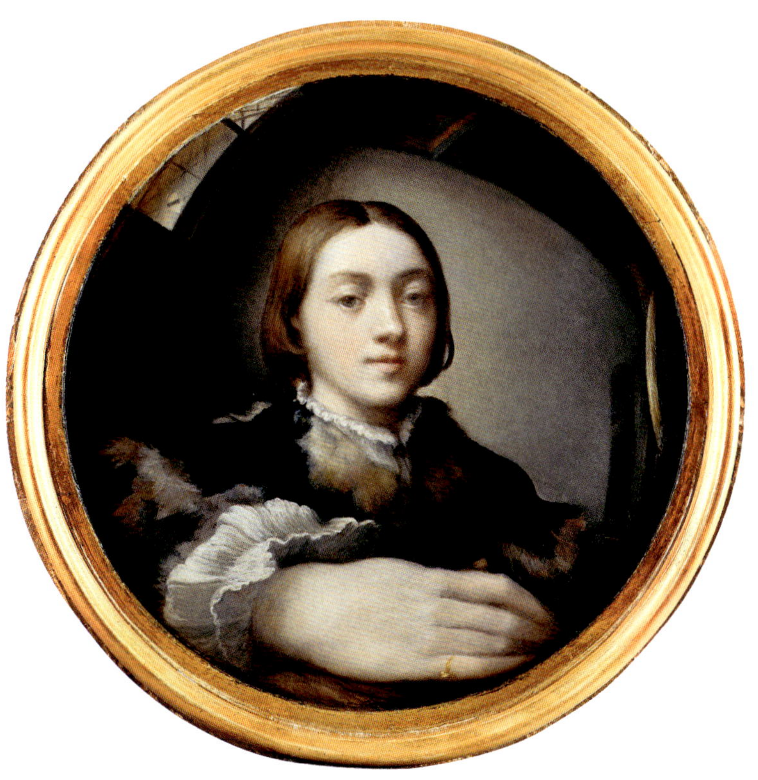

Relatives – including his eldest half-brother Zaccaria and uncles Pier Ilario and Michele, all of whom were artists – served as Parmigianino's guardians after his father died of plague when he was two.[3] By the age of 12, he appears to have been working in the Mazzola family workshop, and by 16 he had produced his first independent altarpiece.[4] His work with Antonio Allegri (active 1494–1534), called Correggio after his neighbouring hometown, on church ceiling decorations in Parma also shaped his craft.[5] In 1521, when Parma became a battleground between the French and papal armies, Parmigianino's uncles sent him about 20 miles north-east to Viadana, where he produced two altarpieces.[6] Plague and war already punctuated his young life as his ambition swelled. At 21, with prestigious local commissions under his belt, he set his sights on Rome.

Artists travelled to Rome from all over Europe to see ancient sculptures such as the recently unearthed *Laocoön* and sites like the *Domus Aurea* (Golden House) of Nero.[7] The latter bears witness to the desire to declare access to antiquity: hundreds of names have been inscribed on its walls. Among them are three versions of 'Zakaria Mazola da Parma', which may record the presence of Parmigianino's half-brother Zaccaria in Rome.[8] A 'Mazola' inscribed in the Domus's room 34 is tempting to identify with Parmigianino himself.[9] Vasari recounts that Parmigianino, too, was eager to study the art of Rome, especially that of Michelangelo and Raphael.[10] The trope of a visit to Rome as a rite of passage for European artists is due in part to Vasari, who wrote that the very air of Rome had the power to transform artistic ability – for better and worse.[11] It would be in Rome that, according to Vasari, the 'spirit of Raphael' would pass into Parmigianino's body.[12]

Rome lies some 300 miles from Parma, on the other side of the Apennine mountains. Parmigianino's uncles advised him to bring 'something by his hand' to gain entrance into Rome's artistic circles; thus he packed two religious paintings and his *Self Portrait in a Convex Mirror* (fig. 2) to take on the journey.[13] Accompanied by his uncle Pier Ilario, Parmigianino likely departed sometime in 1524.[14] Their route is unknown but may have taken them through Florence, given the young artist's interest in Raphael and Michelangelo.[15] Whether he had intended to meet Zaccaria in Rome, or if the brothers overlapped, is unclear.[16] Zaccaria earned little fame, was not mentioned by Vasari and by 1525 was documented in Umbria.[17] Parmigianino likely aspired to succeed in Rome in ways his elder brother had not.

By 1524, the city was home to 'the greatest painters and sculptors' from around the Italian peninsula, and they apparently met at least twice weekly.[18] Some had come in the hopes that the new Medici pope, Clement VII (r. 1523–34), would be as generous with his art patronage as his cousin, Pope Leo X (r. 1513–21), had been.[19] Ultimately, he was not.[20] Introduced to Parmigianino by the papal datary Gian Matteo Giberti (1495–1543),[21] Clement was impressed by the paintings the young artist had brought from Parma and awarded him one of his few papal commissions, the completion of the Sala dei Pontefici at the Vatican Palace; for unknown reasons, however, the work was never carried out.[22] The pope kept one of Parmigianino's paintings for himself and gave the others away, famously gifting the *Self Portrait in a Convex Mirror* to the writer and literary activist Pietro Aretino (1492–1556), the first of its illustrious owners.[23] Vasari lavished several paragraphs of his *Life* of Parmigianino on the *Self Portrait*, detailing how Parmigianino shaped, painted and varnished it to create the illusion that its viewer is looking at the artist's reflection in a barber's mirror, as if to assume the artist's own point of view.

With a papal commission not materialising in Rome, Parmigianino took to making smaller-scale religious works

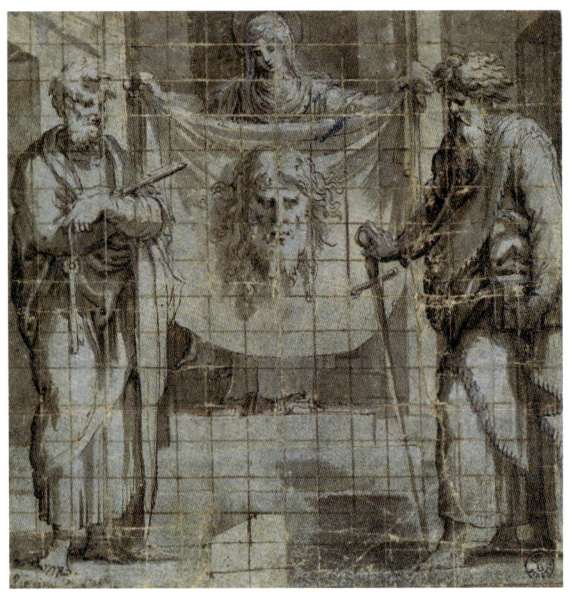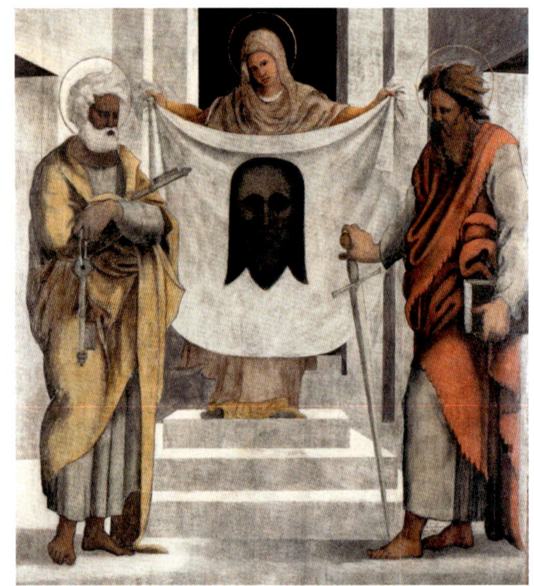



and portraits for private patrons. About a dozen of his paintings have been proposed, on the basis of style, to have been made in Rome, but *The Vision of Saint Jerome* is the only documented painting. He also explored printmaking, perhaps as another way to earn a living and circulate his designs, collaborating with printmakers in all three print processes: engravings with Gian Jacopo Caraglio (about 1500–1565), woodcuts with Ugo da Carpi (about 1480–1532) and possibly learning etching from Marcantonio Raimondi (about 1480–about 1534).[24] His engagement with the network of artists in Clementine Rome – including Sebastiano del Piombo (about 1485–1547), Rosso Fiorentino (1494–1540), Polidoro da Caravaggio (about 1499–1543) and many others – is explored elsewhere in this volume (see pp. 17, 22–5).

A pen-and-wash drawing (fig. 3), squared for transfer of the composition to another, presumably larger, support, connects Parmigianino to one of the most peculiar altarpieces in Rome: Ugo da Carpi's *Saint Veronica* altarpiece for Old St Peter's (fig. 4), the most important church in the papal city.[25] The site remained a partial ruin and largely unchanged until the early 1530s, when work began on the demolition of the old basilica and construction of the new.[26]

Parmigianino's *Saint Veronica* drawing was possibly the first of several that he provided to Ugo for various projects. Derived from prints by Albrecht Dürer (1471–1528) and Marcantonio Raimondi, it presents Veronica, flanked by Saints Peter and Paul, displaying the *Sudarium* (also known as the Veil of Veronica, one of the most important Catholic relics, a cloth believed to bear an image of Christ, miraculously created 'without human hands' when she pressed it to his face).[27] Ugo's altarpiece was made to adorn the structure in which the relic was kept under lock and key (it was shown to worshippers only on rare occasions).

Though no documents for the altarpiece are known, it was presumably commissioned as part of the celebration of the 1525 papal jubilee, for which Clement renovated the Porta Santa, the 'holy door' that welcomed pilgrims to St Peter's and led directly to the *Saint Veronica* altar.[28] It is remarkable that the *Saint Veronica* project was given to a printmaker, even more so because Ugo inscribed it as having been made 'without a brush'.[29] Recent examination suggests that rather than painting it, Ugo took the extraordinary step of printing the altarpiece, pressing woodblocks onto the panel, a process of creating an image 'without human hands' that mimics the alleged mode of creation of the *Sudarium* itself. The altarpiece thus offers the sense of perpetual ostentation of the relic. While the exact circumstances of Parmigianino's involvement with the *Saint Veronica* are unknown, the project resonates with the artist's experiments with vision, illusion and points of view.

As Vasari narrates, Parmigianino was working on the *Vision of Saint Jerome* for his patron Maria Bufalini when soldiers invaded Rome on the foggy morning of 6 May 1527.[30] Thousands of German, Spanish and Italian forces loyal to the Holy Roman Emperor Charles V surged into the papal city, part of an ongoing battle for power in the Italian peninsula (comprising, until 1861, independent kingdoms, dukedoms, republics and states over which various rulers fought for power). The magnitude of the brutality inflicted on the city and its people was exacerbated by months of unpaid soldiers' wages; looting Rome was presented to them as compensation. They tortured scores of men, women and children to extract ransom, pillaged churches and palaces and unleashed unbridled violence on the city for seven days, followed by a nine-month occupation. Letters and pamphlets

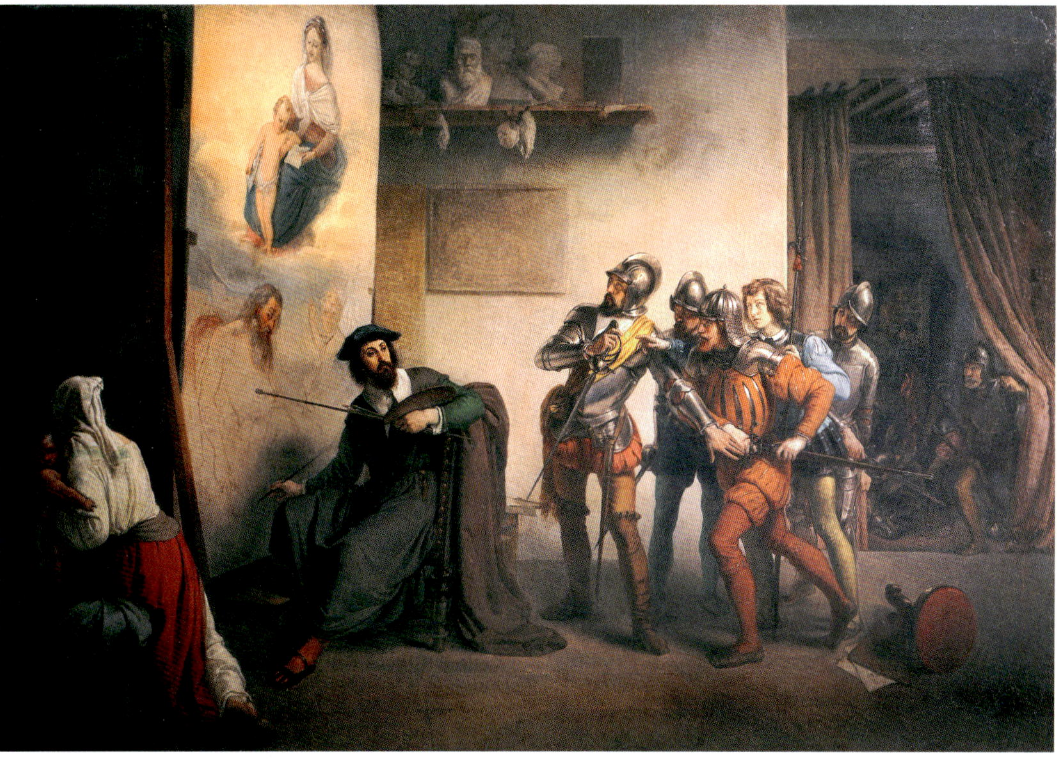



detailing the horrors of the Sack circulated around Europe, a proliferation of 'news' that has been associated with the birth of journalism.[31] Though the exact number of deaths resulting from the violence is not known, by January of the following year, between deaths and those who fled, the population of the city had been halved.[32] Imprisoned in his own fortress, the Castel Sant'Angelo, Pope Clement was forced to capitulate to imperial demands and to pay an enormous ransom, eventually – seven months to the day after the Sack began – escaping in the middle of the night disguised in the clothes of a civilian.[33]

Vasari relates that soldiers who had invaded Parmigianino's studio were so enchanted by the *Vision of Saint Jerome* that they allowed him to continue painting. The story rings of myth, recalling the ancient tale of Protogenes, whose art had the power to divert a war, and it later inspired a painting (fig. 5).[34] While Vasari's accounts are not always reliable – indeed, far from it – his accuracy in this case should be considered alongside the probability that the two artists met shortly after the Sack, when both were in Bologna in early 1530 during Clement VII's coronation of Charles V; Vasari even reports that he purchased one of Parmigianino's paintings.[35] In the first edition of the *Lives*, Vasari identifies Lorenzo Cybo as having initiated the painting for San Salvatore in Lauro, correcting and expanding his text, in the second edition, to name Maria Bufalini as the patron. As is their nature, Vasari's *Lives* offer precious historical information along with frustrating errors, lacunae and mysteries.

According to Vasari's dramatic telling, one soldier forced Parmigianino to pay his ransom by making 'an infinite number' of drawings in pen and wash.[36] None of these drawings has been identified; it is tempting to wonder if any lurk among his surviving sheets and what Parmigianino drew under duress. The idea of making art while soldiers sacked the city has a whiff of Mannerist nonchalance to it, but such a response to the event should be seen in the context of the botched attempt to overthrow Pope Clement just eight months earlier, in September 1526, when soldiers commanded by Cardinal Pompeo Colonna (1479–1532) invaded Rome.[37] Then too Clement fled to the Castel Sant'Angelo, and soldiers looted the Borgo, the neighbourhood around St Peter's. Losses were sustained (including the theft of Raphael's recently completed Sistine Chapel tapestries) but the violence of the Colonna raid was soon contained (and the tapestries restituted).[38] The Sack was different. After Parmigianino's salvation by the power of his painting, he left his studio in search of friends, and a second group of soldiers took him prisoner, forcing him to surrender what little money he had.[39] He may have been among some 400 captives held in the palace of Cardinal Andrea della Valle (1463–1534) on 8 May.[40]

Many artists were beaten or tortured, and some were killed. Parmigianino was not the only one who was forced to make art.[41] No evidence of how the Sack affected Parmigianino's psychological state has come to light, though contemporary writings offer a glimpse of its impact on individual artists.

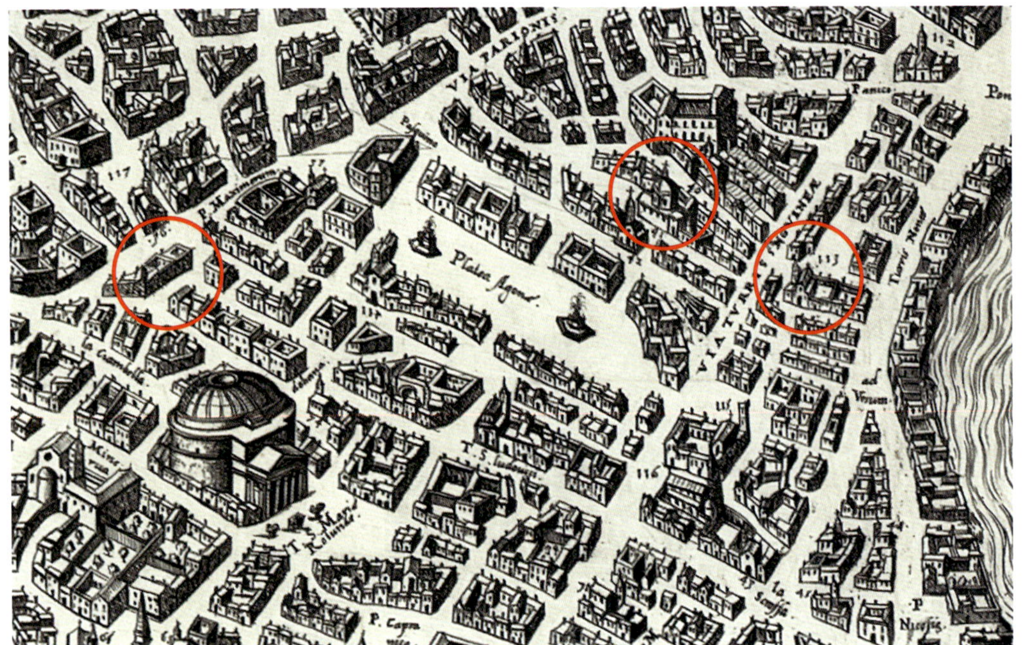



Sebastiano del Piombo, for instance, who was among those besieged in the Castel Sant'Angelo with the papal court, later wrote to Michelangelo: 'As of yet, I do not seem to myself to be the same Bastiano that I was before the Sack; I am still not able to regain my mind.'[42] Vasari described the debilitating effects on Vincenzo Tamagni (1492–after 1529), whose artistic skill degenerated because of the hardships he suffered during the Sack, and on an artist Vasari refers to as Schizzone, who, because of the soldiers' treatment, was made to turn away from art and soon lost his life.[43] Others, however, like Benvenuto Cellini, wrote of the experience with excitement, and Parmigianino's subsequent paintings – especially his much-copied *Madonna of the Rose* – exude an elegance and sensuality that have inspired scholars to judge him as having been 'impervious' to the trauma of the Sack.[44]

Pier Ilario does not appear to have been among those held in the Della Valle palace, perhaps having been separated from Parmigianino in the chaos. Vasari recounts that Pier Ilario mourned his nephew's lost opportunity to achieve fame in Rome and sent him back to Parma, while he stayed behind to deposit the *Vision of Saint Jerome* for safekeeping in the refectory of Santa Maria della Pace.[45] Scholars have rightly questioned Vasari's claim that the Sack prevented Parmigianino from completing the painting which, to modern eyes, does not appear unfinished; as has been suggested, it seems most likely that Vasari referred to his failure to complete the entire chapel decoration.[46] Why the Pace was chosen as a haven is unclear, as neither the Mazzola nor Bufalini family had obvious ties to the church.[47] Very close to San Salvatore in Lauro, for which the painting was intended, the Pace may simply have been

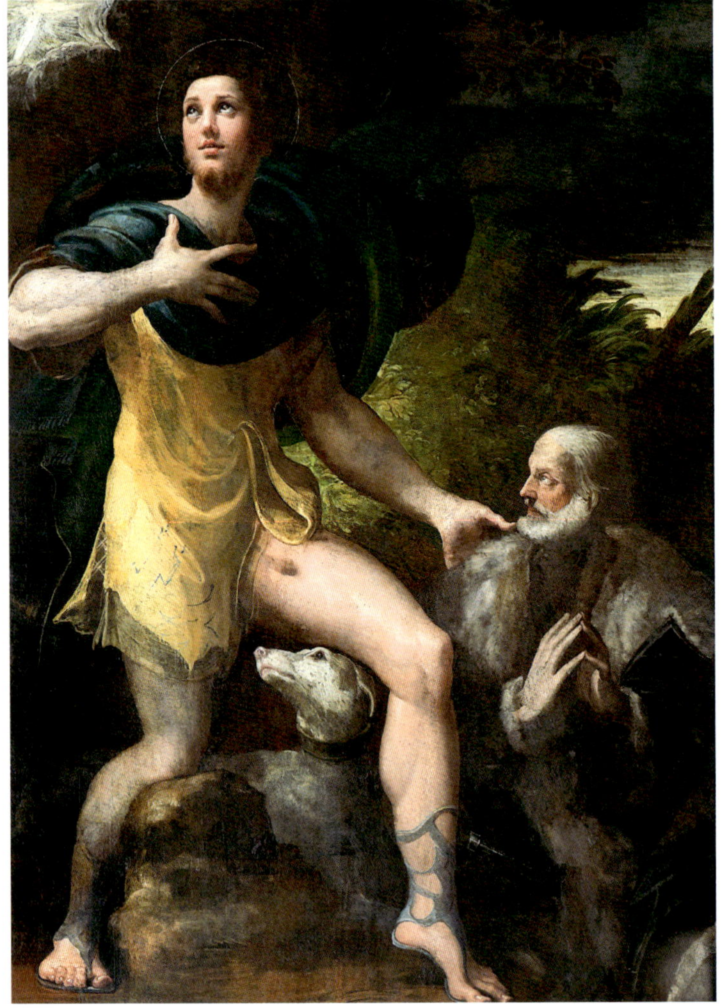

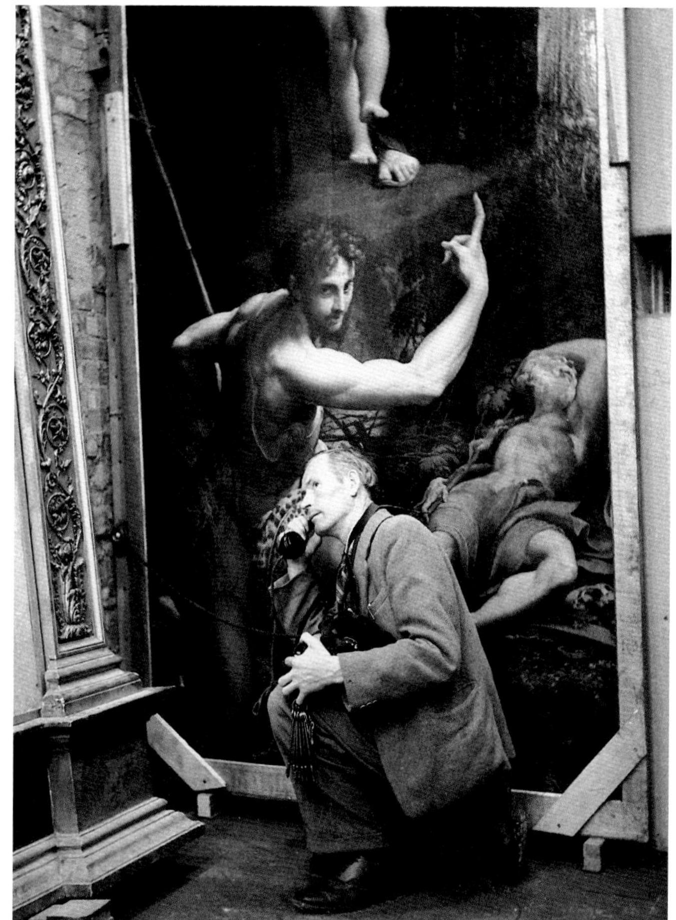

the nearest and most suitable site for such a purpose (fig. 6). If Vasari's account is to be believed, then Parmigianino's studio may have been on these same streets, as Pier Ilario reportedly transported the monumental panel (almost 3.5 metres tall and weighing nearly 100 kilograms) from Parmigianino's studio to the Pace in the midst of the terror.[48]

Contemporary accounts describe in detail the ravaged bodies and buildings on the streets of Rome; it was enough, one eyewitness recounted, to reduce Pompeo Colonna, the very man who had attempted to raid the city in 1526, to tears.[49] Pier Ilario appears to have been heroic in acting to preserve Parmigianino's altarpiece, even if he may have been thinking pragmatically about the panel, for which, according to the contract, he and his nephew were ultimately accountable.[50]

In light of the suffering and destruction in Rome at this time, the misfortune of Parmigianino's never-unveiled painting may seem insignificant. From the perspective of the young artist, however, it was surely a profound disappointment and setback. Perhaps in part because his great Roman painting was hidden away, he invested his next commission – *Saint Roch with a Donor* for San Petronio in Bologna, where he took refuge (fig. 7) – with some of its inventions. The similarity between the twisting Baptist from the *Vision of Saint Jerome* and the exuberant Saint Roch in Bologna has been noted, and Parmigianino explores the figure's reincarnation in drawings for the Bologna painting.[51] He also adds the anachronistic detail of Roman footwear on the medieval Saint Roch, as if the saint – like Parmigianino himself – had just arrived from Rome.[52]

After Parmigianino's Roman misadventure, he acquired status in Vasari's eyes and thus in modern art history, contributed significantly to the graphic arts, especially printmaking, and made portraits and altarpieces for important patrons. He did not, however, attain widespread fame and success. The final chapter of his short life was consumed by the years-long and never-completed project to decorate Santa Maria della Steccata in his native city, which ended ingloriously with him fleeing a lawsuit to Casalmaggiore, where he died of a violent illness in 1540. Enough late works have survived to suggest that he may not have actually devolved into the wild man, obsessed with alchemy, that Vasari describes in his *Lives*, but for whatever reason, the biographer mourned

Parmigianino's wasted talent and the tragic end to a life endowed with such promise and skill.

Incidentally, 400 years later, the *Vision of Saint Jerome* was hidden for safekeeping once again. During the Second World War, German bombing in London prompted the transfer of the National Gallery's paintings – among them Parmigianino's *Vision of Saint Jerome* – to Manod Quarry in Wales, where they remained from 1941 until the end of the war.[53] A photograph records Parmigianino's unframed painting in its refuge, the larger-than-life painted figures dwarfing the guard kneeling before it (fig. 8). The image prompts visions of Pier Ilario mournfully moving the painting to the Pace during the devastation of the city; whatever he hoped would become of it, he too would never see the painting again. The altarpiece would be transferred from Rome to Città di Castello in 1558 and eventually from the patrons' family palace to the National Gallery in London (see pp. 43–5). Today, the long-awaited re-emergence of the *Vision of Saint Jerome* from its conservation treatment draws attention to its preciousness as a relic of the past and to the miracle of its survival. It also compels recognition and reflection upon the human hands that made, moved and have taken care of an object so divine.

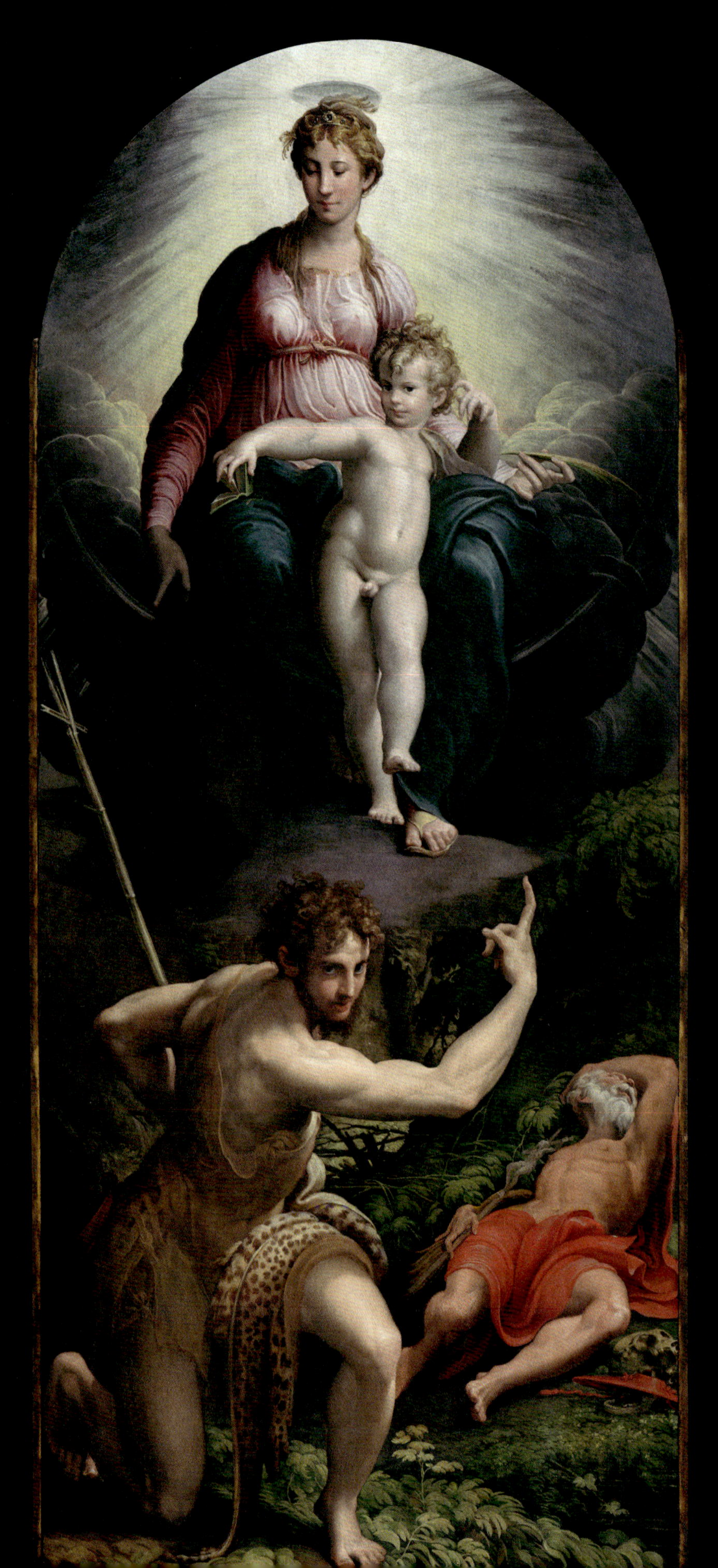

# A VISION OF SALVATION

**MARIA ALAMBRITIS**

*Rome, May 1527.*

Parmigianino places the finishing touches to his altarpiece, oblivious to the imminent arrival of Charles V's looting troops. As told by Giorgio Vasari, so astounded and perplexed were the imperial soldiers by the painting that they allowed Parmigianino to continue working (see p.13). Since this first public audience barrelled its way into the artist's studio, *The Vision of Saint Jerome* has continued to exert such an effect on generations of viewers to date (fig. 9).

Illuminated by an ethereal glow, the figure of John the Baptist emerges from the left. Caught in mid-motion, his left heel has yet to touch the ground. As he comes to kneel, he throws a supernaturally elongated right arm to point upwards and turns his head towards us. Light falls from the right, catching the arc of his arm, the top of his thigh and the rim of his left eye, as he fixes our gaze with his wide eyes. The coiled torsion of his pose intensifies the force of his gesture, as he spirals upwards like a corkscrew. In stark contrast, the dormant form of Saint Jerome reclines into a thick tangle of roots and leaves. His eyes are closed, his neck stretched back as his head nestles into the crook of his left arm. His robes drape loosely around him in ripples, like a languid pool of crimson lapping against the verdant foliage threatening to overgrow him.

The curve of the Baptist's arm is echoed by the torso of Jerome, directing our gaze upwards. Against a blaze of streaming rays and seated on a billow of clouds, a monumental Madonna and Child appear. Dressed in rose and deep blue, the Madonna delicately pinches a palm frond with her left hand, as she reaches down with her right to draw her mantle protectively around her son. He is a buoyant toddler crowned with blond ringlets, who toys with the pages of a book on his mother's lap as he steps towards us. Painted by the artist when he was just 23 years old, this work remains Parmigianino's only

documented commission undertaken during his brief but eventful period in Rome, where he resided from 1524 to 1527.

Vasari's sensational anecdote placing Parmigianino and the painting in the midst of the catastrophic upheaval of the Sack of Rome has historically overshadowed its reception. The title by which it is generally known today – *The Vision of Saint Jerome* – is a nineteenth-century invention, in response to the unusual depiction of the apparently sleeping saint. While attesting to the tenacity of both the painting and its artist's idiosyncratic visual imagination, this critical fortune has to some extent obscured our understanding of the work. This chapter seeks to re-examine Parmigianino's seemingly peculiar formal and iconographic choices within the humanist climate and religious tensions of 1520s Rome. With its towering verticality, exaggerated forms and unusual iconography, in this painting Parmigianino gave form to what Vasari called a 'particular manner' that was uniquely his own.[1] Emphasising visual idiosyncrasy and refined artifice, this mode of expression, later generalised as Mannerism, would diffuse among countless other artists through the sixteenth century.

## The Caccialupi Commission

The years of Parmigianino's Roman stay saw the germination of a vibrant artistic scene in the Eternal City. In the wake of Raphael's death in 1520, his pupils and workshop assistants, including such virtuosic talents as Perino del Vaga (1501–1547) and Polidoro da Caravaggio, channelled their association with him to establish themselves independently. The Venetian Sebastiano del Piombo was the leading painter, while the influence of Michelangelo was felt across sculpture and painting. After the brief and austere papacy of Adrian VI (r. 1522–3), the election of Giulio de' Medici as Pope Clement VII in November 1523 brought with it the promise of a renewed golden age of art patronage, attracting newcomers to Rome such as Rosso Fiorentino and Parmigianino.[2]

With Parmigianino's hopes for papal support failing to materialise, however, he pursued private commissions (see p. 11). The patron for his Roman altarpiece was the widowed Maria Bufalini, who hailed from one of the most distinguished families of Città di Castello. This small but artistically rich town in the central Italian region of Umbria



**Fig. 9**
*The Madonna and Child with Saints John the Baptist and Jerome ('The Vision of Saint Jerome')*, 1526–7
Oil on poplar, 342.9 × 148.6 cm
The National Gallery, London. Presented by the Directors of the British Institution, 1826 (NG33)

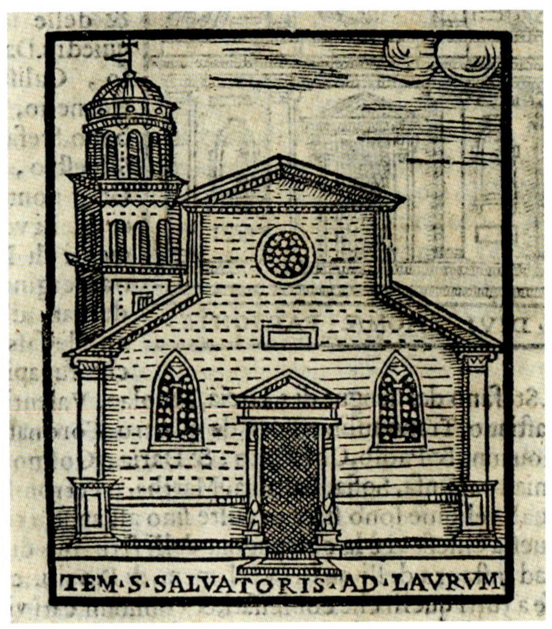

**Fig. 10**
Girolamo Franzini (1537–1596)
*San Salvatore in Lauro*, 1588
Published in *Le cose maravigliose dell'alma città
di Roma* (*The Marvellous Things of the Ancient City
of Rome*), 1600, p. 88.

was then under the dominion of the Papal States.[3] Maria Bufalini's husband, Antonio (1453–1518), and father-in-law, Giovanni Battista Caccialupi (about 1420–1496), from San Severino in the Marches, both worked as ecclesiastical lawyers in Rome.[4] Antonio had purchased a funerary chapel upon his father's death and when he himself passed away, its management and decoration fell to his widow.[5]

The Caccialupi Chapel was located in the church of San Salvatore in Lauro, in the Roman *rione* – or district – of Ponte, located between the river Tiber to the north and Piazza Navona to the south. San Salvatore in Lauro was the Roman home of the Venetian Secular Canons of the Congregation of San Giorgio in Alga ('Saint George in the Seaweed'), who will be discussed later (see p. 20). In 1468, through the support of Cardinal Latino Orsini (1411–1477), Pope Paul II (r. 1464–71) granted the Congregation the church of San Salvatore in Lauro and its attached complex as their seat in Rome.[6] Today the exact location of the chapel within the church is difficult to determine, as the original building was destroyed by fire in 1591.[7] A glimpse of its appearance is seen in the small woodcut of the church facade published in Girolamo Franzini's landmark guide *Le cose maravigliose dell'alma città di Roma* in 1588 (fig. 10).[8] Only briefly described in the text, the church featured a simple layout of three naves without a transept and with a gabled facade.[9] According to Vasari the painting was intended for a chapel close to the entrance.[10] As the light in the painting falls from the right, this suggests the first chapel to the right.[11] The commission for a large-scale altarpiece from a wealthy and noble patron, to be displayed in an important religious complex at the heart of the city, therefore held career-launching potential for the precocious Parmesan.

Drawn up on 3 January 1526, the surviving contract (see p. 84) states the requirement for a 'single panel with an image of the seated Holy Virgin Mary with the Child in her arms; and an image of Saint Jerome, Doctor of the Church, and Saint John the Baptist at the feet of the Virgin'.[12] The inclusion of the Baptist and Jerome, the former the namesake of Antonio's father and the latter the patron saint of the Caccialupi men's shared legal profession, suggests a choice based on familial devotion.[13] The painting was to be completed 'with the colours fully executed, and as much gilding on the frame of the panel as is needed'. The named artists – 'Petrus et Franciscus de Mazola de Parma' –

were to be given a down-payment of 30 scudi of a total of 65 scudi for the work. The 'Petrus' here refers to Parmigianino's uncle Pier Ilario Mazzola.[14]

Yet it soon became apparent that what seemed a straightforward commission would prove far more complicated than expected. Parmigianino swiftly began experimenting with numerous compositional variations in order to best present all four figures as coherently and compellingly as possible (see pp. 29–37). Parmigianino's veneration of Michelangelo and Raphael spurred his journey to Rome.[15] Raphael's *Madonna di Foligno* is frequently noted as one key example to which Parmigianino must have turned (fig. 11).[16] It was then *in situ* on the high altar of Santa Maria in Aracoeli, the same church where the Bufalini had a family chapel that Maria's father, Nicolò Manno (about 1450–1506), had commissioned Pintoricchio (active 1481; died 1513) to fresco in 1486.[17] While not specified in the contract, the *Madonna di Foligno* would have been known to the patron and perhaps even suggested by her as a model.[18] As this was Raphael's own first commission in Rome and the only altarpiece he painted for a Roman church, it seems apposite that Parmigianino would take from this example.

Following Raphael's design, Parmigianino organised his composition with the Madonna and Child above and attendant saints below. However, the panel on which Parmigianino had to work was of unusually narrow proportion, especially in comparison to Raphael's. To maintain the marked division, rather than dramatically reduce the scale of both saints, his solution was an asymmetrical arrangement, with one figure – Jerome – placed sharply foreshortened on the ground and seemingly asleep.

Various sources have been proposed for Jerome, including the Saint Roch in Correggio's *Madonna of Saint Sebastian* (1523–4)

**Fig. 11**
Raphael (1483–1520)
*Madonna di Foligno*,
about 1511–12
Tempera grassa on canvas
transferred from wood,
308 × 198 cm

Vatican Museum, Vatican City
(inv. 40329)

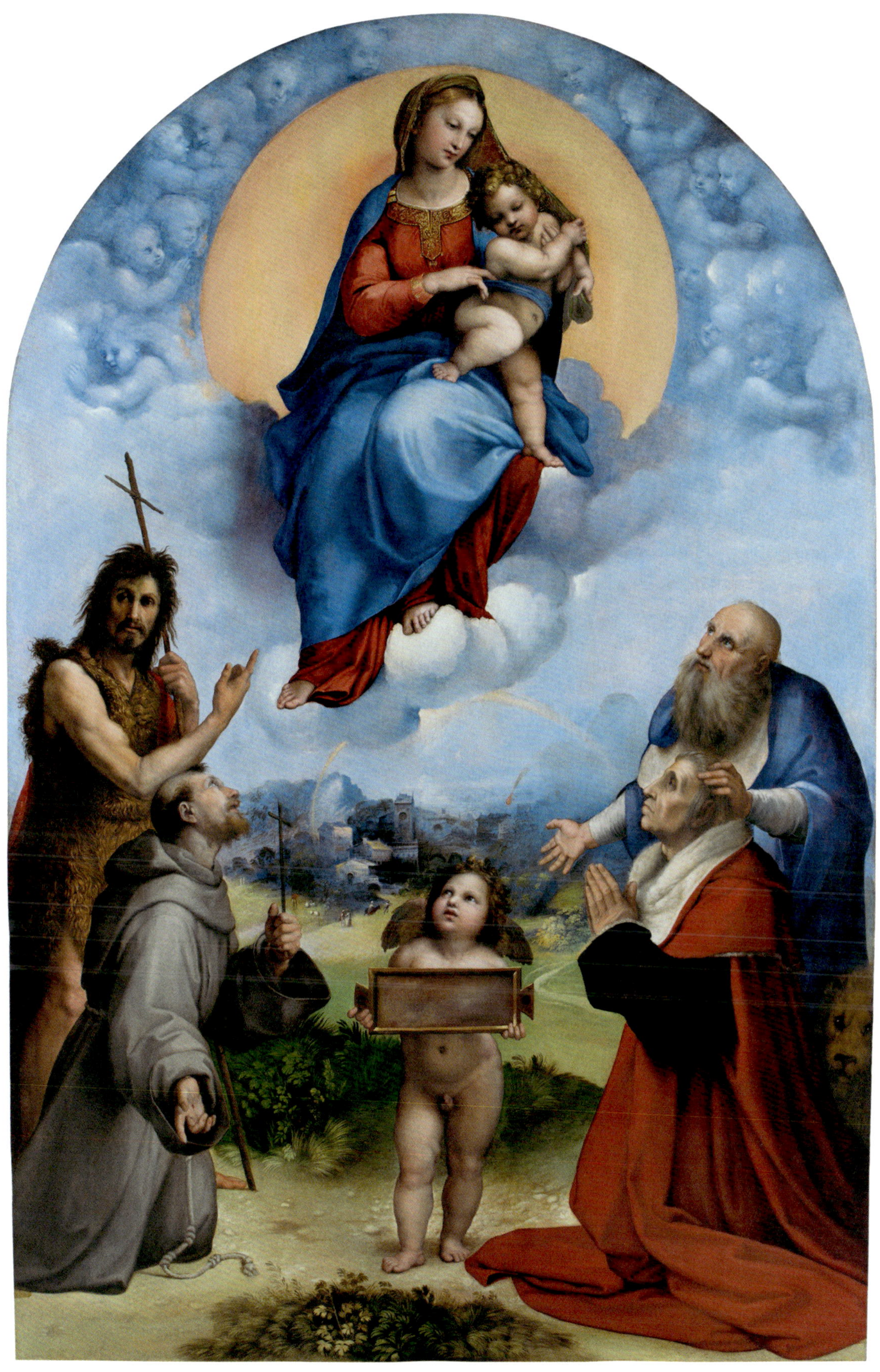

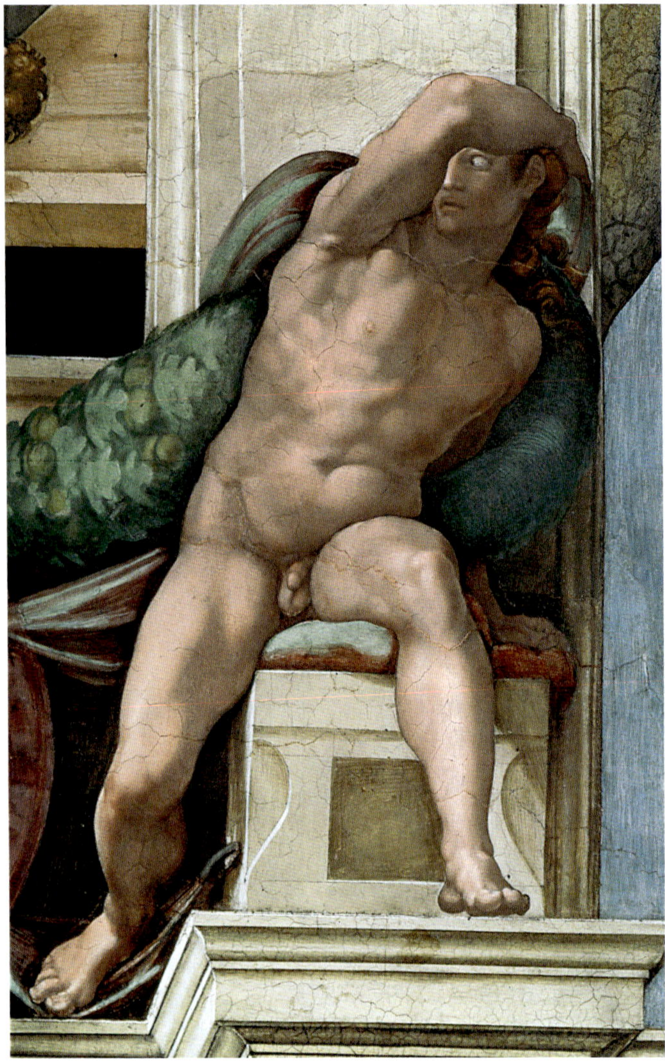



and the central figure in the same artist's *Venus, Cupid and Satyr* (1524–7).[19] Michelangelo's idealised male nudes from the Sistine Chapel ceiling, known as *ignudi*, may also have provided inspiration for the saint's muscular, reclining body (fig. 12).[20] The dormant Jerome has puzzled scholars for centuries, because no scriptural source describes the sleeping saint experiencing a vision of the Madonna and Child and nothing in the contract states this. Some have suggested the unusual composition is simply the logical solution to a formal problem.[21] The difference in scale between the figures has been interpreted on the one hand to mark Jerome as the 'real' figure experiencing the vision.[22] For others, the commanding position of the Baptist identifies him as the prophetic figure, while Jerome is detached and dreaming.[23] Another theory reads the presence of Jerome through his role as an advocate for widows, with the painting acting as a source of guidance for the patron herself.[24] Returning to the context of Parmigianino's Roman milieu can help elucidate the artist's formal and iconographic choices.

## San Salvatore in Lauro and the Secular Canons of San Giorgio in Alga

In the early decades of the sixteenth century, the intellectual and religious climate in Rome was riven with tension, caused by pressing calls for religious reform. The provocation came from the German theologian Martin Luther (1483–1546), who in 1517 published his 95 theses, condemning the Roman Catholic Church for corruption and catalysing what would become the Protestant Reformation.

The Secular Canons of the Congregation of San Giorgio in Alga were among the most influential reform-minded organisations in the fifteenth and sixteenth centuries. Founded in 1404 in Venice, the Congregation was named after the small lagoon island where its mother church was located.[25] The Canons counted illustrious figures such as Lorenzo Giustiniani (1381–1456), first Patriarch of Venice (the bishop of the Archdiocese of Venice), and Gabriele Condulmer, who became Pope Eugenius IV (r. 1431–47), among their founding members.[26] Known for their erudition (prior to its destruction by fire, the library at San Giorgio in Alga was admired as the most extensive in Venice), they espoused a return to the fundamental teachings of the Church to counter corruption, while maintaining deference to the pope.[27] They proliferated rapidly through the northern Veneto and further afield, and were so successful in their reform efforts that the Venetian Senate named them its 'Trojan horse'.[28] Their political sway was demonstrated clearly in 1524, when Clement VII beatified Giustiniani, thereby licensing his cult as bishop-confessor.

Debates about Church teaching and dogma implicated the use of religious imagery. This only became more heated after 1517, as the Protestant schism gained traction. The Canons actively commissioned works of art as tools of religious reform and often acted as intermediaries in commissions for their houses.[29] Known as the 'Celestini' or 'Turchini' after the dark blue of their skullcaps and habits, the Canons were devoted to the Virgin Mary as their protector and intercessor.[30] Given this active involvement, it seems plausible that Parmigianino sought to engage the sophisticated intellectual milieu sustained at San Salvatore in Lauro. With his patron's wishes in mind, this must have informed the innovative iconographical narrative the artist finally developed.

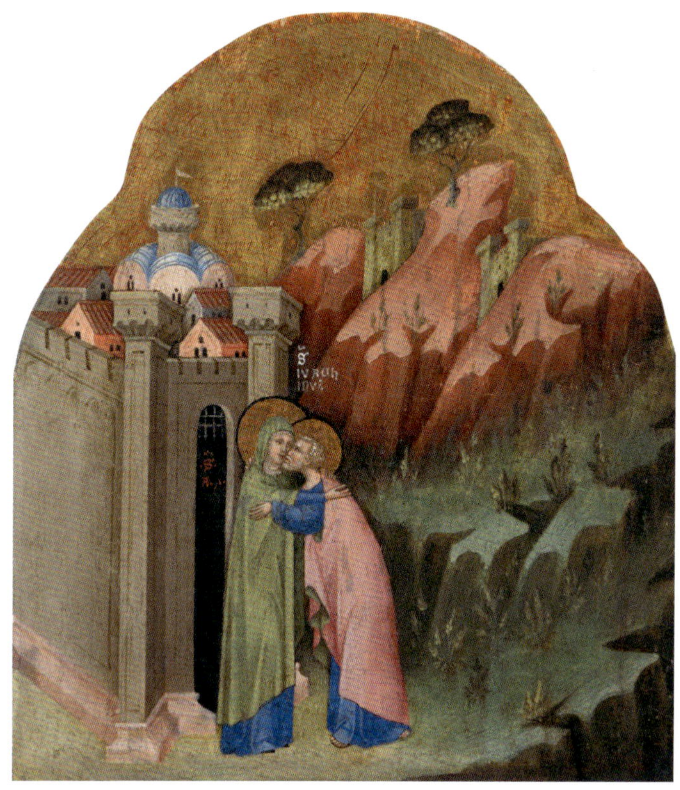

## An Immaculate Conception?

Parmigianino's Madonna is illuminated against a radiant source of light. Numerous fine, linear brushstrokes denote a fan of rays that almost fill the upper zone of the painting and pierce the dark underside of the clouds. Around her head, a perfect circle – drawn in a darker pigment just visible beneath the upper paint layers – forms a blazing centre, suggestive of the sun (see p. 23). Another circle is formed by the continuation of the arched top of the panel with the semicircle of the throne of clouds and the sliver of the crescent moon beneath her. The depiction of the Madonna holding the Child in her arms, enveloped by the sun behind her and the moon beneath her, was understood to represent the Woman of the Apocalypse, as described in the Book of Revelation 12:

> And there appeared a great wonder in heaven;
> a woman clothed with the sun, and the moon under
> her feet, and upon her head a crown of twelve stars …
> And she brought forth a male child, who was to rule
> all nations.[31]

Since the twelfth century, the Woman of the Apocalypse had been regarded as a symbol of the Church and an iconographic type of the Virgin Mary.[32] The representation of the Virgin in this guise was well established from the 1480s as a way to communicate belief in her Immaculate Conception.[33] This doctrine held that Mary was exceptional among humankind in being free of original sin, the state into which all human beings are born according to Christian belief. Parmigianino's contract specified that the main panel of the altarpiece was to be accompanied by lateral images. While it is unclear if these were intended as painted panels or fresco decoration within the chapel itself (neither of which has survived today), they were meant to depict on the one side Saints Joachim and Anne, the parents of the Virgin Mary, and on the other a scene of the Conception of the Virgin (i.e. Birth; see p. 84). The most common depiction of Saints Joachim and Anne together was that of the Meeting at the Golden Gate, showing the pair embracing outside an entrance to Jerusalem and representing the moment in which Anne miraculously conceives Mary in her womb (fig. 13).[34]

The subjects of the Meeting at the Golden Gate and the Conception of the Virgin were derived from the *Protovangelium of James*, an apocryphal text composed during the second or third century AD and one of the most important and earliest surviving sources focusing on the life and character of the Virgin Mary. The *Protovangelium* foregrounds Mary as exceptional in her purity.[35] Images such as the Meeting at the Golden Gate were often combined with that of the Woman of the Apocalypse to convey Immaculist meaning.[36] Together with the central panel, this focus on the Virgin's predestination, her sinless birth and her role in bringing redemption to humanity in the form of Christ conveyed a special Marian context for the commission. The message of salvation and triumph over death was particularly fitting for the funerary context of the Caccialupi Chapel.

The doctrine of the Immaculate Conception was the subject of intense debate between the two most important mendicant religious orders – the Franciscans, who supported it, and the Dominicans, who vehemently opposed it.[37] The doctrine received its first semi-official approval when the Franciscan Pope Sixtus IV (r. 1471–84) sanctioned a feast day on 8 December and commissioned two related offices – liturgical texts – from the Veronese canon Leonardo Nogarola in 1477 and the Milanese Bernardino de' Busti in 1480. This was significant given that the Immaculate Conception would not be accepted as Church dogma until 1854.[38]

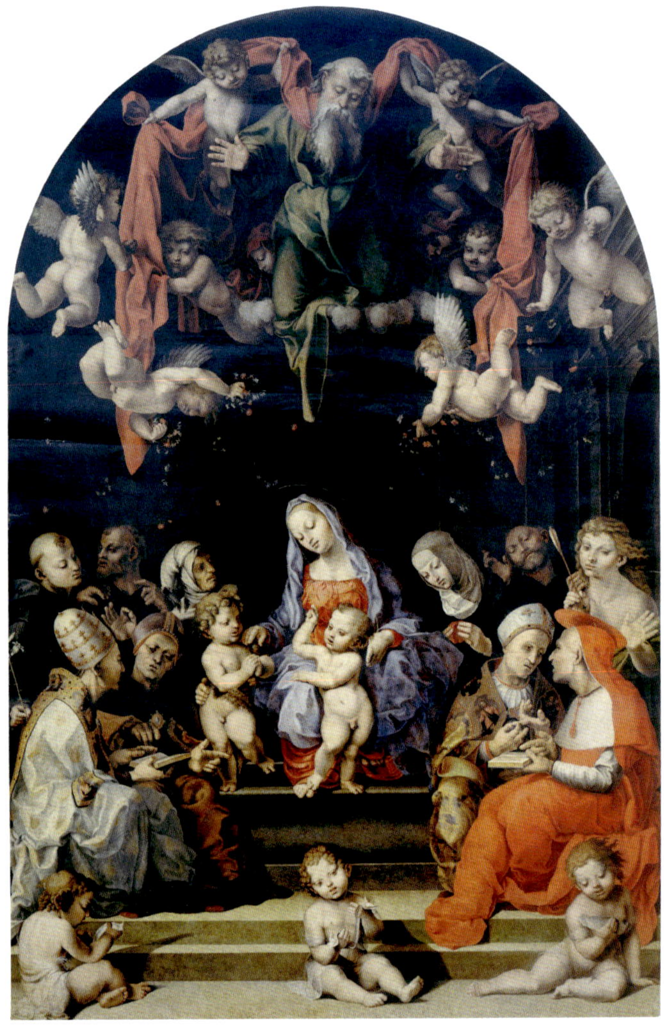

By the time of Parmigianino's arrival in Rome, the debate on the Virgin's purity had escalated from an internal dispute into a bitter polemic between the Catholic Church and the Protestants. Luther in particular was vociferous against this sanctification of the Virgin.[39] Therefore, despite Sixtus IV's partial approval, there was a reticence in Rome towards the commission and public display of definitive Immaculist images.[40] In the city of the pope and seat of the Church, outright endorsement of this heavily contested belief required careful mediation. In the early decades of the 1500s, few images of this kind circulated in Rome and its environs, in comparison to Tuscany, Umbria, the Veneto and the Marches, where the pro-Immaculist Franciscans had a powerful presence.[41] Moreover, with no set iconographical tradition, artists experimented with how to convey most effectively a subject that was inherently immaterial and visually elusive.

Other artists in Parmigianino's circle were employed on projects in Rome with similarly complex iconographical requirements that engaged with Immaculist symbolism. Around 1520, Perino del Vaga began work on a fresco cycle of scenes from the life of the Virgin for the Cappella Pucci in Trinità dei Monti, including the Meeting at the Golden Gate and Birth of the Virgin.[42] The same year that Parmigianino began work on the Caccialupi Altarpiece, Sebastiano del Piombo was engaged with the altarpiece for the funerary chapel of the wealthy papal banker and patron Agostino Chigi (1465–1520) in Santa Maria del Popolo. This project was originally commissioned from Raphael and intended to depict an Assumption of the Virgin; when Sebastiano took over, he attempted a complex reworking of Raphael's original idea. Arranging the ascending Virgin and attendant saints into two distinct groups, he incorporated the explicit Immaculist symbol of the crescent moon.[43] The eventual transformation of the design into a Nativity of the Virgin suggests the risk and suspicion such imagery attracted in Rome.[44]

The inclusion of the Christ Child with the Virgin Immaculate conveyed the justification for Mary's exemption from original sin and the result of it – the Divine Incarnation, God becoming human in the form of Jesus Christ.[45] After numerous trials, Parmigianino decided to liberate the Christ Child from his mother's embrace and stand him between her legs. Michelangelo's *Bruges Madonna* (about 1501–6) has been often cited as the source for this motif, which symbolically represents Christ's first steps towards acceptance of his fate (see p. 34).[46] While Michelangelo's Christ still clings to his mother's hand and looks down cautiously, Parmigianino's steps forward unhesitatingly, expressing a greater sense of independence. This fervency is shared with his counterpart in an altarpiece painted by Girolamo Genga (1476–1551) in 1516–18 for the church of Sant'Agostino in Cesena (fig. 14). Bernardino de' Busti's office, which informed Genga's altarpiece, held particular influence in Emilia and Romagna.[47] The Virgin's parted legs and Christ's placement between them is a particular expression of Immaculate Conception iconography for this time, accentuating her role in bringing Christ into the world, an affirmation of her utmost purity.[48]

Parmigianino's Christ is framed by the palm his mother holds to his left and the book he rifles through to his right. The former is a symbol of his future sacrifice, the latter of the Incarnation and the glory of the 'Word become flesh' (John 1:14).[49] He disrupts his mother's reading, alluding to her foreknowledge of his fate and recalling images of the Annunciation, where the arrival of the Archangel Gabriel likewise interrupts Mary reading. Below, the Baptist's 'heaven-indicating gesture' is the same as that frequently employed for depictions of Gabriel, with both connoting the primacy of metaphysical knowledge (fig. 9).[50] The glimmer of water at the lower left corner suggests the River Jordan in which John will baptise Jesus, emphasising his role as the precursor to Christ. Hovering at the threshold between us and the spectacular appearance of the Virgin and Child beyond, the Baptist makes an appeal to the viewer to focus the attention of their gaze upwards, towards the vision of salvation.

Christ's gleaming nudity is reminiscent of the idealised beauty of classical sculpture, speaking to a 'purification on the iconographical level' particular to the early sixteenth-century atmosphere of reform and the humanist culture fostered in the papal city.[51] The loose trail of the Virgin's veil that falls over his shoulder is suggestive of the burial shroud in which he will later be bound, while his flawless, radiant body connotes the triumph of the divine over death. The Virgin in turn appears more majestic than motherly. The heavy draperies such as those in the Vienna study (pl. 13) are exchanged for revealing diaphanous pleats and a jewel-encrusted tiara, from which golden strands of hair escape. Such elements imbue the painting with an unexpected sensuality that may seem irreverent, but in fact intensifies its religious import by employing overwhelming divine beauty as a means to provoke spiritual sublimity.[52] This elision of the sensual and sacred marked the emergence of a new means of visualising the divine, which came to fruition in Rome, stimulated by the rediscovery of classical works of art.

## The Allure of the Antique

Around the turn of the sixteenth century, archaeological excavations in Rome unearthed a plethora of antique statuary, architectural fragments, carved reliefs and sarcophagi, which were eagerly collected and displayed by wealthy patrons. These remnants wielded an irresistible allure for contemporary artists, who sought to infuse their work with the resonance and grandeur of the city's glorious past.[53] This influenced the development of religious imagery, as artists pursued new ways

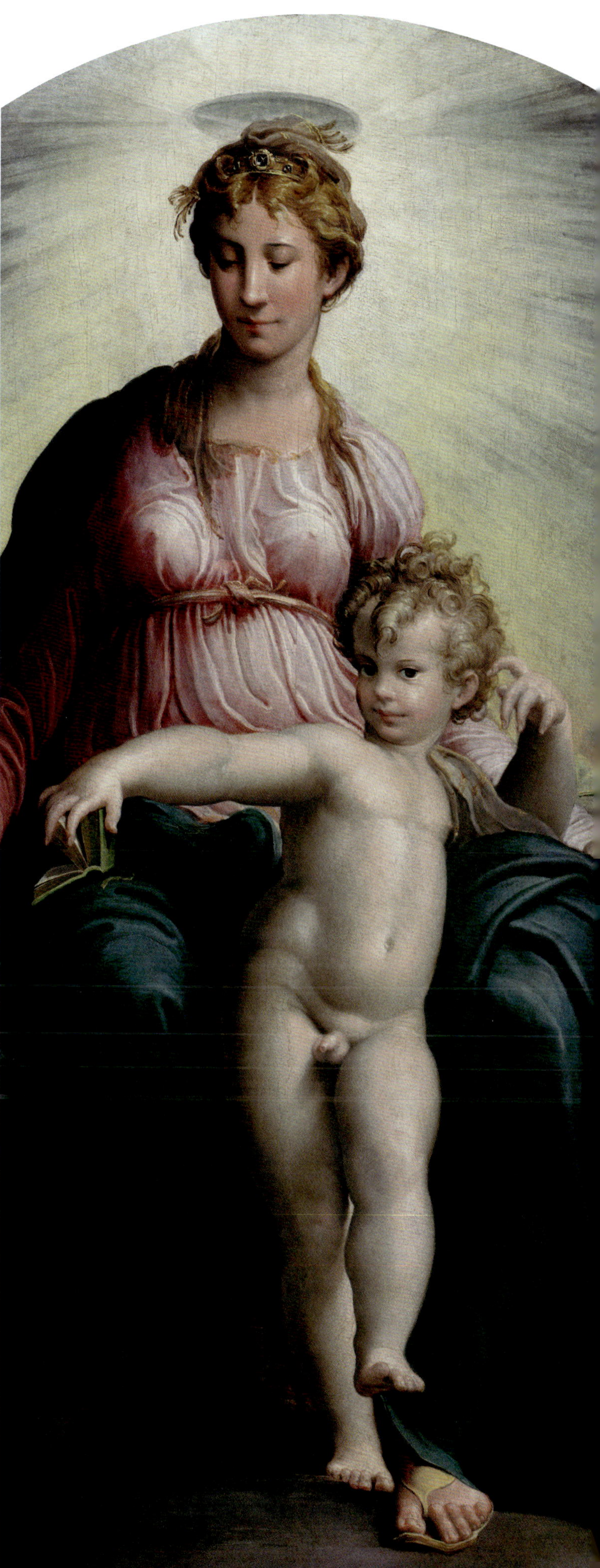

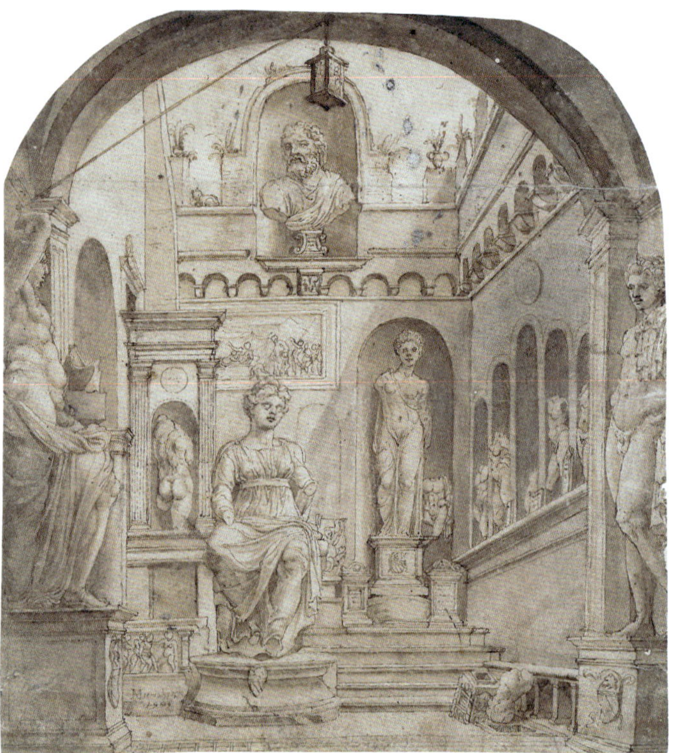

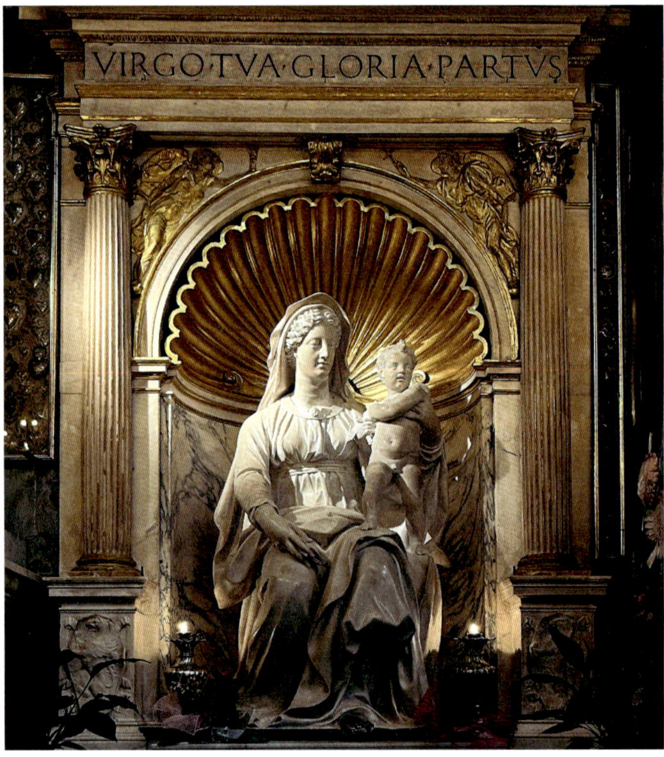

to portray the idealised sacred body. This was a Rome in which the publication of the *Modi* (1524) – a catalogue of sexual positions designed by Giulio Romano and engraved by Marcantonio Raimondi – was possible. Even though it was promptly censored, it attested to the taste for a classicising eroticism encouraged by the humanist culture at Clement VII's court, to which artists responded.[54] Combined with the increasing practice of studying from the live model, this informed the palpable sensuality of Parmigianino's altarpiece.[55]

One of the most revered collections of antiquities then in Rome was that owned by the brothers Ippolito and Benedetto de Sassi displayed in the courtyard of the Casa Sassi in the *rione* of Parione, close to San Salvatore in Lauro (fig. 15). Parmigianino knew of and copied from this collection.[56] Surviving drawings show the artist citing such classical fragments directly, before incorporating this source material in a modified form in his final paintings.[57]

The repetition and reuse of copies from a select group of antique sources became a common feature in the practice of artists working in Rome. Vasari described the new 'manner' of painting as deriving from the frequent 'copying of the most beautiful things … adding them together to make a figure of as many beauties as possible'.[58] One example of this fusion of the classical with the contemporary was the Florentine sculptor Jacopo Sansovino's (1486–1570) *Madonna del Parto* (fig. 16). Sansovino's source was a Casa Sassi sculpture today in the Museo Archeologico, Naples, known as the *Apollo Citharoedus*. In the early sixteenth century it was understood to represent *'Roma trionfante assisa'*, an allegorical seated female figure of Rome triumphant. With its connotations of nurturing and abundance, the *Roma trionfante* was likely considered an appropriate model for the Virgin Mary.[59] Parmigianino must have known the *Madonna del Parto*, which was installed in 1521 in the Martelli Chapel in Sant'Agostino, where it remains to this day.

Parmigianino's Baptist wears his traditional animal garment, which here is a distinctive leopard-skin pelt draped in heavy folds over his thigh. The contemporaneous interest in this sartorial choice is attested to by works such as Raphael's *Madonna dell'Impannata* (1511–12) and Perino del Vaga's *Holy Family with the Infant Saint John the Baptist* (fig. 17).[60] In the latter, the infant John wears a leopard-skin tunic and a wreath of grape leaves crowns his head, accoutrements more in keeping with a Bacchus than a Baptist. This conflation of pagan and Christian symbolism was a characteristic Florentine convention for Baptist imagery, which found popularity briefly in the early sixteenth century.[61] While Parmigianino's altarpiece reveals no Florentine connection, he evidently took to this feature, perhaps imported by the Tuscan Perino to Rome.

The traditional depiction of Jerome in the wilderness is drawn from his own account of the four years he spent in penitence as a hermit in the Syrian desert. This was widely disseminated in the Renaissance through texts such as Jacopo de Voragine's *Golden Legend* (about 1260).[62] In the painting, Jerome is not beating his breast in self-mortification; neither does he gaze upon a cross, but instead is seemingly asleep. Among frequently depicted sleeping figures in Greco-Roman art that of Ariadne was particularly popular, one of the most celebrated examples being the Vatican's *Sleeping Ariadne*, acquired by Pope Julius II (r. 1503–13) in 1512 for his Courtyard of Sculptures (fig. 18). Given Parmigianino's frequent copying from antique sculpture in Rome, it is likely that he knew of this work. Indeed, its influence can be seen especially in the Louvre red chalk study, with the motif of both hands raised over the head, one tucked under the other (pl. 23r).

A liminal state, sleep blurs the boundaries of consciousness and enhances connection to the divine.[63] The transposition from Ariadne to Jerome reinforces the idea of a profound sleep approaching that of mystical abandon.[64] In his influential *Theologica Platonica* (*Platonic Theology*, written 1469–74, printed 1482), the eminent Florentine philosopher and theologian Marsilio Ficino (1433–1499) described the state of sleep as a *vacatio animae* – a 'wandering of the soul' – away from the confines of the body and in closer proximity to the divine.[65] The *Theologica Platonica* remained in

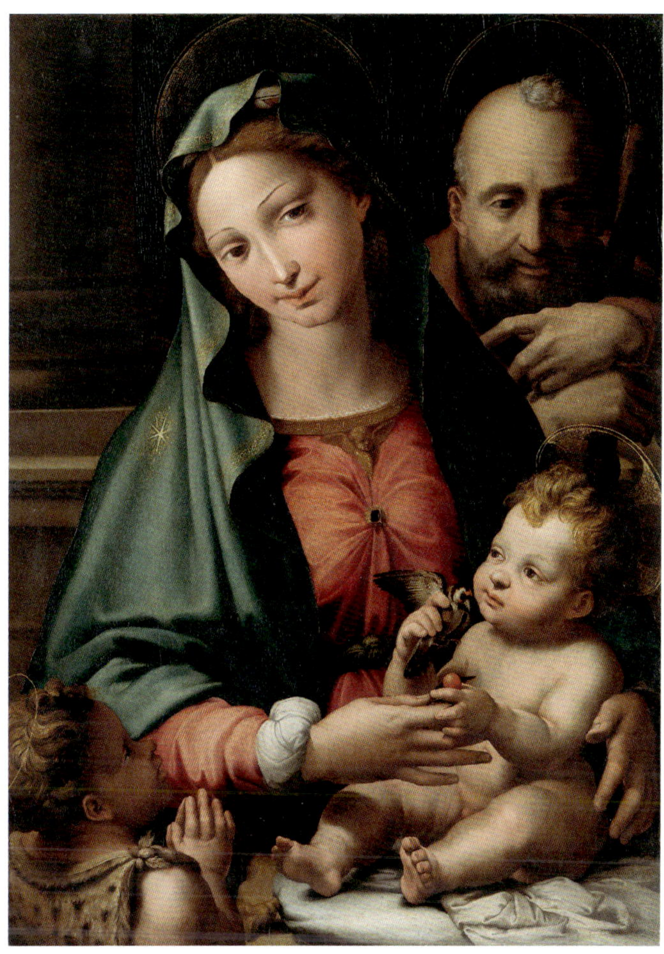

circulation through the early sixteenth century, with a new edition published in 1524.[66] Parmigianino's interest in the visionary potential of the sleeping figure is evident from his many studies of the dormant Jerome, ensconced and isolated in the wilderness (pl. 27). With crucifix and flagellum entwined tightly in his fingers, he appears to be possessed of a fitful rather than restful sleep. Jerome's contorted pose conveys the agitation of ecstatic realisation. The skull to his left is angled in a way that echoes the saint's own head. With his cardinal hat lodged distinctively between the jaw and cranium, it suggests a call to *meditatio mortis* – the contemplation of death and

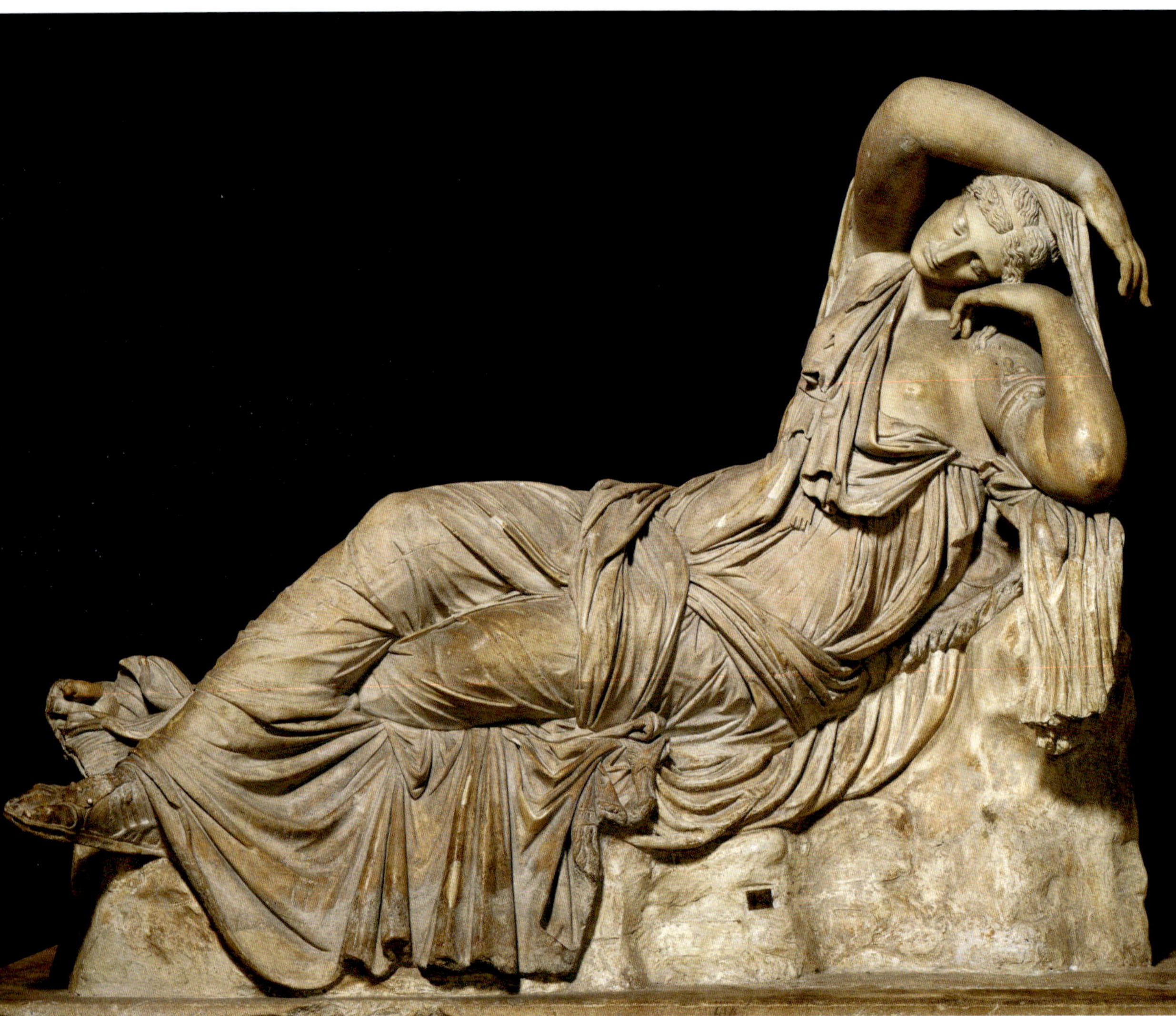



the vanity of worldly trappings. In his *Theologica Platonica*, Ficino draws on this Platonic concept, which posits such contemplation as an aid to the liberation of the soul from the body, a process that culminates in death.[67] Parmigianino painted the skull over the existing foliage, suggesting a late addition to emphasise the connection between sleep, death and the struggle of the soul to free itself from its corporeal cage, appropriate for prayers given up in a funerary chapel context.[68] The puzzling lack of specific reference to the known events of Jerome's life can therefore be read here as intentional. As has been noted in relation to broader experiments in artistic production across northern Italy in the 1520s and 1530s, ambiguity was employed deliberately to emphasise the artist's capacity for invention and to encourage active religious engagement.[69]

Without doubt, Vasari's anecdote presents an unforgettable narrative. It also lends an anti-Protestant gloss to one of the most vivid descriptions of the Sack in the *Lives*: a miraculous

Madonna that stuns the looting soldiers into submission and moves them to an act of mercy.[70] With his eloquent attenuated forms, cultivated synthesis of sources and sinuous brushwork, Parmigianino created an image of divinity that spoke to the fecund intellectual and artistic milieu of pre-Sack Rome. While his Roman masterpiece was intended for the salvation of the Caccialupi men's souls, as the soldiers broke into his studio in May 1527, Parmigianino would soon realise it would be the source of his own.

**Detail from fig. 9**

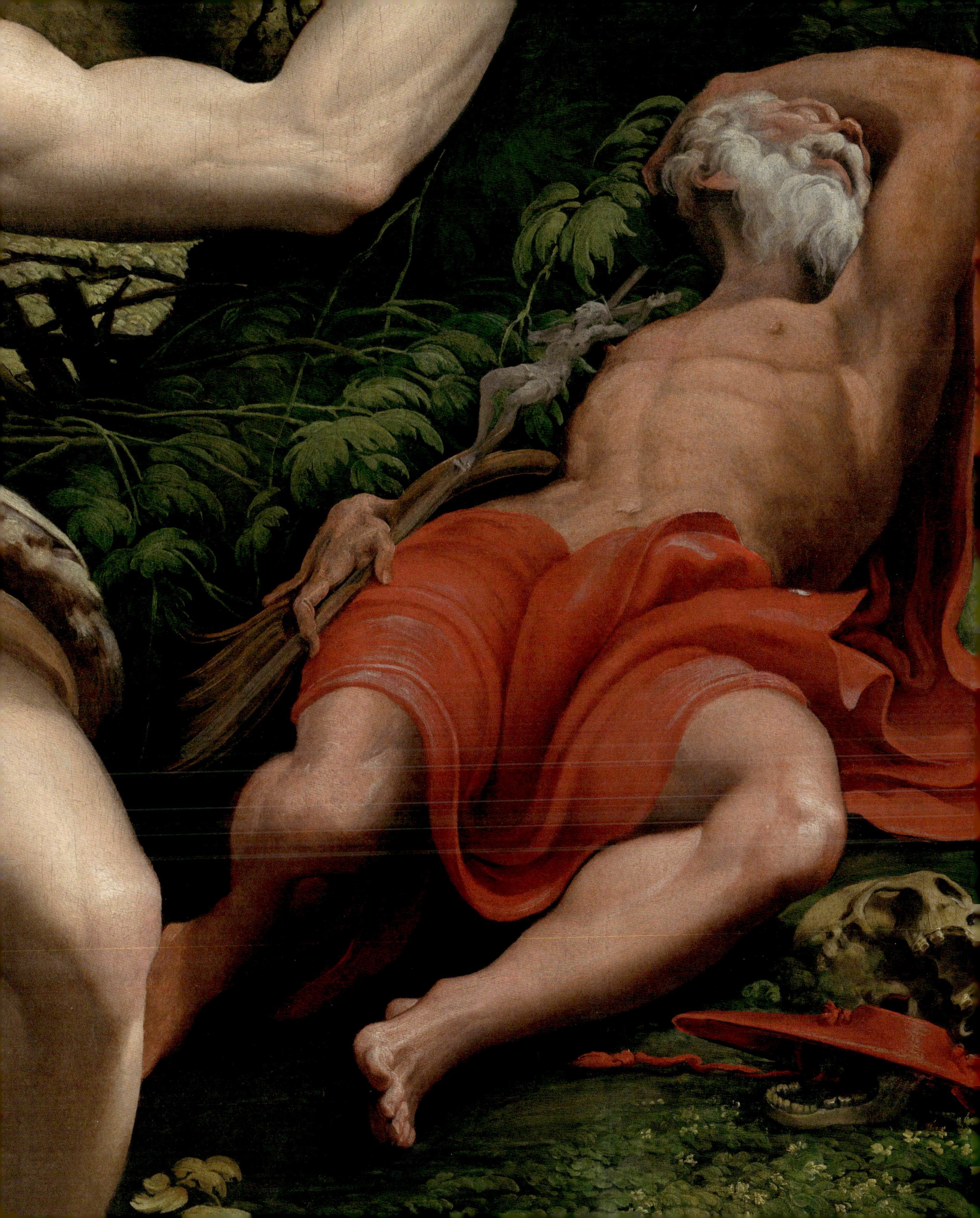

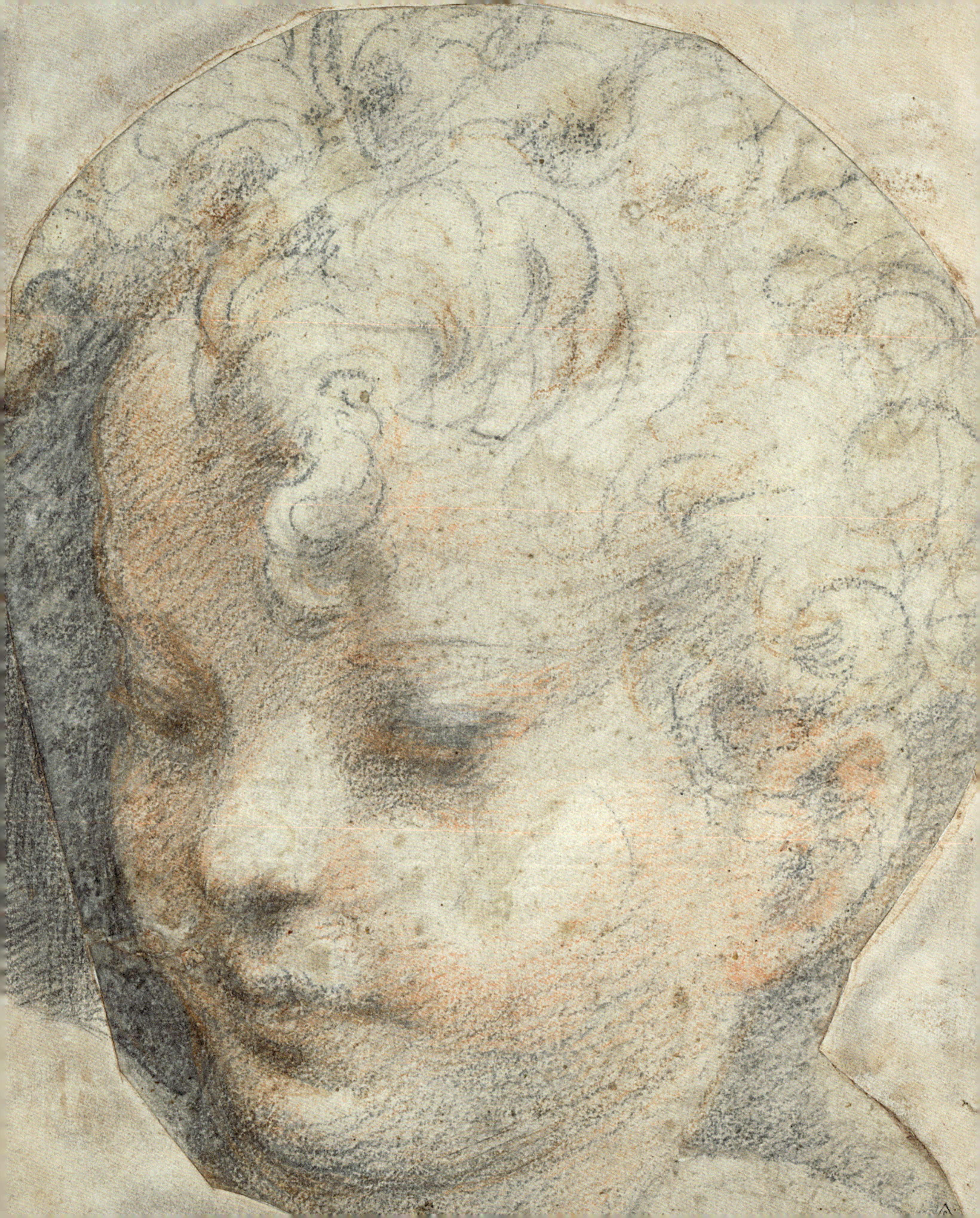

# DRAWING 'THE VISION'

**MATTHIAS WIVEL**

Francesco Mazzola was one of those kids who sat in the back of their writing class, doodling instead of paying attention. This is a quintessential origin story of visually creative people and it appears already to have been a cultural trope when the artist and writer Giorgio Vasari inserted it into the second edition of his biography of Parmigianino, published in 1568.[1] Whether authentic or not, it captures perfectly the artist as we know him from his drawings.

Around a thousand sheets from Parmigianino's hand survive. They vary greatly in style, finish and media – ink and wash and red and black chalks dominate. A study of their purposes and interrelations leaves no doubt that an exponentially larger number has been lost. The fact that we have around 30 preparatory drawings – surely out of dozens more that have disappeared – connected to the National Gallery's Caccialupi Altarpiece is in itself testament to this. Parmigianino drew all the time.

When drawing, he effectively merges structure and spontaneity. The coherence of even his most loosely rendered compositional studies indicates a pre-established, general idea of the whole that he opens to improvisation, yielding revelatory variation and innovation in the process. His line flows, swirls, bends and curls across the paper, describing form as part of an evolving continuum. It connects figures in mutual, melodic interdependence, spirit and matter intertwined.

Contours coil with force and unfurl in release, punctuated as they ebb and the artist lifts his hand to pick up their flow with renewed energy (pls 1r, 5). Shape and texture are obtained through hatching, pooling wash or smudged chalk. The fall of light is evoked by the white of the paper in areas left untouched and sometimes enhanced in white gouache or chalk (pl. 11r). And while figures such as Saint Jerome in the Caccialupi Altarpiece may be dramatically foreshortened, Parmigianino usually maintains a fairly shallow depth of field, concentrating our attention on the essential. Tonal coherence unites individual compositional elements across the paper, as if in a sculptural relief carving.

Vasari describes the 'loveliness', 'sweetness' and 'elegance' (*venusta*, *dolcezza* and *leggiadria*) and notably the 'grace' (*grazia*) of

Parmigianino's work, reporting that it was said in Rome that the spirit of the recently deceased Raphael had passed into young Mazzola's body.[2] 'Grace' is applied more than any other term to Raphael's art. It covers a complex of qualities having to do with his eloquence of expression, his ability to make the contrived seem natural and the pleasing – indeed elevating – effect this has upon the viewer. There is a spiritual overtone to this: the artist reflecting, in his own particular way, the Grace of God.[3]

The notion of Parmigianino as 'Raphael Redivivus' – the spiritual reincarnation of the great Raphael – had a long afterlife in art historical literature, despite many obvious differences between the two artists.[4] Vasari himself (who never knew Raphael, but likely met Parmigianino in Bologna in 1530) takes pains to differentiate their personalities. He portrays Mazzola as a nervous fantasist who lost his way in alchemical experiment, pursuing the gold of the philosopher's stone to the detriment of his art, and dying – inevitably, it is implied – at the young age of 37. This is in contrast to the polished yet passionate genius of Raphael, whose death at the height of his powers, also at age 37, is cast in terms of unexpected tragedy.

More to the point, Raphael was concerned with idealised but accurate anatomy and the credible placement of the figure in three-dimensional space, while Parmigianino distorted anatomy in his exploration of what can best be described as *inner* space.

The Caccialupi Altarpiece is an arrangement of figures out of scale with each other, situated in a vividly rendered natural environment that is only partially defined in spatial terms. They are elongated beyond anatomical reality, stretching to the height of nine heads (against the traditional and more accurate seven); their limbs swell and contract as they flex and relax, their distended fingers bending in accentuation.[5] Parmigianino's figures are built from ovalising, almost urn-like shapes and attain monumental proportion from the swelling and tapering of contours.[6] In other words, he subverts the rules of physics as well as physiology, shaping reality in his own emphatic manner, with an intensity of conviction that lends a sense of spiritual uplift to the picture, in step with its visionary theme.

This is consistent with the emerging understanding in the period of personal style as an inevitable, constituent part – and increasingly valued aspect – of art. The artist's style was coming to be seen as expressing something uniquely his, often a direct



"

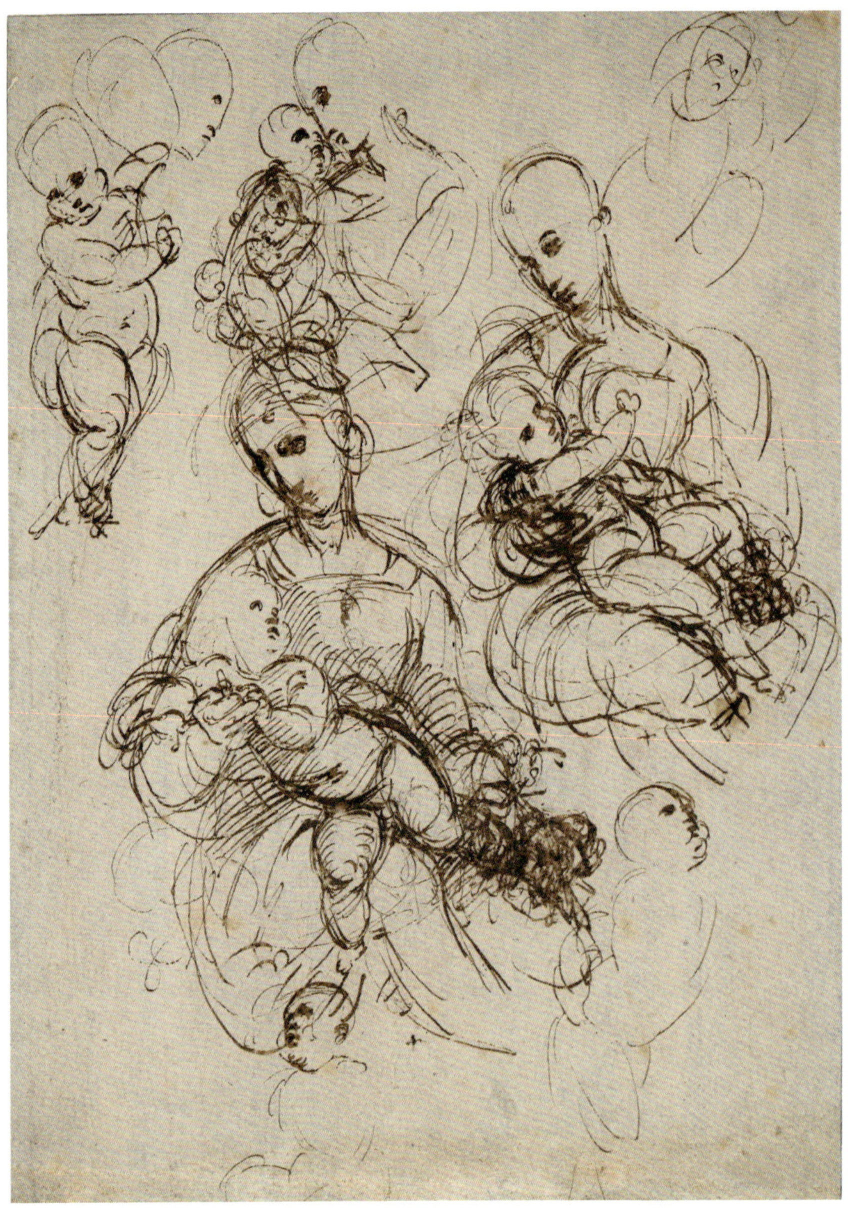

extension of his personality. It is the foundation of what Vasari describes as the 'third manner' in his analysis of the evolution of art, the manner 'which we would call modern'.[7] It is at the root of the problematic modern term 'Mannerism' (see p. 9).

Vasari's *Life* of Parmigianino is in part a cautionary tale of a supreme talent whose troubled personality ultimately hindered its full realisation. It is the story of the delicate balance between creative success and personal oblivion so familiar to creative people, surely before, but especially since it became a literary trope in the sixteenth century. Through his biographies of artists of this modern manner, notably those of Jacopo Pontormo (1494–1557) and Rosso Fiorentino, Vasari analyses the flipside of this new personal freedom of expression. Elaborating upon it in the 1580s, the Milanese artist and art theorist Giovan

Paolo Lomazzo (1538–1592) suggested that Parmigianino became trapped in his manner, losing sight of the variety of life and producing similar-looking figures by adhering to typologies and stylistic imperatives.[8]

However, both Vasari and Lomazzo, as well as many later critics, emphasised the grace, loveliness and elegance of Parmigianino's work as transcendent elements – an unquantifiable *non so che* ('I know not what') that animated his art.[9] Ultimately, Parmigianino's reinterpretation of Raphael is not so much in his direct, and by all accounts, avid study of the older master's work but more fundamentally in his artistic temperament, his will to grace.

As with Raphael, everything is interconnected in Parmigianino's art: his lines move in arabesque rhythm;

*Virgin and Child*, about 1526
Pen and brown ink with brown wash
on paper, 19.2 × 9.4 cm

Devonshire Collection, Chatsworth (inv. 1072)

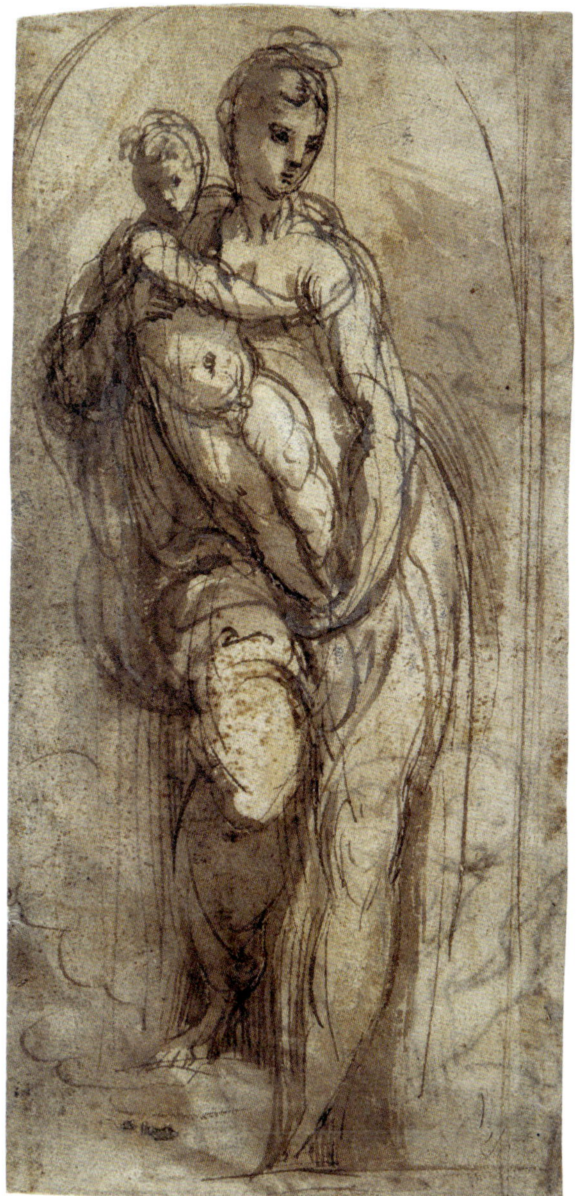

forms transmute one into the other, animated in a flow of unified energy (fig. 19). Raphael's circular and curving motion of the hand finds more smoothly extended, ovalising and dynamically curled parallels in Parmigianino's compositions. For both artists, it is this open-ended approach to mark-making from which their inventions spring – a curve is the beginning of a shape which eventually leads to form.[10] There is a profound harmony to their work, analogous to music, but where Raphael's form is driven by a moral imperative – a reflection of the harmony he senses in the world and projects onto human interdependence – Parmigianino's is more abstract, expressive of individual vitality and spirituality.[11] In broad (and inevitably reductive) terms, Raphael's vision is universal where Parmigianino's is personal.

The process of shaping described above occurs across Parmigianino's drawn oeuvre and is exemplified vividly by the drawings relating to the Caccialupi Altarpiece. Surely imposed by the architecture of the chapel at San Salvatore in Lauro, rather than being a creative choice, the unusually narrow format of the altarpiece and the contract's mention of the decoration to extend to the 'chapel's architectural framing' set certain parameters (see pp. 18–21).[12] Another result of pre-existing conditions was the direction of the light in the painting – from the right – which must reflect its intended location in the church. This helps identify drawings related to its creation.[13]

The extant drawings for the Caccialupi Altarpiece are hard to insert into a strict chronology, as Parmigianino would work on different visual solutions in parallel. He clearly decided at an early stage to dispense with the stipulation in the contract that the Virgin be seated – surely his prerogative, as long as he included the requisite figures. He may have chosen to do so better to accommodate her figure to the narrow format of the altarpiece, but it might also have had to do with the emerging iconography at the time of the Immaculate Virgin as standing on a cloud cover against a field of heavenly light (see p. 21). A pen-and-ink sketch in the British Museum swiftly outlines the Virgin looking downward to her right. She props the Child against her extended left leg and he looks to his left. Curving outlines and parallel hatching define the figure. Mary's hair is suggested by

a few twirly strokes of the pen, while the Child's tufty locks are flicked off the top of his head in suggestion of his inquisitive energy (pl. 2).[14]

Parmigianino routinely developed compositions across projects, with ideas and themes cross-pollinating. An example at Chatsworth has the Virgin in a similar pose to the British Museum sketch, but with her right leg bent and the Child more relaxed at her right side (fig. 20).[15] This is loosely derived from Raphael's Sistine *Madonna* (1512–13, Gemäldegalerie, Dresden). Although a cloud cover is suggested, she is placed in a narrow niche that does not correspond with the shape and size of the Caccialupi Altarpiece and thus must reflect a discrete project. Her outlines are indented, indicating transfer to a different sheet for further elaboration.

A complex drawing at Chantilly, clearly cropped at top and right, includes a similar pen-and-wash study of a seated Virgin and Child placed in a niche atop a shield carried by putti (pl. 6r).[16] As we shall see, this sheet carries on its verso preparatory studies for the Caccialupi Altarpiece, but the niche arrangement must be distinct and perhaps relates to the same project as the Chatsworth drawing. A sheet in the Louvre carries a pen-and-wash drawing of the Virgin and Child in a similar position to that at Chatsworth, if at slightly smaller scale and flipped (pl. 3). Whether this is for the same project as the Chatsworth drawing, but lacks the niche, or for the Caccialupi Altarpiece, or neither, is difficult to say.[17]

That these experiments fed into the Caccialupi commission is established by a compositional drawing for the altarpiece in the British Museum, in which the Virgin and Child appear in broadly similar positions (pls 1r, 1v). They are positioned within a clearly demarcated field drawn in proportion (1:2.3) to the National Gallery panel. On the recto, executed in pen, ink and wash, the Virgin gazes down to her right at John the Baptist, while the Child looks and gestures to his left, as in the Louvre drawing. The indication of the picture's frame in red chalk shows Parmigianino's awareness of its narrow format. This may have contributed to his decision to dispense with the traditional *sacra conversazione* arrangement with the saints arrayed in a semicircle around, or below, the Virgin – a convention he had previously deployed on several occasions.[18] This, then, was the arrangement that he initially settled on for his composition.[19]

Having energised the Virgin and Child by standing her up, he similarly activated the saints by crouching them, which also helped to fit them into the space available. John performs a challenging bodily turn simultaneously to address the viewer and – as he traditionally does in his role of precursor of Christ – to indicate the apparition of the Child. He is executed loosely but confidently, with adjustments to his head and contours made along the way. The lack of major revisions, however, suggests prior sketching. Jerome is relegated to a more passive if still dynamically torqued counterpoint, leaning against his crucifix, head turned towards John. Less resolved, he is established with curving movements of the pen: Parmigianino equivocates between a bent and a stretched position of his left arm, shifts both legs to the right into a

tighter crouch and revises an initial, frontal presentation of his face to a profile view.

He subsequently turned the sheet over and drew a new version of the composition in red chalk, building on the figure of the Virgin on the recto as seen through the paper but keeping her oriented in the same direction (pl. 1v).[20] He cropped the saints along the bottom edge the better to fit and enlarge them to scale with the Virgin and Child. John is in front, almost leaning out of the picture, his head turned to greet us while pointing upwards to the sacred presence. Jerome leans away in foreshortening, turning in attention to the apparition above.

Two drawings of the saints demonstrate that this arrangement was perfected separately.[21] Whether they are developments upon the British Museum sheet or precede it is difficult to determine, but they articulate the arrangement more clearly, showing the saints in half-length, turning in counterpoint to each other. In a red chalk drawing in the Getty, we see John from behind more fully than in the London drawing, although his head is turned towards the viewer as he indicates the holy presence (pl. 4r). Jerome is similarly posed to his counterpart in London, but has his head turned upwards; his crucifix is sketched in several positions. Behind them are four ghostly heads, presumably saints, arranged in two pairs; one wears a bishop's mitre. The drawing is clearly cropped along the top, as well as the sides, and may once have included the Virgin and Child.

The verso carries a study of the standing Christ Child, identifiable as such by the Virgin's hand steadying him under his right arm, as well as a crucifix – presumably Jerome's – and two greyhounds unrelated to the altarpiece (pl. 4v). These latter correspond in posture, and such detail as the chain link collar one wears, to those Parmigianino frescoed in 1523–4 in a room in the castle at Fontanellato outside Parma, three years prior to undertaking the Caccialupi commission (fig. 21). This presents a challenge to a linear understanding of his development and is emblematic of how ideas and motifs interweave and recur in his work across time.

There is nothing material on the sheet to indicate two separate drawing campaigns: the quality and hue of the chalk are the same throughout, and John and Jerome were not drawn atop the figures behind them.[22] Thus, if the drawing was made at Fontanellato – and its soft focus and roundedness of form are

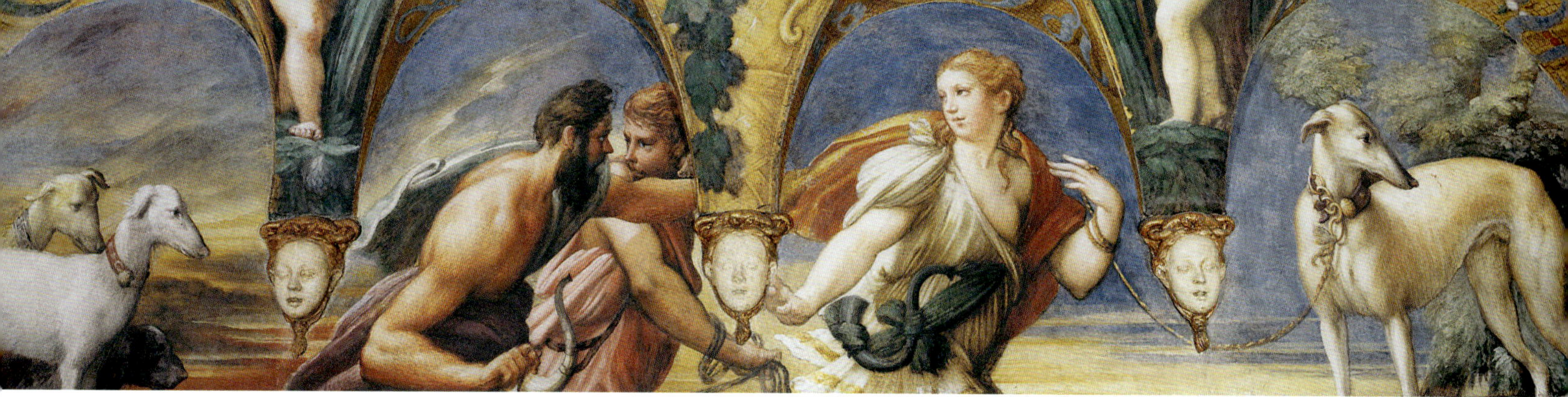

not incompatible with the artist's pre-Roman drawing style – it would mean that he worked on a configuration of Virgin and Child with Saints John and Jerome, perhaps along with four other saints, that was very close to the Caccialupi commission years prior to arriving in Rome.[23] This seems unlikely.

The alternative is that the drawing was indeed a preparatory sheet for the Caccialupi Altarpiece to which Parmigianino added the other saints' heads, perhaps spontaneously, perhaps in pursuit of a different idea.[24] This would make the hounds a recollection, for reasons unclear, of those at Fontanellato. This does not seem impossible: the fact that they overlap differs from their placement at Fontanellato and the way the body of the hound in front is outlined, with its head absent and its legs only suggested, indicates repetition of an existing design. This scenario too is challenging, but somewhat less reliant on coincidence and thus more acceptable.

Parmigianino varied slightly the arrangement of the two saints in a tiny thumbnail in pen and ink, today in Frankfurt, perhaps as a clarification of the design (pl. 8). Regardless of the precise chronology, these drawings mark a step on the way to the final arrangement. On the verso of the sheet in Chantilly (pl. 6v), he sketched in an alternative configuration of the saints kneeling in full figure, facing us: John gesturing backwards and Jerome lost in contemplation of scripture. Parmigianino explored this idea further in an atmospheric red chalk sketch where he applied it to a figure of the Baptist, wearing fur. Next to it, his head is studied in profile. The sketch is lit from the left, however, so probably intended for a different project.[25]

Returning to the Chantilly sheet, it carries to the right of the compositional study a cropped sketch of John very close to how he would appear in the painting: his upper right arm is shorter, the drapery falls slightly differently, his reed cross is missing and he is not carrying the baptismal bowl on his hip. In all essentials, however, this is the final design. In an outline drawing in Buenos Aires from around the same moment (pl. 7),[26] Parmigianino tried out this figure of John with the variation of Jerome as he appears on the British Museum recto.

As demonstrated by Maria Alambritis, the Chantilly drawing was part of the same sheet as a *Virgin and Child* in the Ashmolean Museum (pl. 5; see pp. 38–41). Here Parmigianino returned to the idea of a seated Virgin, drawn as if emanating from the cumulus in

a succession of squiggles and swathes of brown wash that combine to articulate her forms. Areas of the paper left blank convey the brightness of divine light; a few lines denote radiation at the left. Standing, the Child straddles the Virgin's powerful left thigh, looking at us.

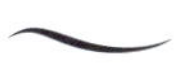

Several drawings by Parmigianino of the Virgin and Child seated on clouds survive from this period, but it is often hard to judge how closely they relate to the Caccialupi commission.[27] Two presentation drawings for wall tombs datable to the artist's Roman years, in the Metropolitan Museum and the Louvre respectively, for example incorporate the Virgin seated with the Child standing on her lap, the former with a cloud cover.[28] It is conceivable that a tightly cropped, elegantly notational and historically much-admired pen drawing at Chantilly, which shows Mother and Child looking in opposite directions, is for one of these projects (pl. 9).[29] Very close in style to this sheet and to the Ashmolean *Virgin and Child*, and thus likely contemporaneous, is a pen drawing with the Child lying across his mother's lap (pl. 10), much as Parmigianino would later arrange him in his so-called *Madonna of the Rose*, today in Dresden.[30]

In the double-sided Chantilly drawing, the cropped design on the recto shows an arrangement with a more unruly Child struggling for balance on his mother's right thigh (pl. 6r). This seems related to the already-mentioned Virgin and Child in a niche at right, but the crossover between it and the Caccialupi Altarpiece is simultaneously evident.[31] Parmigianino explored this more mobile Child in a series of drawings, one of which is also in the Ashmolean. On its verso are sketches of legs, one in red chalk by Parmigianino, others in pen by a lesser hand. It also contains a sketch in pen and ink with corrections in white bodycolour of the Child twisting over his mother's knee (pl. 11v), which demonstrates awareness of Michelangelo's so-called *Taddei Tondo* (about 1504–5).[32]

On the recto of this same sheet, Parmigianino studied in black and white chalks a voluminous swathe of drapery, folding over the lap of a nude female figure (pl. 11r). Parmigianino was here likely drawing on antique as well as contemporaneous sources (see pp. 23–5), but the pliably bending lower legs and

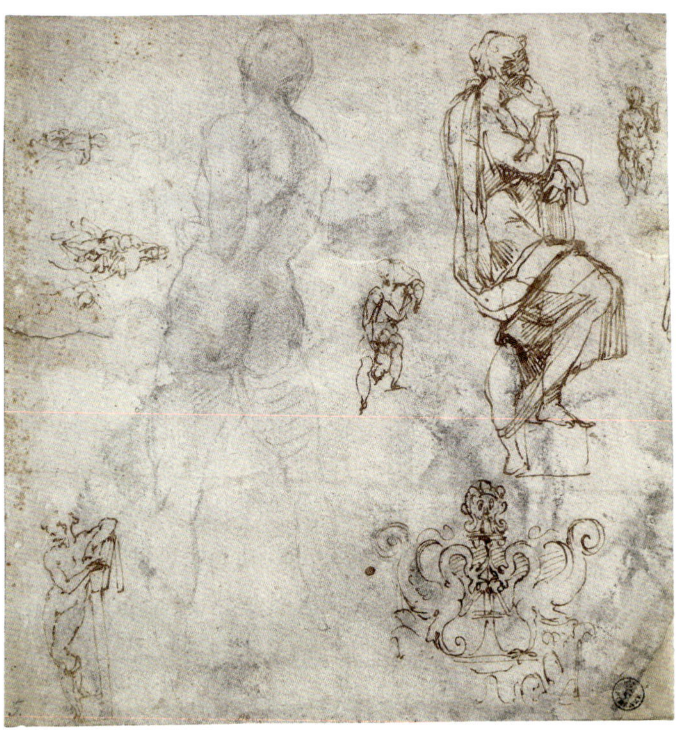

tapering ankles, however, are emphatically Parmigianino's own interpretation, as is the even, linear hatching used to model the figure against the light falling from upper right to almost relief-like effect. Most notable is the spirited furling of the drapery, especially at the centre, where it sensually suggests what it conceals. With this drawing, the Virgin's monumental form as it appears in the painting decisively began taking shape.[33]

Following this, Parmigianino moved the Child to a standing position between his mother's legs, which emphasises both Mary's maternal loins and Christ's first step away from her, into the world and towards Golgotha. We see this in two red-chalk drawings, at the Ecole des Beaux-Arts in Paris and in a private collection (pls 15, 16).[34] They imbue the Child with a monumentality akin to that of the Ashmolean drapery study. In the privately owned drawing he holds a bird, perhaps the goldfinch symbolic of his Passion or possibly a dove suggestive of his spirit. The Child's lower body is very close indeed to the final arrangement, down to the sway of his hip and his leg extending towards the viewer.[35] His upper body is unfixed, however: he looks up to his mother, while two alternative positions are indicated for his right arm.

In the Paris drawing, Parmigianino solidifies the Child further through careful hatching. His playful upward gaze is emphasised by his raised right arm, which holds not a bird but the palm frond, symbolic of life after death, which would be transferred to the Virgin's right hand in the painting. His left arm rests against his mother's knee in a position close to that of his right in the final picture. Parmigianino retained the pose of his lower body in another red chalk study now in the Beaux-Arts, drawn mostly in outline with minimal modelling. He also maintained the left arm in more or less the same position, but bent the right behind the Child's head, now gazing downwards, a step closer to the painted version (pl. 17).[36]

During this process, Parmigianino appears to have taken a cue from preparatory drawings for Michelangelo's so-called *Bruges Madonna*, or copies after such drawings (the sculpture had been dispatched to Flanders in 1506). Small notational sketches by Michelangelo at the upper left and right edges of a sheet in the Uffizi record an abandoned design for the Bruges Child that is very close indeed to Parmigianino's final

arrangement, if in reverse (fig. 22). It seems likely that more elaborate drawings of this design once existed. Michelangelo was living in Florence at this time but maintained a house in Rome. Perhaps Parmigianino met him in Florence, somehow established long-range contact or gained access to drawings in free circulation.[37] In any case, the combination of the outstretched arm and raised leg in Michelangelo's design is so particular that coincidence is unlikely. Another contemporaneous sketch for the Bruges group in the British Museum also aligns with Parmigianino's design, albeit in more general terms.[38] A damaged red-chalk drawing of the Virgin with the Child between her legs in the Museo di Capodimonte in Naples seems to be Parmigianino's direct development from Michelangelo's model (pl. 12).[39]

Around this same time, Parmigianino completed a highly finished Mother and Child in pen and wash over a rough black chalk outline, today in the Albertina (pl. 13).[40] It is painterly in its elaboration, with contoured wash shading setting the figures off against the divine light, and with white gouache taken beyond highlights in places softly to dissolve contours and define form. In contrast to the final design, the Virgin wears a more traditionally Christian wimple, but also a distinctly classicising band across her chest. She has an air of melancholy that Parmigianino would eventually eschew. Christ sticks his right foot forwards, crossing over his left leg as he looks down to our left, while his arms are more or less in the positions they would assume in the painting. A small fragment in Naples shows us his left hand almost exactly as it would be painted (pl. 14).[41]

Parmigianino concurrently studied the head of the Virgin in what was presumably a series of drawings. In an intimate red chalk study in a private collection, he models the features of a young woman carefully, capturing a pensive aspect (pl. 18). This was likely drawn in connection with the Caccialupi Altarpiece. Another, more worked-up red chalk drawing, cropped at top and probably at right (once and perhaps still in the Krugier-Poniatowski Collection in Geneva) unequivocally prepares her head as executed on the panel, with the wimple removed and with a suggestion of her eventual diadem and halo (pl. 19).[42]

Parmigianino had still not fully resolved the figure of Saint Jerome, who was becoming a variation on his favoured motif of the wise hermit experiencing insight or even revelation.[43] A rough pen-and-ink sketch in Parma – drawn on the verso of a sheet of head studies and a remarkably palpable drawing of a dead mouse – provides an indication of where he was by this point (pl. 20). The finalised figure of John as developed on the Chantilly sheet is on the left, while on the right, sadly cropped, is a quick notation of an almost finalised arrangement of the Virgin and Child. She looks to our left and slightly downwards, as in the two red-chalk head studies; the Child's lower body is as established on the Paris sheets, while his arms are developed on the basis of the Albertina design towards the final arrangement seen also in the Naples fragment. His head, oriented towards our left, differs from the painting's direct gaze, however. Between these sketches is a summary indication, at smaller scale, of Jerome as he would be painted.[44]

The eventual opening of the painting's depth of field, with Jerome situated in complex foreshortening towards its middle ground, allowed for the presentation of the Baptist on a larger scale. It was a compellingly original idea, with Jerome's arched body and swirling red garments accentuating his disturbed sleep.[45] Whether the Parma thumbnail sketch reflects Parmigianino's initial breakthrough towards this arrangement or a slightly later essay in placing the two saints in relation to each other is hard to say, but it is clear from the surviving drawings that he developed the figure of Jerome with care and attention.

Foreshortening the human form came naturally to Parmigianino, who had come of age creatively working on vaulted ceilings in Parma in close proximity to Correggio, who mastered such designs.[46] Parmigianino would routinely pose his models outlandishly, asking them to maintain impossible positions. The fluidity with which he grasped the flex and bend of the prostrate model is evident from a study sheet in the Louvre in which he translates what he sees into cascading curves of muscle, sinew and flesh (pl. 21).[47]

In a more detailed, small study from the live model in pen and brown wash with white heightening on blue paper, today in a private collection, we find Parmigianino developing Jerome's sleeping form (pl. 22).[48] He regularly used blue paper to provide a dark mid-tone to accentuate his modelling. This had been standard practice in Venice since the fourteenth century and Parmigianino had employed it in Parma. Here he studies a youthful, muscular body posed on a ledge or raised platform, leaning back, feet to the floor. The saint's conventional bearded features are indicated summarily at top, with tufts of hair vaguely suggestive of horns. The right arm and hand are very close to the final arrangement.

More or less simultaneously, Parmigianino posed a model fully prostrate and nude on a blanket and sketched him in red chalk on a sheet in the Louvre (pl. 23r).[49] The articulation of the chest is unresolved and the head remains a mere suggestion. In contrast to the drawing on blue paper, both of Jerome's arms are bent above and behind his head, the right in a position eventually used for his left.[50] The verso reveals that the sheet was cropped at least slightly, containing as it does a fragment of a larger study of the saint's right leg, bent at an angle and supported on the forefoot with the toes characteristically marked in quick dashes of the chalk.[51] It is carefully modelled with cross-hatching, lending it a sense of neat, even finish (pl. 23v).

That the leg may not have attached to a more complete study since cut from the sheet, but was drawn in isolation, is indicated by a cropped pen-and-ink sheet in the Uffizi, which contains a number of separate arm and hand studies, including one of Jerome's right leg drawn at the same angle and with the same cast shadow (pl. 24).[52] This may have been imported freehand from the Louvre sheet. It is tightly arranged

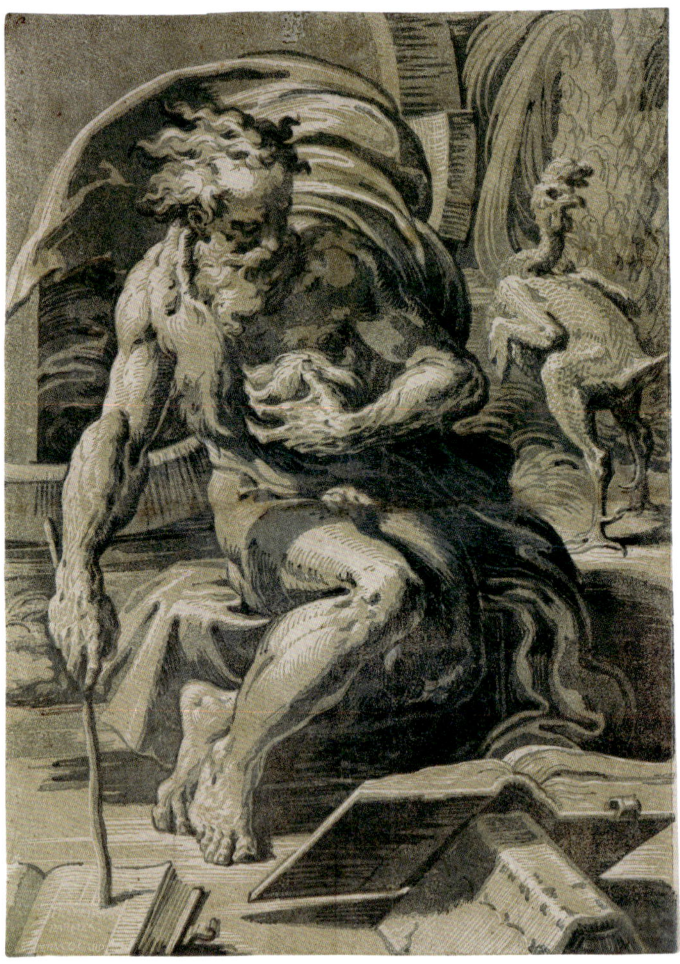

alongside other fragmentary studies, including one of a head of hair seen from above as well as a humorous caricature. This suggests a sheet used to refine designs laid out elsewhere. Everything is executed with neat, cross-hatched strokes, resulting in an even, clear, almost diagrammatic effect, similar to the Louvre verso.

Interestingly, the arm and hand studies on the upper part of the sheet correspond closely to Parmigianino's most famous design of a wise hermit, the monumental *Diogenes*. This was first engraved by Jacopo Caraglio and subsequently turned into a chiaroscuro woodcut by Ugo da Carpi, both of whom reversed its orientation, as tends to happen in prints (fig. 23).[53] This is evidence that Parmigianino was developing Jerome and Diogenes at the same time. The third hand study, which is close to the right hand of the figure in the drawing on blue paper and indeed Jerome's right hand as finally painted, features a pair of dividers and a sheet of geometrical diagrams, inscribed *giometria*. This indicates an allegorical figure and further instantiates the equivalence between scientific insight and spiritual vision that so preoccupied Parmigianino. The Uffizi sheet thus exemplifies lucidly how the creative cross-pollination between his projects unfolded on multiple levels, from the figurative to the thematic.

He developed the figure of Jerome in greater detail on a sheet now in the Getty, cropped at top (pl. 25).[54] He was probably still working from a posed model, now in pen and ink, refining in linear terms his suggestive Louvre red chalk study and articulating the difficult foreshortening of the body along the way. There is a frank eroticism to the way he not only exposes but exhibits the saint's genitals, exemplifying his ability to root visionary ecstasy in sensual physicality.[55] Such explicit imagery was presumably inappropriate for the painting, for which the traditional nudity of Christ would in any case have taken precedence.

At any rate, Parmigianino covered Jerome's genitals with drapery. He developed this in a black and white chalk drawing on low-grade blue paper at Windsor (pl. 26).[56] This is rougher but similar in both concept and execution to the Ashmolean drapery study for the Virgin. In addition to the main study, which applies the drapery to the posed figure, he examines its fall between the saint's legs separately and at larger scale

to the left. Jerome is here arranged almost exactly as in the painting and is cropped by a line drawn freehand at right, indicating the edge of the panel. This demonstrates that Parmigianino drew this sketch after he had begun work on the panel itself, perhaps during the laying-in phase and possibly even after he had started painting.

⌣

X-radiography of the Caccialupi Altarpiece reveals that the artist made very few corrections to the design while painting (see p. 50). For all his equivocation and experimentation while preparing it, Parmigianino thus started working with his brushes only once his composition was more or less fully established.

Infrared reflectography does not detect the kind of systematic underdrawing of forms one might expect of a work of this size with so few corrections. For comparison, the unfinished Courtauld *Virgin and Child* (about 1527–8; see fig. 38) and Louvre *Mystic Marriage of Saint Catherine* (about 1529) appear to have been executed on the panel *alla prima*: that is, effectively laid in and built up directly in paint. The former was painted with reference to a compositional study today in the Albertina and it seems likely a similar drawing existed for the latter.[57] Neither exhibits much, if any, preliminary underdrawing.

The scale of the Caccialupi Altarpiece and the precision of its execution make it unlikely to have been painted *alla prima*. One would assume, at the very least, a process analogous to that adopted for the Louvre panel, if not execution based on transfer from cartoons (full-scale prepared outline drawings). Close scrutiny of the infrared reflectogram reveals what might be at least partial underdrawing in the Child's head, and even if it is not, none of this means that Parmigianino did not draw on the panel: he may have used a material that does not contain carbon and is therefore invisible to infrared light.

A drawing of the Child's head in the Albertina, executed in black stick material (either chalk or charcoal) with red chalk and irregularly cut from a larger sheet, is a rare surviving cartoon-like drawing from Parmigianino's hand (pl. 28).[58] It is to scale with the Child as painted and carries a few indentation marks, but none that follow the contours, so they were not made with transfer to the panel in mind. It differs in important aspects from the painting in which the Child sports a more elaborate coiffure than he does in the drawing and looks straight at the viewer. In the drawing he expresses a discrete self-awareness, while his direct gaze in the painting is provocatively confrontational. Infrared reflectography of the painting reveals minor adjustments to the Child's face, notably the mouth and left eye, which may have been laid in closer to how they appear in the drawing.[59]

None of this evidence is conclusive, however, and it seems highly unlikely that the drawing was transferred wholesale. It could conceivably have been used rather loosely as an auxiliary cartoon, that is a full-scale drawing, derived from the actual cartoon, used as reference while painting. More likely, however, it reflects the final phase of preparation, helping us understand two things about Parmigianino's process: firstly, that he did indeed prepare cartoons for larger paintings such as the Caccialupi Altarpiece. Secondly, that he was revising his compositions significantly on paper even at late stage such as this and at full scale.

We have no drawings specifically for the landscape or ancillary elements, but Parmigianino surely drew upon studies made independently but with a view to being applied to painting. We have a few spectacular landscape drawings from the period, most relevantly a drawing in the Uffizi. Lushly rendered in pen, ink and painterly white bodycolour on blue paper, it evokes the movement of wind through foliage with shimmering touches and liquid contrast, as if impressed upon our artist's memory after awakening from a dream (pl. 29).[60] Surely such drawings informed Parmigianino's dense natural environment in the Caccialupi Altarpiece. Similarly, a sensitive red-chalk drawing of a skull seen at an angle from below, also in the Uffizi, which probably predates his arrival in Rome, is the kind of observational study that would have informed his clever and morphologically credible rendition of the death's head with its split jaw around Jerome's cardinal's hat in the painting.[61]

⌣

The wealth of drawings that Parmigianino produced for the Caccialupi Altarpiece speaks to an irrepressible creativity, if perhaps also one driven by doubt, and evidences an incessant openness to alternatives. There is a nervousness, even an anxiety, to his creative process that tempers the astonishing facility of his craft. His very inventiveness forestalled resolution. From what we have learned of his work on the Caccialupi Altarpiece and know about his technique more generally, it seems logical that his paintings contain few in-process revisions. The painting, as the final product, appears to have had to be conclusive in order properly to crystallise his flow of ideas. It follows naturally that as he grew older, his painting became increasingly polished, premeditated and perfectionist, to the point – at the church of Santa Maria della Steccata in Parma – where it finally crushed him (see p. 15).

Visions, as generally described by the holy men and women who experience them, come to their recipients vivid and fully formed. Visualising them, which appears to have been one of Parmigianino's chief concerns, required management of his percussive flow of inspiration in order for the salient image to materialise before us. The Caccialupi Altarpiece appears to have been a breakthrough in this respect.

# A REUNITED STUDY FOR THE CACCIALUPI ALTARPIECE

**MARIA ALAMBRITIS**

Among Parmigianino's surviving drawings for the Caccialupi Altarpiece, the British Museum double-sided sheet is to date the only intact study for the whole composition (pl. 1).

However, two other sheets today housed in separate collections are here reunited for the first time as a proposed new full compositional study (fig. 24). Both the *Virgin and Child* in the Ashmolean Museum, Oxford and *Three Studies of Saints* in the Musée Condé, Chantilly, have long been acknowledged as preparatory studies for Parmigianino's only documented Roman altarpiece.[1] The visual and historical connections between them, however, have so far gone unnoticed.

## The Composition

The recto of the Ashmolean drawing depicts the Virgin and Child seated among clouds (pl. 5). The Virgin turns towards her right as she reaches across with her right arm to support her son, who balances standing on her leg with the precarious wobble of an infant. Framing lines at the top edge of the drawing indicate the arched top of the panel, and a group of loose dashes to the left of the Virgin's head mark rays of light emanating from behind. Both of these elements are also present in the British Museum full study. The Ashmolean Virgin's right foot dips down into the nebulous swirl beneath her, but stops abruptly just before her toes, where the sheet has been cut along the bottom edge. It has been suggested previously that this drawing may have formed the upper part of a full composition, which was later separated into two.[2]

Turning to the Chantilly sheet, its verso is divided into two: on the left is a pair of kneeling saints recognisable as John the Baptist and Jerome (pl. 6v). On the right, Parmigianino has drawn the Baptist again, in a pose very close to that of his counterpart in the final painting. He is, however, cut-off at the shoulders where the sheet was later cropped, and now missing the top right corner. Just visible on the left at the very top edge of the Chantilly study is a tiny semicircular set of piano key-like marks – Parmigianino's distinctive manner of delineating toes. Inevitably, these must belong to a foot, like that of the Virgin of the British Museum recto, whose foot extends down towards the Baptist's head. These seem to be the toes missing from the Ashmolean Virgin's foot and, along with the Chantilly pair of saints, complete a full compositional study.

The framing lines above the Ashmolean Virgin and Child stop where the drawing has been trimmed along the sides. Following the lines as they would continue downwards, it is possible to join them with the outermost vertical framing lines enclosing the pair of Chantilly saints. The faces of the Ashmolean Virgin and Child and Chantilly Jerome and Baptist are all described with the same teardrop-shaped head and quick-dash notation for eyes, nose and mouth. Both sheets are drawn in pen and brown ink, with brown wash. They share Parmigianino's swirling calligraphic lines to describe drapery and softly curved scalloped limbs. The light falls from the right in both drawings, with dappled placement of wash to render the dramatic play of light and dark.

This reunited composition shows Parmigianino's attempts to arrange the required figures within a triangular format, with the Virgin and Child at the apex and the two saints forming the base below. It can therefore be placed at an early stage of the design process, alongside the British Museum study. In both, the Christ Child is held to the Virgin's left, with her right arm reaching across her torso to steady him. In the Chantilly study, both the Baptist and Jerome kneel facing outwards. The Baptist lunges forward, his left arm draped nonchalantly over his thigh, his right curved upwards. Jerome nestles his head in his hand, dozing off into the sleep that will eventually render him recumbent on the ground. The pose recalls that of the philosopher Heraclitus in Raphael's *School of Athens*, hunched moodily over his knees (fig. 26).[3] Suggestive of reclusive interiority, it demonstrates how the idea of Jerome in a subliminal state formed part of Parmigianino's early thinking for the composition and was not only a practical consequence of reducing this figure in scale to accommodate the narrow panel.

## The Paper and Mount

The Ashmolean drawing has been laid down onto a secondary support that now cannot be removed, and the original reverse is concealed. The chain and laid lines are visible under transmitted light, although the vertical, widely spaced chain lines belong in fact to the mount paper; it is not possible to see those of the original drawing.[4] Transmitted light also reveals a fragmentary watermark on the Chantilly sheet (fig. 27). There is no visible trace of watermark on the Ashmolean sheet where one would expect it to continue.[5] However, the Baptist's

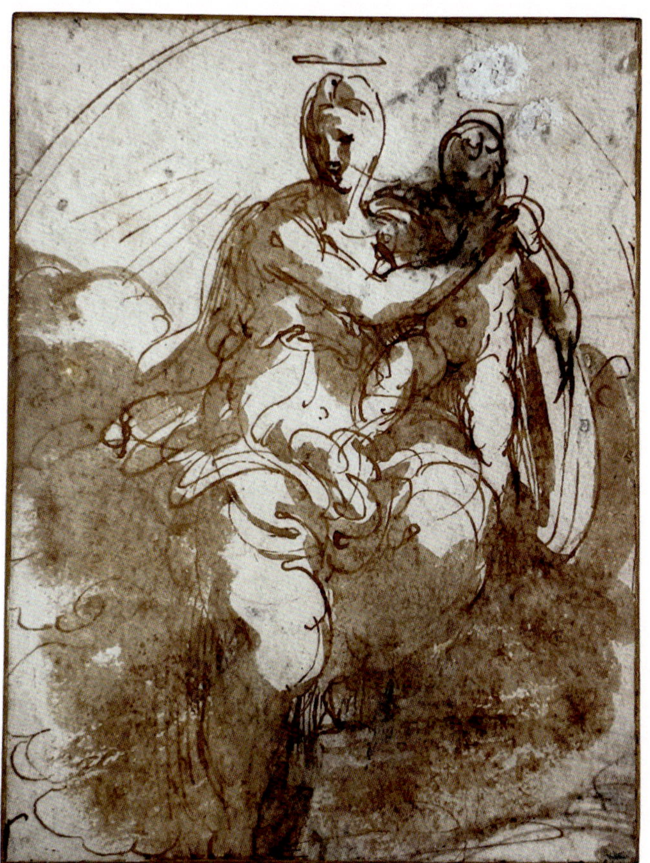

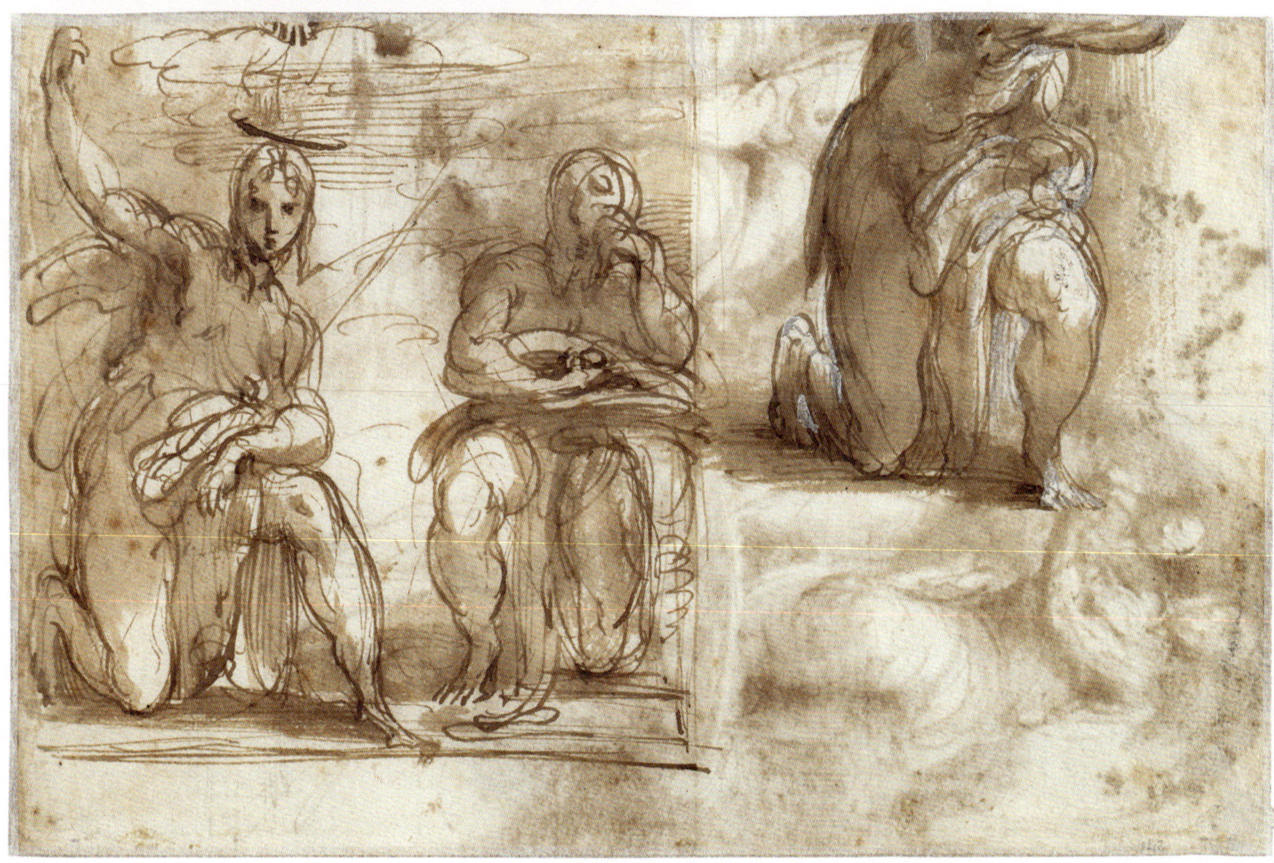

Fig. 24
Reconstruction of the Ashmolean–Chantilly composition

(top) *The Virgin and Child* (recto), 1526
The Ashmolean Museum, University of Oxford (WA1949.212)

(bottom) *Three Studies of Saints* (verso), 1526
Musée Condé, Chantilly (inv. 142)

**Fig. 25**
Reconstruction of the Ashmolean-Chantilly composition

(top) *The Virgin and Child* (verso), 1526,
in transmitted light
The Ashmolean Museum, University of Oxford (WA1949.212)

(bottom) *Two Studies of the Virgin and Child* (recto), 1526
Musée Condé, Chantilly (inv. 142)


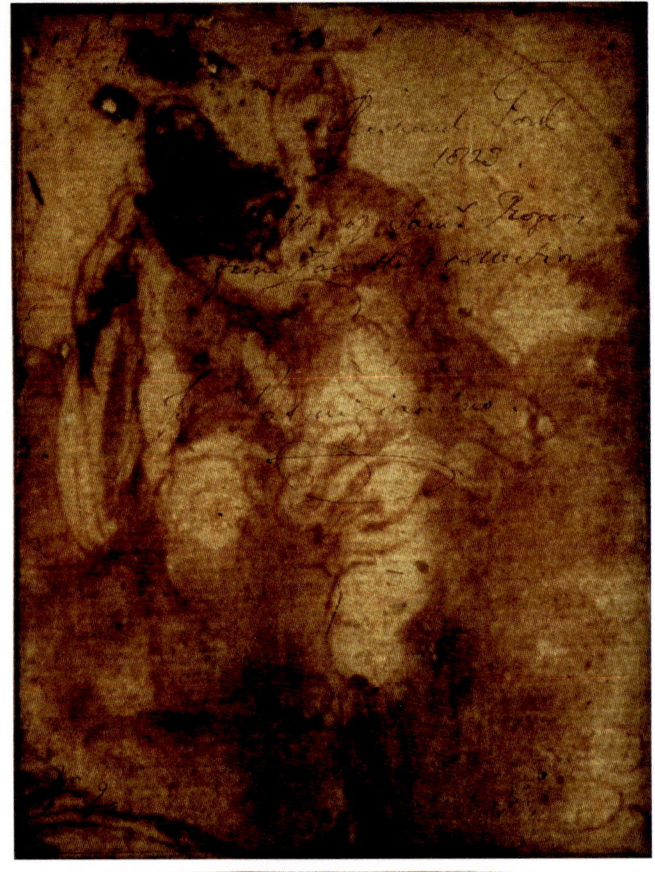

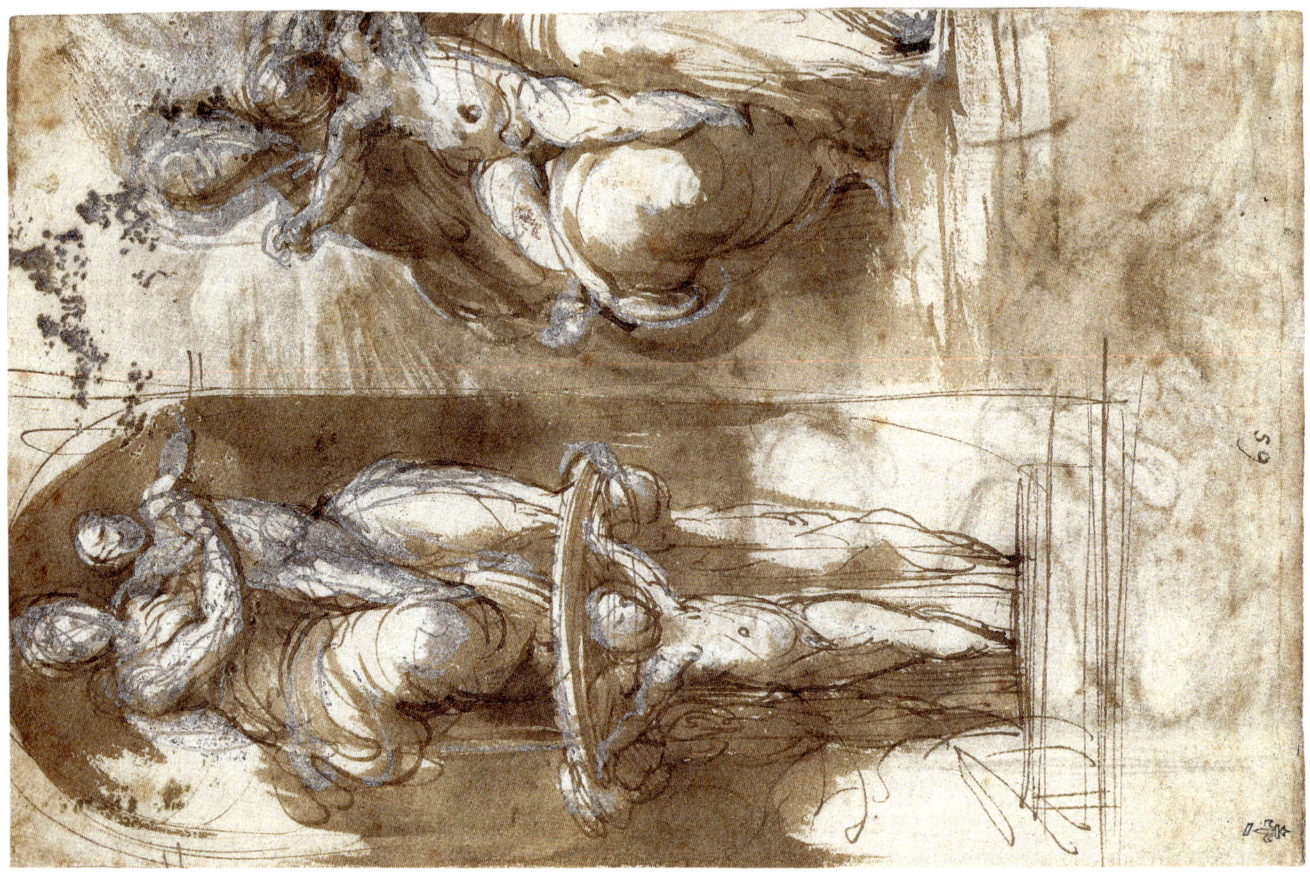

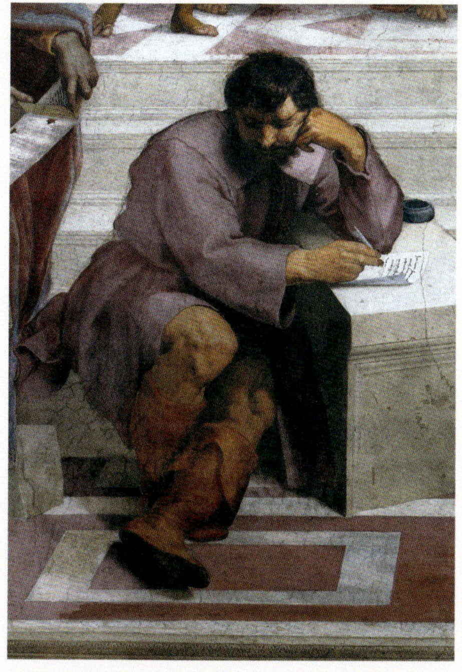

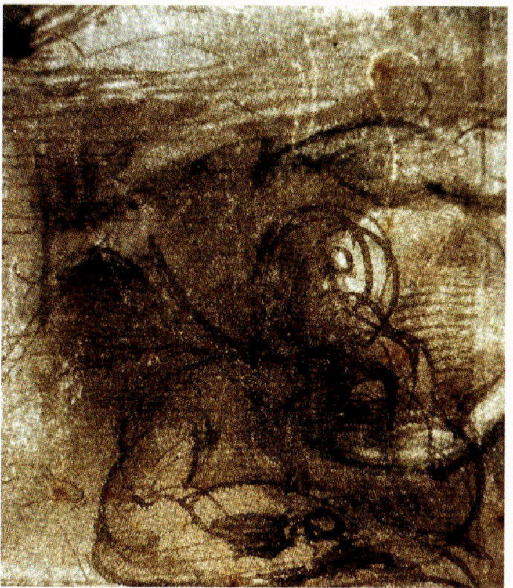

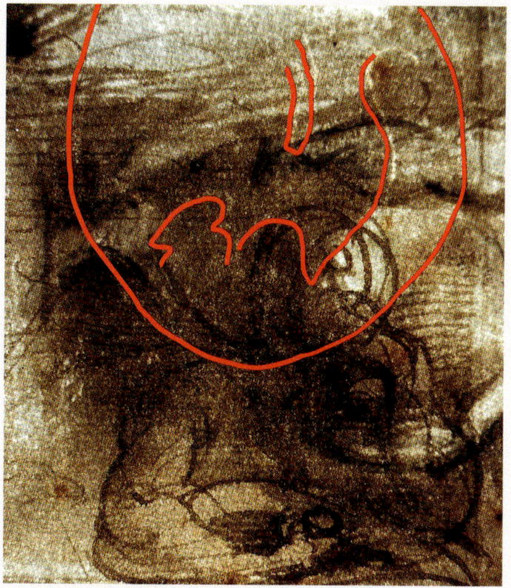

**Fig. 26** (left)
Raphael (1483–1520)
Heraclitus in *The School of Athens*, 1511
Fresco
Stanza della Segnatura, Vatican Palace, Vatican City

**Fig. 27** (above)
The Chantilly watermark in transmitted light (left);
watermark outlined (right).

extended pointed finger is also missing, indicating that the sheet must have been trimmed at the point of separation. The watermark measures 40 millimetres in diameter and as the majority of it appears on the Chantilly half, this suggests that the remaining sliver was lost when the sheet was cut.

With the naked eye it is possible to see a group of oblong looped lines in the lower right corner of the Ashmolean recto. Examination under magnification confirms that these lines are not present on the surface of the paper and instead appear to be drawn on the verso.[6] They appear smooth and flowing, which suggests they were made with an aqueous medium, presumably iron gall ink. Over time, the ink has been absorbed by the paper and today shows through on the recto. Ending at the edge of the sheet, these lines presumably continued part of another drawing, before the sheet was cut.

Turning to the recto of the Chantilly sheet, this depicts two studies for the Virgin and Child: the pair on the left shows the Virgin seated with knees slightly angled to the right within a niche, atop a type of pedestal supported by putti or angels; on the right, she is seated with hips facing forward, one foot placed in front of the other (pl. 6r). This right-hand group is now cropped where the sheet has been trimmed. When the Ashmolean verso is viewed in transmitted light, it is clear that the looping lines correspond with and continue the missing fall of drapery from the lower left leg of the Chantilly Virgin (fig. 25).

### The Shared History

The Ashmolean and Chantilly sheets share the same early provenance. Both can be traced to Thomas Howard, Earl of Arundel (1585–1646), one of the most important British collectors.[7] The earl's Parmigianino drawings were believed to be those notoriously stolen from the artist by Antonio da Trento (active 1527–1540s) after the Sack of Rome in 1527.[8] In 1720, the esteemed Venetian collector, dealer and connoisseur Antonio Maria Zanetti the Elder (1680–1767) travelled to London specifically to search for Italian old master prints and drawings.[9] He came across the Arundel Parmigianino drawings, one of the greatest finds of his career. The earl's son wished to sell, so Zanetti seized on the opportunity to acquire all of the approximately 130 drawings.[10]

After Zanetti's death, his heirs began to sell off the collection. The Parmigianino drawings were widely renowned and attracted the attention of eager collectors.[11] Two figures in particular seeking to secure these drawings were the Venetian collector and dealer Giovanni Antonio Armano (active 1777–1823) and the French diplomat and first director of the Louvre, Dominique-Vivant Denon (1747–1825). Between late 1788 and early 1789, Denon acquired around 40 of the Zanetti Parmigianino drawings, including the Chantilly sheet. Later that year, Armano succeeded in purchasing some of Zanetti's remaining drawings, including the Ashmolean *Virgin and Child*.[12] It is plausible that the sheet was cut at the time of the sale, with the intention of dividing it into individual studies that would be more appealing to collectors.

Despite the limitations of technical evidence posed by the Ashmolean secondary support mount, the coherence of the composition and the continuity of drawn line across the two sheets, as well as the shared provenance, nonetheless suggest the intriguing connection between them.[13]

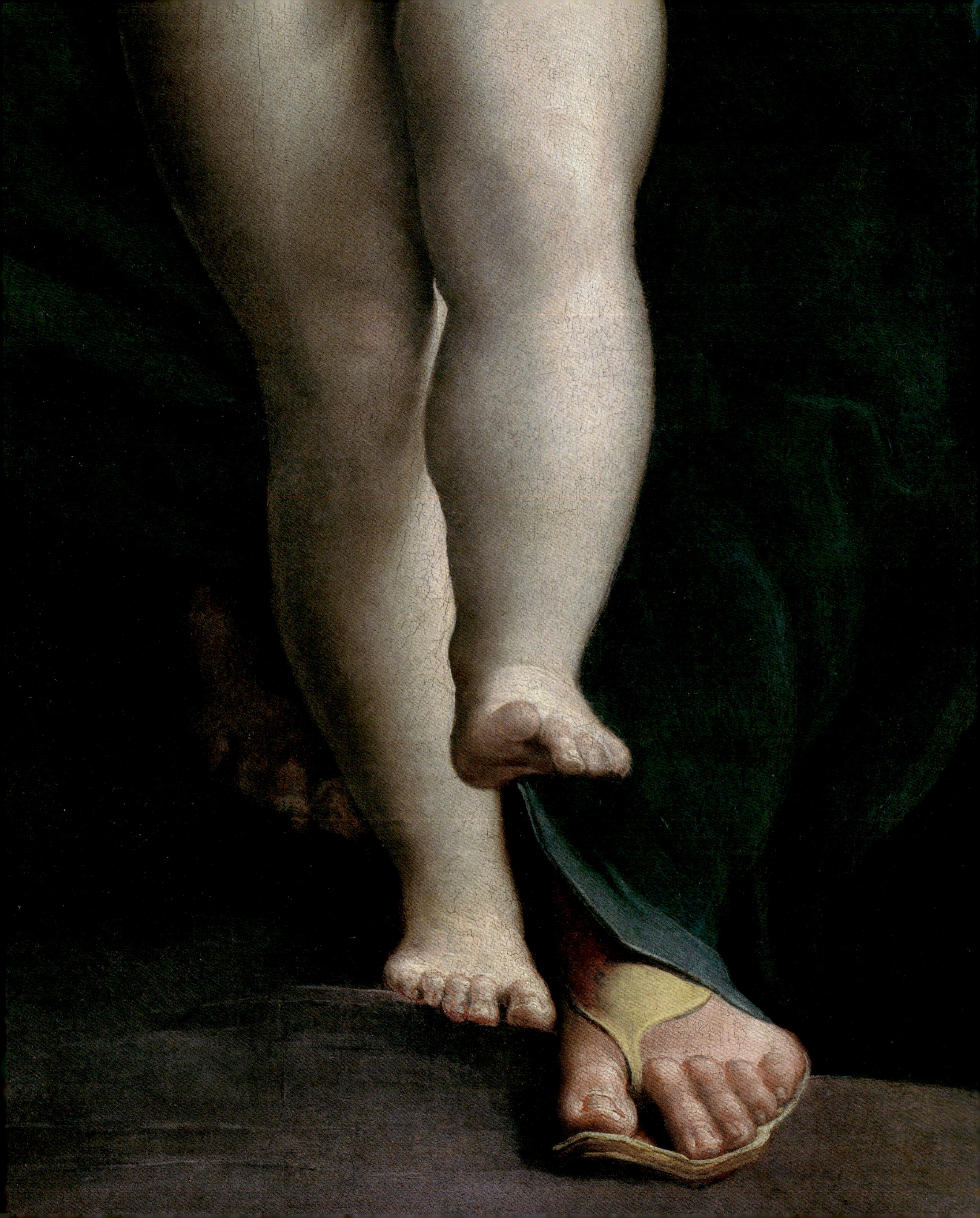

# FROM ROME TO LONDON

**MARIA ALAMBRITIS**

On 15 July 1528, soon after Charles V's nine-month occupation of Rome had ended, Maria Bufalini drew up her will. Among the property and possessions allocated to various family members, she instructed her heirs to pay the remaining fee for the painting intended for the Caccialupi Chapel and to request the painter frame and install it on the altar (see p. 84).[1] Yet Parmigianino had settled in Bologna and would not return to Rome.[2] Maria had no children to lay claim to the painting and it seems neither her Bufalini nor Caccialupi relatives took interest in restoring it to San Salvatore in Lauro. It remained in the refectory of Santa Maria della Pace, where Parmigianino's uncle had secured it for safekeeping (see p. 14). It was there, less than a decade after Parmigianino's death, that the Venetian writer and publisher Michelangelo Biondo (1497–1565) recorded seeing the 'very wonderful painting of the Madonna'.[3] At least another 30 years would pass, however, before Parmigianino's Roman masterpiece would finally be put on public display.

### Parmigianino in Città di Castello

It was Maria's great-nephew, Giulio Bufalini I (1504–1583), a noted diplomat and captain in the service of France's King François I (r. 1515–47), who arrived in Rome to retrieve the altarpiece from the Pace in 1558. By this time, the altarpiece – together with its maker – had achieved significant renown. A year after Biondo's recollection, the publication of Giorgio Vasari's first edition of his *Lives of the Artists* featured a biography of Parmigianino and discussion of the painting.[4] Giulio eschewed placement in San Salvatore in Lauro altogether, perhaps spurred by the wish to repatriate an important work of art to Bufalini family ownership. His actions inadvertently saved the painting from the fire that destroyed the interior of the church in 1591.

From the grandeur and bustle of Rome, Parmigianino's painting travelled to the picturesque Umbrian city of Città di Castello, which lies enveloped in the verdant expanse of the Upper Tiber Valley.[5] There, Giulio had it installed in the Bufalini Chapel in the church of Sant'Agostino in August 1558.[6] The chapel was located in a primary position, in the transept to the right of the altar.[7] The painting was displayed in a 'majestic golden ornament [frame], accompanied all around with various figures of Prophets … and various Arms of the House of Bufalini intertwined with those of the Vitelleschi of Corneto'.[8] The latter was the family into which Giulio's sister Maddalena had married, which suggests that the painting may have been repurposed to commemorate this union.

Once transferred to Sant'Agostino, it wielded an impact on artists in Urbino almost immediately. Federico Barocci (1533–1612), who likely saw the painting during a visit to Perugia in 1567–9, and local artist Giovanni Battista Pacetti (1593–1670) both drew on the figure of the Baptist as a model.[9] At least one other full-size copy was produced.[10] In 1627, the local Franciscan Angelo Conti affirmed there was 'never enough praise' for the painting.[11] In Sant'Agostino, it was in the company of other much-admired pictures, including Raphael's Baronci Altarpiece (1500–1; later dismembered, surviving only in fragments) and Luca Signorelli's *Adoration of the Magi* (1493–4) and *Nativity* (about 1493).[12] After his appointment as cardinal and bishop of Ancona, Giovanni Ottavio Bufalini (1709–1782) embarked on a renovation of the Palazzo Bufalini in 1767, including the enrichment of its collection display.[13] Parmigianino's eighteenth-century biographer Ireneo Affò (1741–1797) recorded that by the time of writing, the Caccialupi Altarpiece was 'already reduced to a deplorable state' and 'rather rotting and flaking'.[14] This may well have informed Cardinal Bufalini's decision to transfer the original to the family palazzo around 1772, replacing it with a copy in Sant'Agostino.[15]

### Arrival in England

Once more, the Caccialupi Altarpiece escaped ruin when on 30 September 1789 an earthquake destroyed the church of Sant'Agostino. Shortly after the Bufalini heirs sold the work to the English history painter James Durno (about 1745–1795), who also acted as an art agent in Rome.[16] Durno soon found a buyer in John James Hamilton, first Marquess of Abercorn (1756–1818), who purchased the painting for 1,500 guineas.[17] The latter's cousin, Sir William Hamilton (1730–1803), negotiated the sale on his behalf. In December 1791, Durno wrote to confirm the painting had reached Livorno and was ready to be shipped to London:

Detail from fig. 9

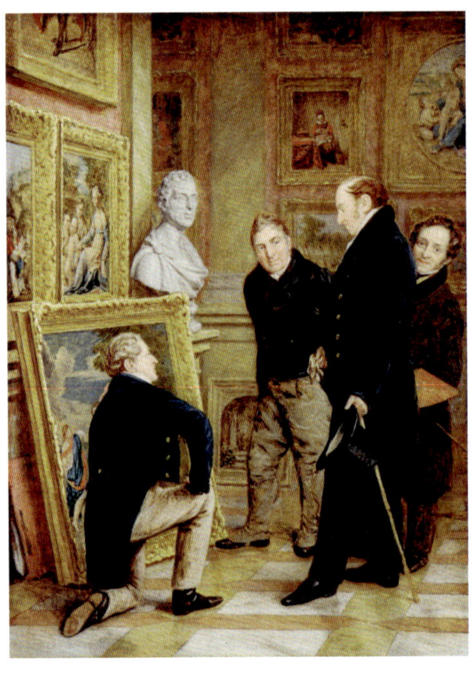



> Sir believe me when this Picture was remov'd from my
> appointments I was Malencholy [*sic*] for some time and
> lamented my situation of being oblig'd to part with so fine a
> Picture … it is universally esteemed one of the finest pictures
> that has been sent to England where I hope it will arrive safe.[18]

The sale was the subject of discussion among the cognoscenti.
The art collector Sir Abraham Hume (1749–1838) wrote that
'an English gentleman has finally purchased a most beautiful
painting by Parmigianino, which a few years ago formed an
altarpiece at a convent of a city not far from Perugia'.[19] The
departure of the work from Città di Castello was keenly felt, as
attested by continuous reference in local guidebooks and art
publications. Almost 30 years after the sale, it was described
as a 'celebrated painting' that was sold for the 'outlandish price of
7,700 piastre', the author asserting that 'in the opinion of anyone
half-intelligent, Parmigianino never made a more beautiful work'.[20]

The number of Parmigianino paintings then in England
demonstrates his popularity among wealthy collectors and
connoisseurs. The *Pallas Athene* (about 1531–8) in the Royal
Collection was presented to King Charles II in 1660; a *Madonna
and Child* acquired by Nathaniel Curzon in 1758 hung at
Kedleston Manor (about 1529);[21] the *Saturn and Philyra* (early
1530s) painted for Francesco Baiardo, the artist's principal patron
in Parma, was owned by Joshua Reynolds until 1791 and passed
through the hands of distinguished collections, including those
of John Julius Angerstein and Ramsay Reinagle RA;[22] and the
*Virgin and Child with Saint John the Baptist and Mary Magdalene*
(about 1535–40) graced Sudeley Castle.[23]

This last painting was inherited by George Watson Taylor
(1771–1841) and his wife, Anna Susannah Taylor. In 1815, Anna
had acquired huge wealth on the death of her uncle, Simon
Taylor, who own several large plantations worked by enslaved
labourers in Jamaica. The Watson Taylors' subsequent
management of these plantations provided the profits by which
they built up one of the most significant private art collections
of the time, which was displayed in their London townhouse in
Cavendish Square.[24] By 1819, this included his purchase of the
Caccialupi Altarpiece.[25] That same year, the painting was

exhibited publicly in England for the first time when Watson
Taylor lent it to the British Institution.[26] Pieter Christoffel Wonder's
(1780–1852) *Study for 'Patrons and Lovers of Art'* featured the
Sudeley Madonna and Child (fig. 28). Commissioned in
celebration of the various benefactors who had contributed to
the foundation of the National Gallery in 1824, it depicts Watson
Taylor kneeling in front of Titian's *Bacchus and Ariadne* (1520–3).[27]
To the immediate right is the Reverend William Holwell Carr
(1758–1830), who was instrumental in securing the Caccialupi
Altarpiece for the national collection. Carr purchased the work
on behalf of the British Institution at the sale of Watson Taylor's
collection, on 14 June 1823, where it fetched the highest price
of the sale at £3,202, exceeding even that of Rubens's *Rainbow
Landscape* (about 1636).[28] The purchase was acknowledged in
the press as 'more than worth any sum that a further competition
might have advanced it to'. However, Parmigianino's painting
was seen to stand out mostly for its 'theatrical' aesthetic merits
and 'surprising force', and deemed 'a production of one of the
most successful followers in the track of M. Angelo, Rafaelle,
and Correggio', suggesting a shift in the tide of taste.[29]

## Parmigianino and Nineteenth-Century Art Critics

Parmigianino's drawings and prints were always much coveted
by collectors and connoisseurs.[30] Yet by the mid-nineteenth
century, when the idealised serenity of Raphael and grandeur of
Michelangelo were admired as the zenith of sixteenth-century
art, Parmigianino's style was often perceived as too idiosyncratic
for contemporary tastes. This was particularly noticeable in the
negative comparison made between Parmigianino and his fellow
Emilian master, Correggio, who then enjoyed enormous popularity.

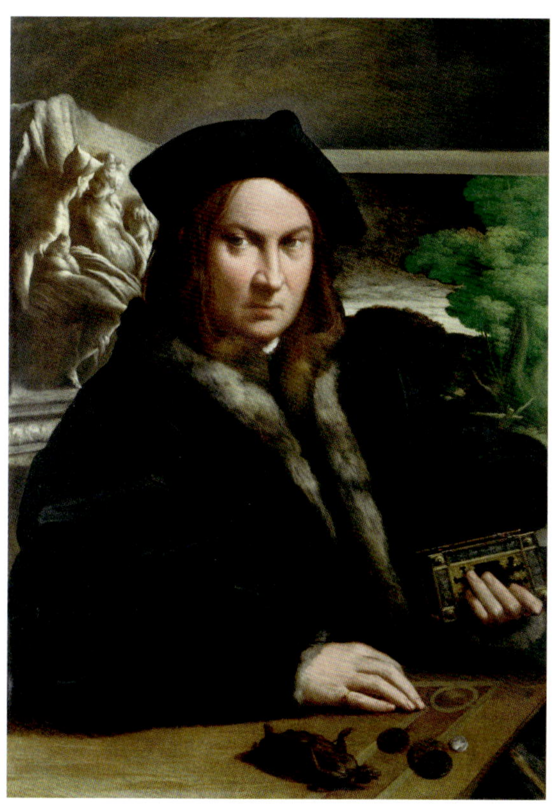

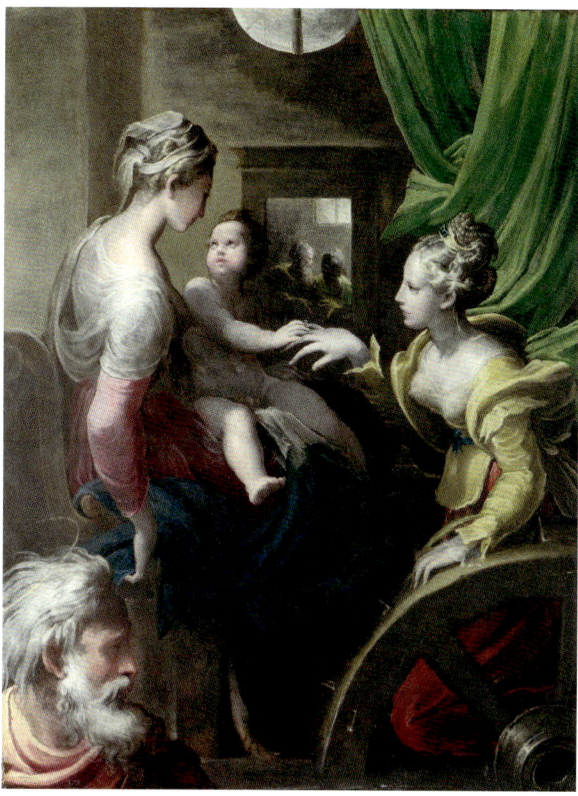



Despite Vasari's clear favouring of Parmigianino as a herald of the new *bella maniera* alongside Leonardo and Raphael, he would be reduced to a second-class status in this period.[31]

In regards to the Caccialupi Altarpiece, the sleeping figure of Saint Jerome was one cause of particular consternation. Throughout its critical reception prior to its removal from Italy, the painting was referred to in Italian literature as Parmigianino's painting of 'San Giovanni Battista'.[32] However, as noted in 1897 in local historian Giovanni Margherini-Graziani's (1852–1924) guide to Città di Castello, the painting was by then 'generally recognised [as]… the Vision of Saint Jerome'.[33] The origin of this much-debated latter title resulted from the change of audience and function for the painting. As an altarpiece commissioned for a funerary chapel, the patron saint of the deceased – to whom Parmigianino gave prominence over Jerome – wielded significance. Removed from its familial connection and placed in a gallery, the unusual presence of the sleeping Jerome came to dominate discussion and interpretation.

The opinions of two respected authorities on art written only three years apart capture the painting's changing fortunes. In his *Descriptive Catalogue of the National Gallery* (1833), the author and collector William Young Ottley (1771–1836) described the painting as 'sublimely conceived' and 'perhaps a work of more genius, and in a greater style, than any that the artist afterwards produced'.[34] Ottley was an important advocate for Parmigianino, having purchased around 1800 the artist's *Portrait of a Collector*

and *The Mystic Marriage of Saint Catherine*, both now in the National Gallery (figs 29, 30).[35] However, the noted German art historian Johann David Passavant (1787–1861) dismissed the painting in his *Tour of a German Artist in England* (1836) for its 'stiff and highly mannered vision' of 'distorted figure[s]' and 'unpicturesque attitudes', its fame 'more attributable to its defects than to its beauties'.[36]

The then-leading Anglo-Irish art writer Anna Jameson (1794–1860) found a conscientious middle ground between the two. Both well informed on the current opinions of her art critic counterparts on the continent and dedicated to educating and engaging a mostly Anglophone Protestant audience on the works of Italian painters, she posited:

> This picture is an eminent example of all the beauties and faults of Parmigiano [*sic*]. The Madonna and the Child are models of dignity and grace … the play of the lights and shadows, in delicate management, worthy of Correggio: on the other hand, the attitude of St John the Baptist … is altogether forced and theatrical; while the foreshortened figure of St Jerome in the background is most uncomfortably distorted. Notwithstanding these faults, the picture has always been much celebrated.[37]

Jameson's account captured the general attitude towards artist and painting for much of the nineteenth century. The altarpiece was certainly studied with great interest by British artists. John Constable (1776–1837), for example, described its striking power in his first encounter with it in 1814: 'I have never seen any picture (not a landscape) that had so much the power of taking me from the present scene – it is entirely enthusiasm'.[38] According to the tenets of early nineteenth-century British art practice, however, this 'enthusiasm' rendered the painting unsuitable as an example to follow. In his second lecture at the Royal Academy, Henry Fuseli (1741–1825) warned that the elegance characteristic of Parmigianino's art was 'nearly always obtained at the expense of proportion'.[39]

The dismissal voiced by the American art historian Clara Erskine Waters (1834–1916) in her popular art *Handbook* characterised the fall from grace that both artist and painting had suffered by the end of the century:

> Perhaps the best that can be said of [Parmigianino] is, that he was the most excellent of the imitators of Correggio. His religious subjects are not enjoyable … The 'Vision of S. Jerome', in the National Gallery, is one of his celebrated works, and is open to much criticism.[40]

The noted connoisseur and dealer Bernard Berenson (1865–1959) allowed Parmigianino 'but a word' in his monograph *North Italian Painters* (1907), criticising him for exhibiting 'too overmastering a bent for elegance'.[41] His response was typical of the pejorative reception of artists associated with the style that came to be known as *maniera* or Mannerism. By the seventeenth century, such artists were disparaged for 'abandoning the study of nature' in their conscious cultivation of individual style, the results of which were deemed artificial, distorted and antithetical to good practice.[42] In his *Storia Pittorica della Italia* (1795–6), Luigi Lanzi (1732–1810) split the development of sixteenth-century Italian art in two, ostracising those artists working in the wake of Leonardo, Michelangelo and Raphael as symptomatic of the decline of art. The distaste for this period of art would continue into the twentieth century.[43]

**Towards the 'Modern Manner'**

It was not until the publication of the first monograph on the artist, *Parmigianino und der Manierismus* (*Parmigianino and Mannerism*; completed in 1918 and published in 1921), by the German art historian Lili Fröhlich-Bum (1886–1981), that work to recuperate the artist's reputation began.[44] Fröhlich-Bum

attributed to Parmigianino the creation of a new ideal of beauty, of 'easy grace, perfection of limbs and spirituality of expression'.[45] She rooted this development in Parmigianino's attention to the elongated forms and linear purity of antique art, anticipating the landmark publications of Craig Hugh Smyth and John Shearman, for whom Mannerism 'first reared its beautiful head in Rome about 1520'.[46]

In his Preface to the third part of the *Lives*, Giorgio Vasari expressed his idea of the *maniera moderna* or 'modern manner' of painting, as emerging in the work of sixteenth-century artists and setting them apart from what had come before.[47] Artists such as Leonardo, Giorgione (1473/4–1510), Raphael, Andrea del Sarto (1486–1530) and Correggio distinguished themselves from their predecessors through the manifest display of *grazia* (grace) in their artworks.[48] This quality was associated more frequently with Parmigianino than any other of his contemporaries. In his *Dialogue of Painting* of 1557, the Venetian man of letters Ludovico Dolce (1508–1568) drew on Vasari's concept, transmuting grace into *vaghezza*, an alluring beauty inherent in Parmigianino's art, which 'made anyone who looked upon it fall in love with it'.[49] In Vasari's reading, this sensual overload of *maniera* marked the shift of painting from a mechanical practice replicating the natural world to a divinely inspired medium for spiritual connection and transformation. The qualities of vividness, variety and individuality inherent in *maniera* imbued images with a living presence that could provoke an audience's empathetic participation and exert spiritual transformation.[50]

Having survived a war, a fire and an earthquake, Parmigianino's Roman masterpiece exhibits in both its facture and its history the marvellous diligence for which the painter was renowned.[51] Parmigianino's sensibility for tapered extremities to intensify the harmony of pose and gesture, his refinement of ornamental detail and his silvered chromatic palette, as well as his sophisticated play of space and perspective to enhance the emotive impact of the painting, demand our active engagement rather than quiet contemplation. As the painting returns to public display after a decade, this is a moment to celebrate its significance and to enable a new generation of viewers to encounter, and become enamoured with, the transformative 'light of grace' of Parmigianino's art.[52]

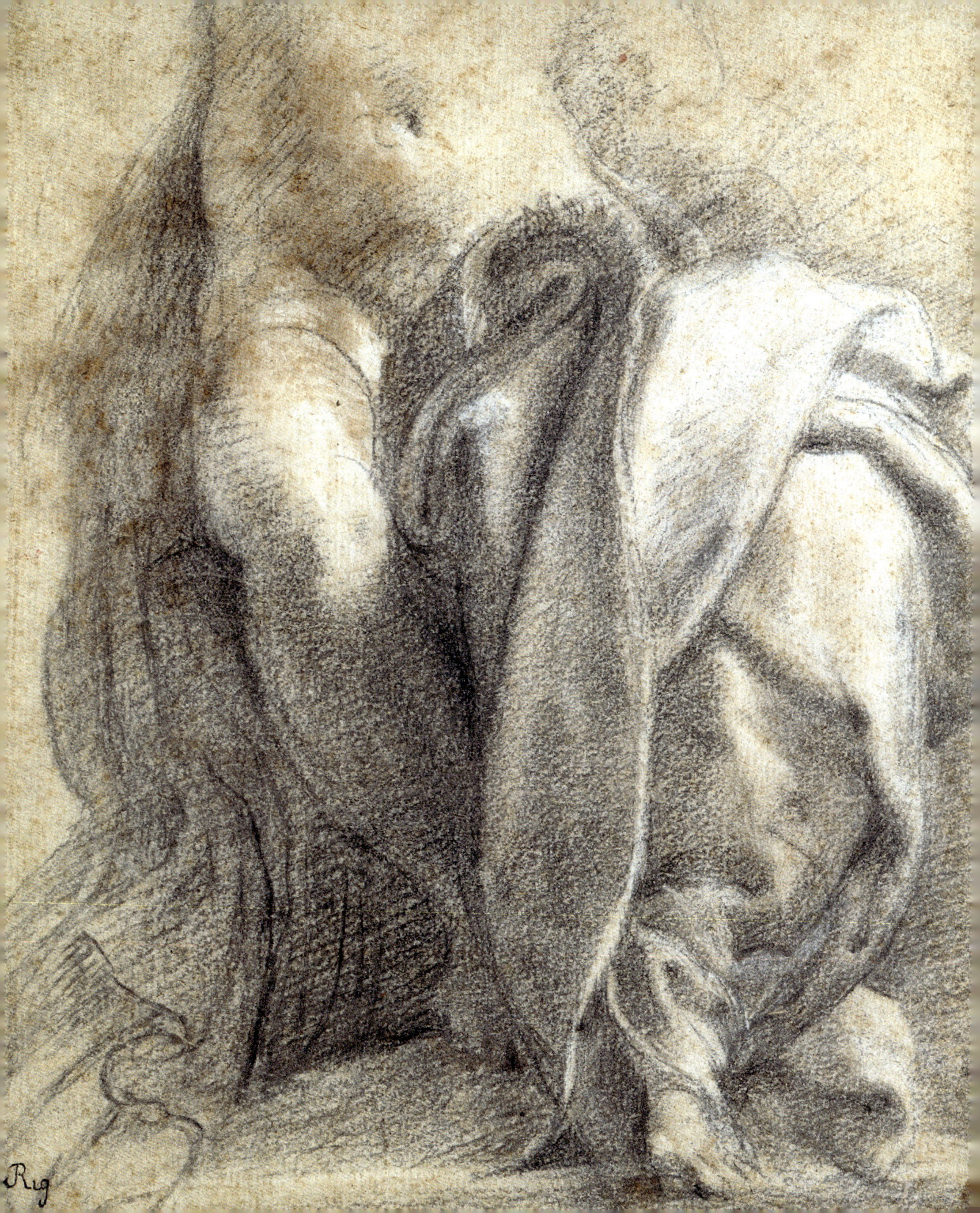
Rig

# RESTORATION, CONSTRUCTION AND PAINTING TECHNIQUE

**LARRY KEITH**

Parmigianino's great panel for the Caccialupi Altarpiece was among the first works added to the nascent National Gallery collection and remains among the most monumental works of the Roman Renaissance within it. The painting's recent conservation treatment has allowed us to consider anew the artist's methods and materials. The panel stands nearly 3.5 metres tall. It was constructed from seven rather narrow poplar planks which run the full height of the work, reinforced by three original dovetailed cross-grain pine battens.[1] Given all the movements it experienced before entering the National Gallery, it is not surprising that at some stage the panel seems to have got very damp, and almost certainly suffered other extreme shifts of temperature and relative humidity (see p. 43). These have resulted in several local areas of loss of paint caused by movement of the wooden support in response to those shifts – though the surviving paint, which is by far the greater part of the image, remains in excellent state for a work of this date.

Remarkably, the panel reverse retains its cross-grain battens and original roughly hewn surface (fig. 31). The recent structural treatment consisted of removing several pieces of timber which had been added to the reverse in a misguided attempt to reinforce it, followed by a campaign of realignment and glueing of old splits and joins and re-establishing more free movement of the original dovetailed battens.

There are three documented campaigns of cleaning since the painting came to the Gallery, and it is presumed that these were preceded by other treatments during the nearly three centuries between the painting's creation and its acquisition by the Gallery. Perhaps daunted by the scale of the undertaking, previous restoration campaigns often reused existing larger-scale retouchings from previous treatments, working on top of them and producing ever larger areas of restoration – some of which were rather crudely applied. The panel was last cleaned in 1938, and so the yellowing of the varnish applied then and the poor cumulative effect of the expanded old retouchings led to the latest decision to restore the work – this time also painstakingly removing the majority of the accumulated older retouching layers.

While most of the damage to the original paint was localised and straightforward to retouch, there were areas of loss extensive enough to require some degree of reconstruction during the restoration phase – reconstructions which would require a high

**Fig. 31** Panel reverse of *The Vision of Saint Jerome* after restoration.

**Fig. 32** *The Vision of Saint Jerome* with new frame.

**Fig. 33** X-radiograph of *The Vision of Saint Jerome*.

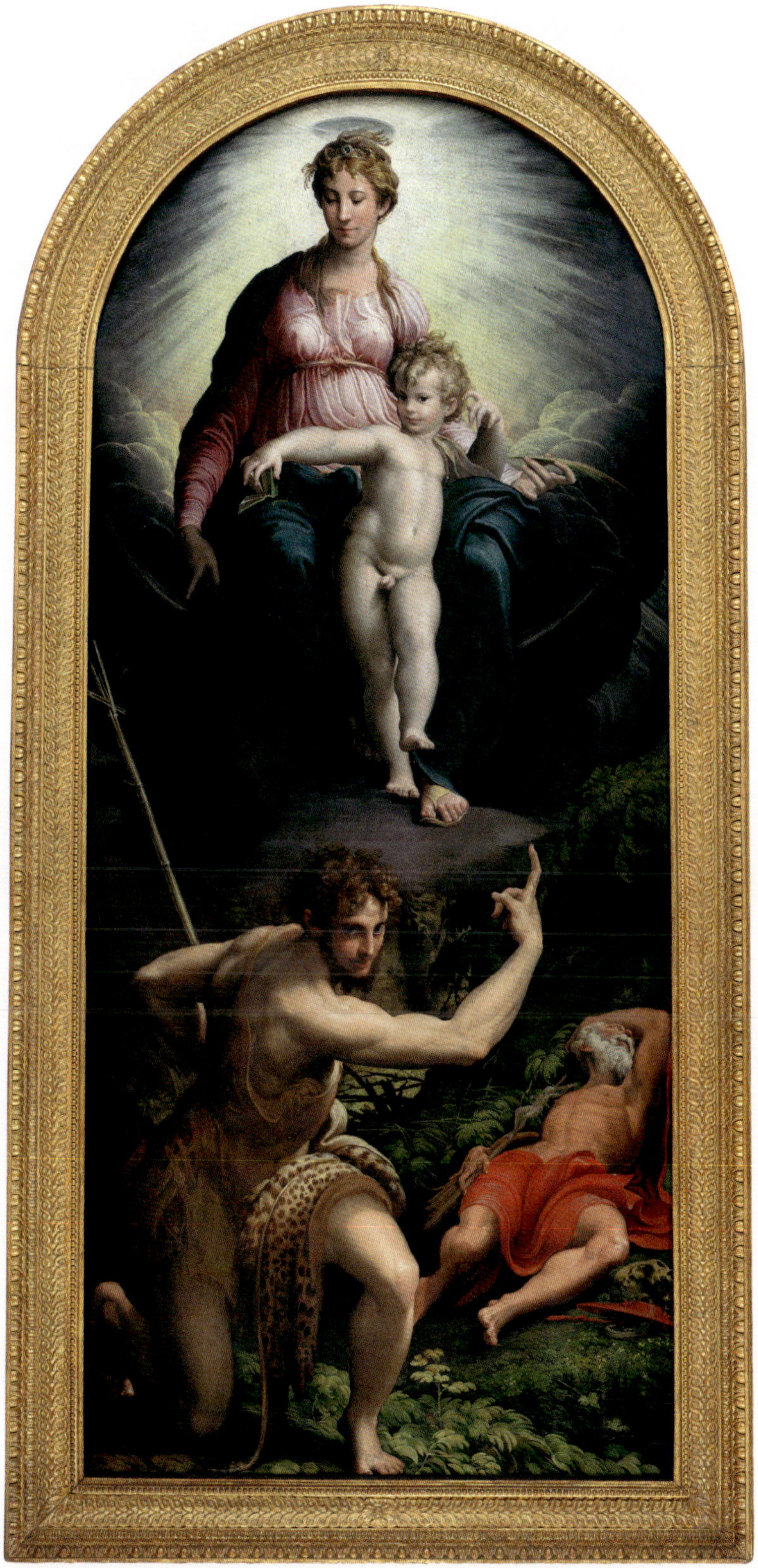

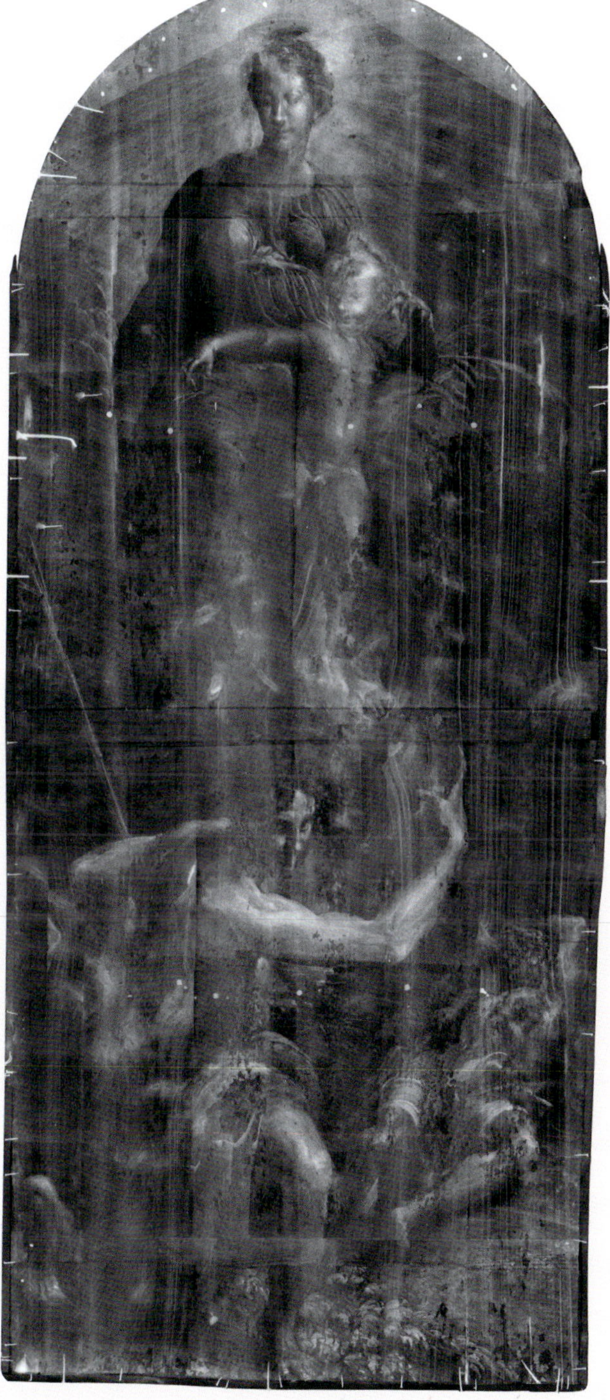

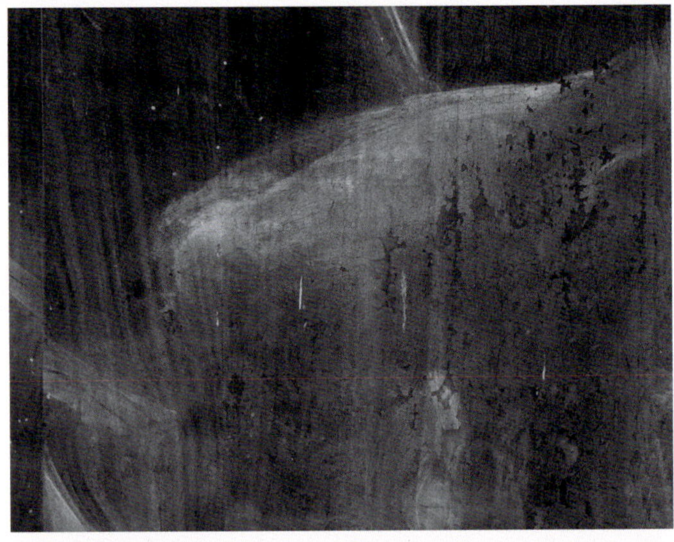

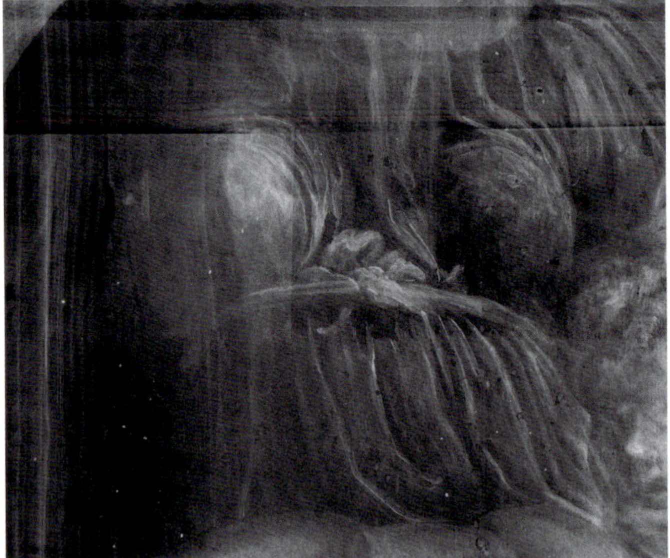

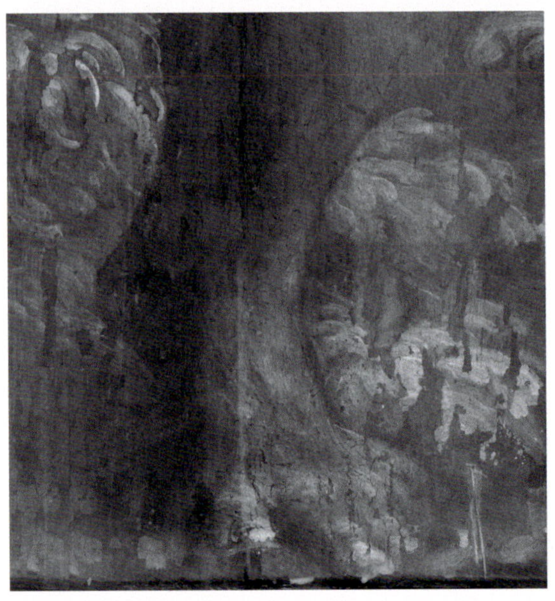

degree of finish, in keeping with the excellent state of preservation of the majority of the image. Retouching of these areas generally followed the reconstruction of the earlier restorations, refined in some areas by additional information taken from Parmigianino's related drawings, or other secondary sources such as the near-contemporary engraving made after the painting by Giulio Bonasone (about 1500/10–after 1574; fig. 37).[2]

The restored painting has been given a new frame made by the Framing Department at the National Gallery: a carved and gilded moulding based on surviving contemporary examples, a solution that suggests its original ecclesiastical setting while working within the Gallery's display (fig. 32).

Given the extraordinary invention within the composition – the radical projections and foreshortenings within the poses of the saints, and the dramatic lighting contrasts and perspectival shifts between the upper and lower tiers, elements that seem so dynamic and improvisatory – the work was made with surprisingly few major changes undertaken during the course of painting. The changes that are apparent, such as the adjustment of the pose of the Baptist's arm (fig. 34), are more revision than radical reinterpretation. Overall, the X-radiograph makes clear that by the time Parmigianino had come to paint the panel he had more or less fixed upon the composition we now see.

The lengthy process of making preliminary drawings to test his ideas and work them up, whether of specific details or larger compositional relationships, was the real crucible of Parmigianino's creativity. The complex evolutionary process from rough sketch to the transfer of a finished design to the support for painting using a full-scale cartoon was a mainstay of central Italian theoretical writing later in the century, and the trail of Parmigianino's drawings and studies associated with this painting shows his broad adherence to this method. While for *The Vision of Saint Jerome* there is no visible, physical trace of the use of full-scale cartoons, the lack of major changes, as revealed in the X-radiograph (fig. 33), and the well-defined painting reserves (unpainted areas), suggest otherwise. The landscape elements in the background, for example, are painted around the principal figures and not underneath them. This inability to see underdrawing may be in part due to the use of materials for the laying-in of the composition which are not easily detected within the paint layers. There is a full-scale drawing by Parmigianino of a bishop saint

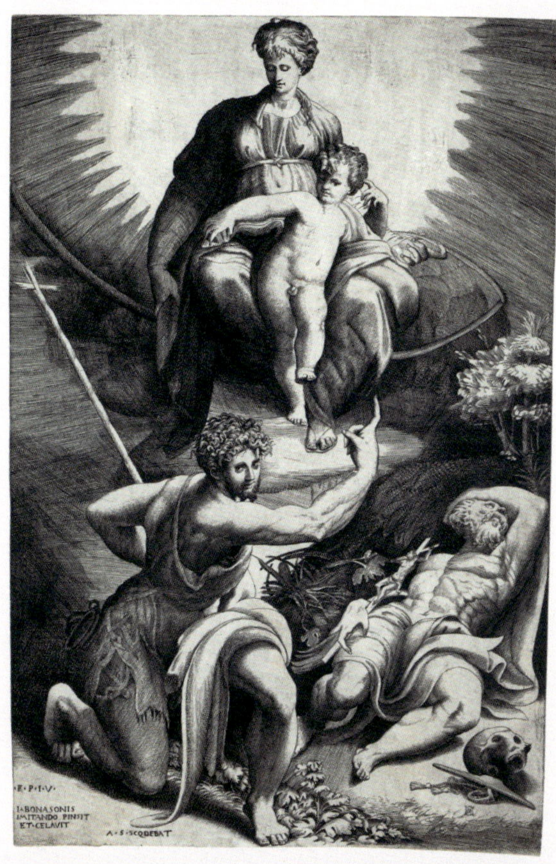

(now in the Metropolitan Museum, New York) associated with the *Saint Margaret* altarpiece in Bologna (see p. 36). The Met drawing may have been intended to have a cartoon-like function for that painting (although in the finished altarpiece the figure is significantly different from the pose depicted in the drawing), and it seems reasonable to suppose that similar drawings were made for the National Gallery panel.[3]

However thoroughly worked out the composition may have been, the paint handling itself shows a remarkably lively quality. For all the painting's debt to Parmigianino's study of the Roman Renaissance of Raphael and Michelangelo – notable in the monumental scale of the Baptist and the learned complexity of his pose – the rich colours and loaded brushwork are qualities particular to Parmigianino.

An unfinished *Virgin and Child* now in the Courtauld Gallery (fig. 38), which dates from near this time, shows him working freely on top of the darker tonal undermodelling with bold calligraphic strokes to establish the highlights, gradually building up the opacity and richness of the colour while maintaining an almost improvisatory quality to the brushwork. A slightly later work from the National Gallery, the *Mystic Marriage of Saint Catherine* (about 1527–31; see fig. 30), also demonstrates this method of the gradual refinement of a loose laying-in of light and dark values, gaining solidity and opacity as the areas are developed but maintaining the same lively handling as the forms gain solidity and mass. The darker underlayers allowed him to achieve the desired opacity relatively easily; an X-radiographic detail of the chest of the Virgin from *The Vision of Saint Jerome* shows that Parmigianino kept the freedom and surety of his handling in a highly finished work (fig. 35).

The Caccialupi Altarpiece exhibits a high degree of finish across the whole of the panel, with little trace of underlayers showing through. For the most part, the flesh paint is quite opaque, with carefully blended modelling transitions. It nonetheless keeps a typically animated surface, with bold flickering highlight strokes sitting alongside carefully blended gradations, and the dynamic, almost playful depiction of foliage where Parmigianino let his brush run most freely. He gives us a rare and pleasing combination of the extraordinary powers of invention of a born draughtsman together with a wonderful fluency with the brush.

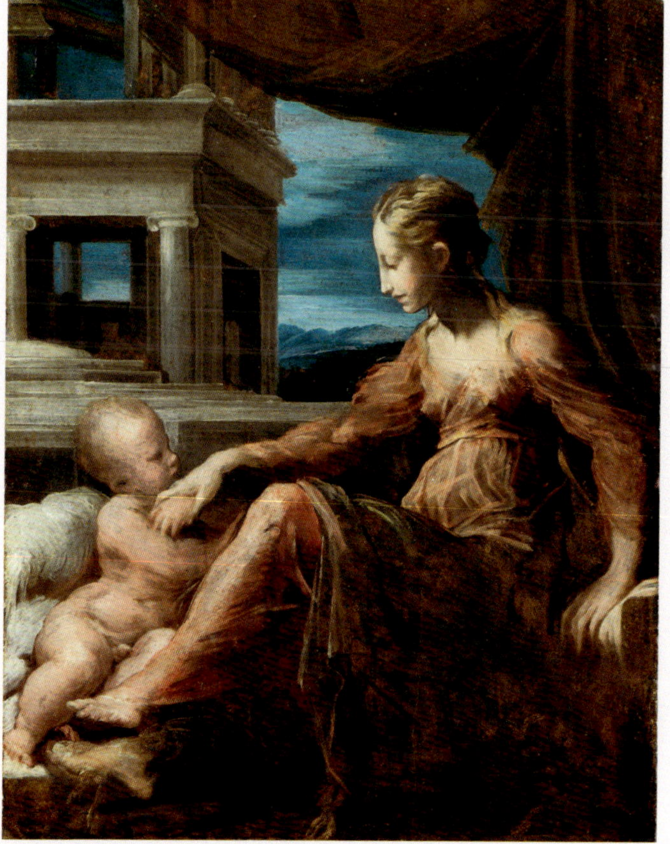

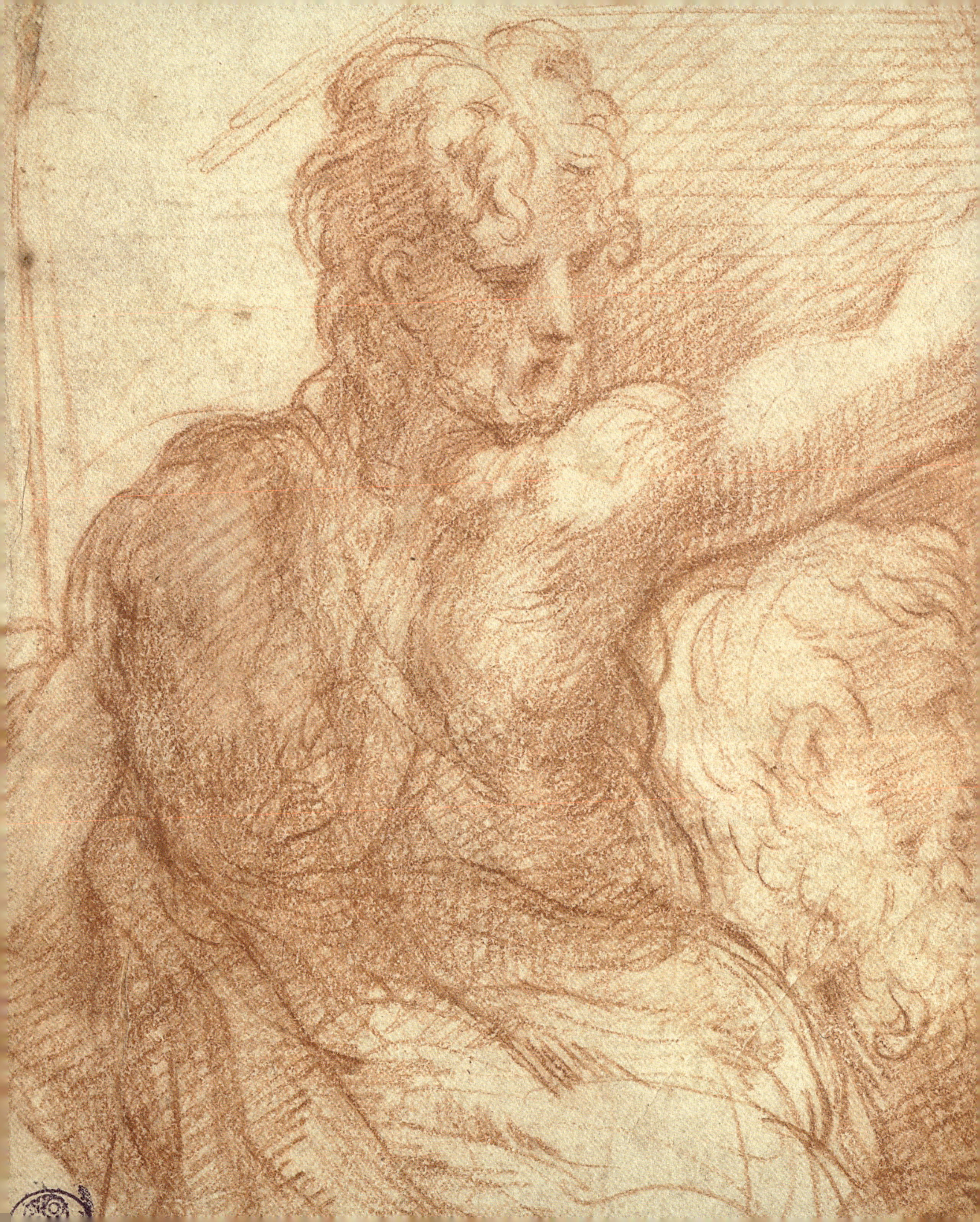

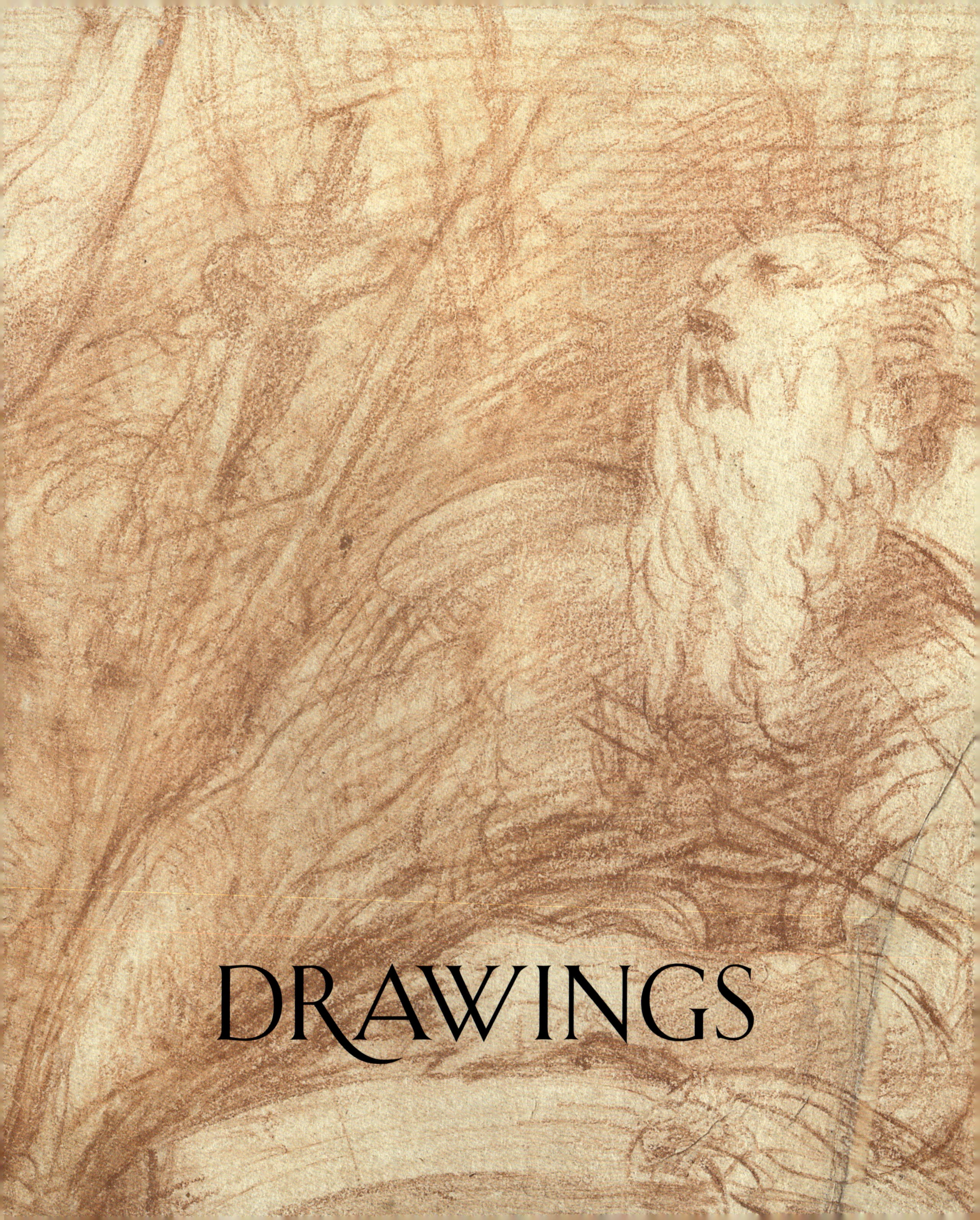
DRAWINGS

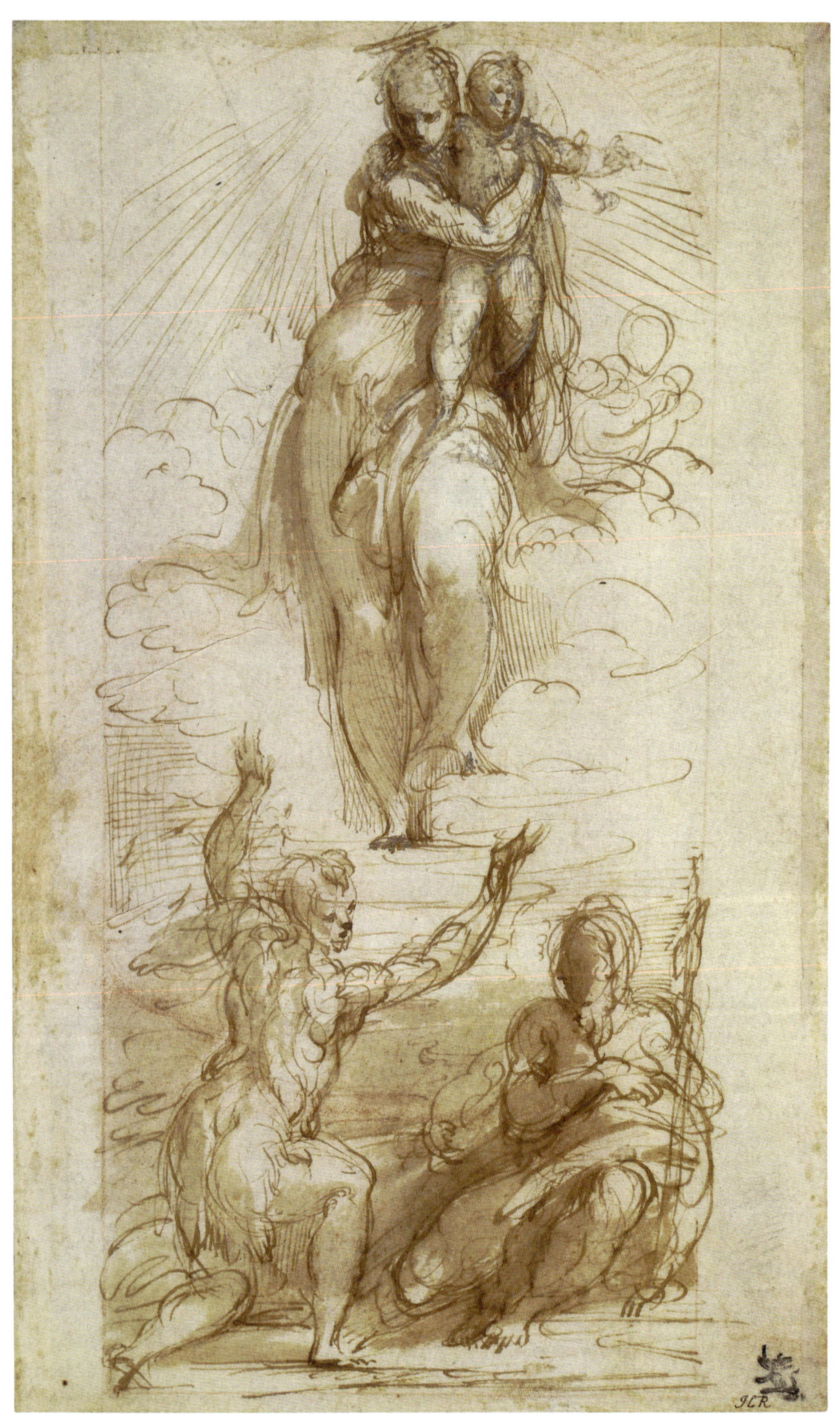



**1r**
*Study for a Composition of the Virgin
and Christ Child with Saint John
the Baptist and Saint Jerome below*
(recto), 1526

Pen and brown ink, with brown wash,
with white heightening (oxidised),
over red chalk on paper, 25.8 × 15.6 cm
British Museum, London
(1882,0812.488)

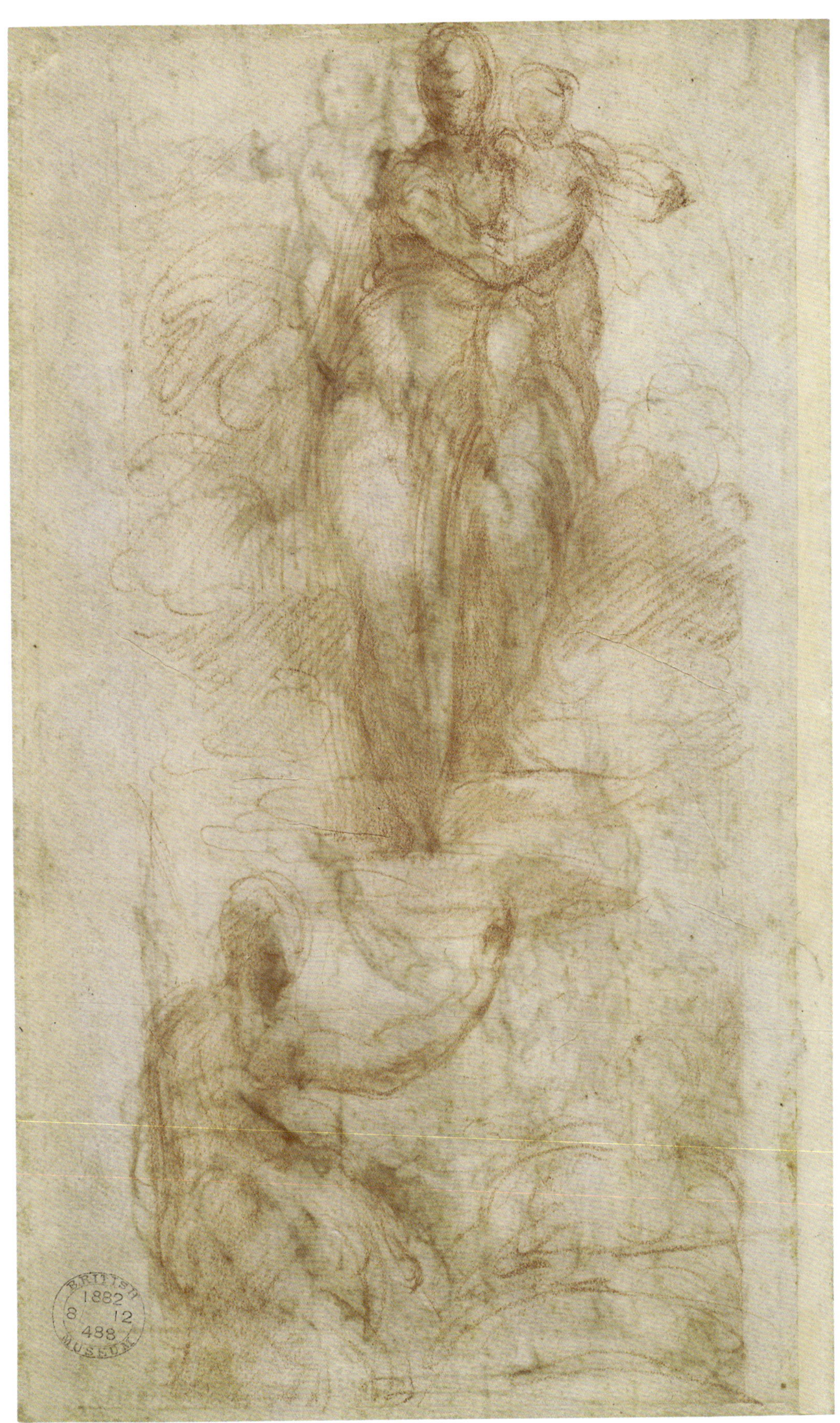



**1v**
*Study for a Composition of the Virgin
and Christ Child with Saint John
the Baptist and Saint Jerome below*
(verso), 1526

Red chalk on paper, 25.8 × 15.6 cm
British Museum, London
(1882,0812.488)

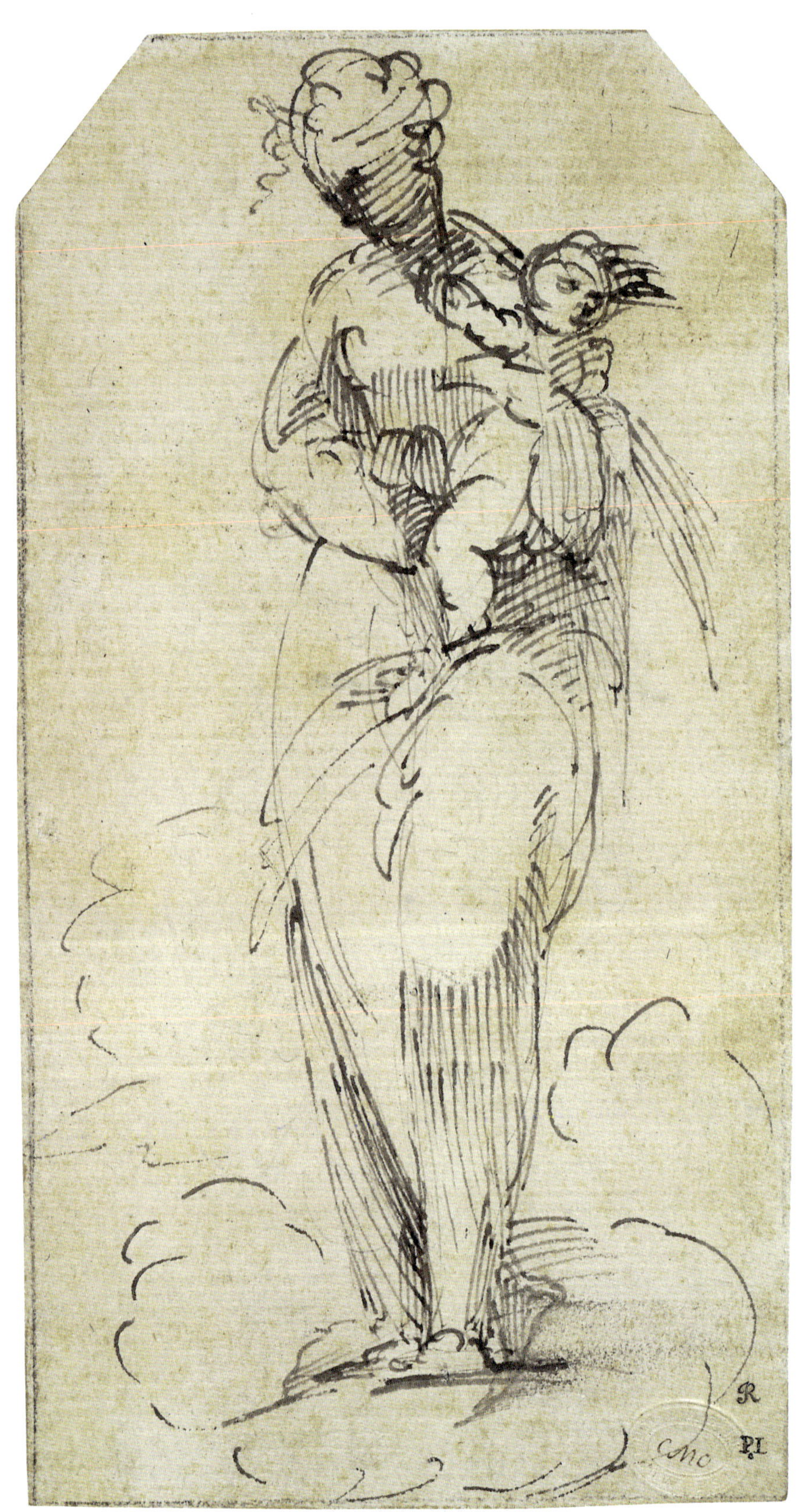



**2**

*The Virgin standing on Clouds holding the Child,* about 1526

Pen and grey ink on paper, 21.6 × 11.5 cm (actual size) British Museum, London (Ff, 1.94)

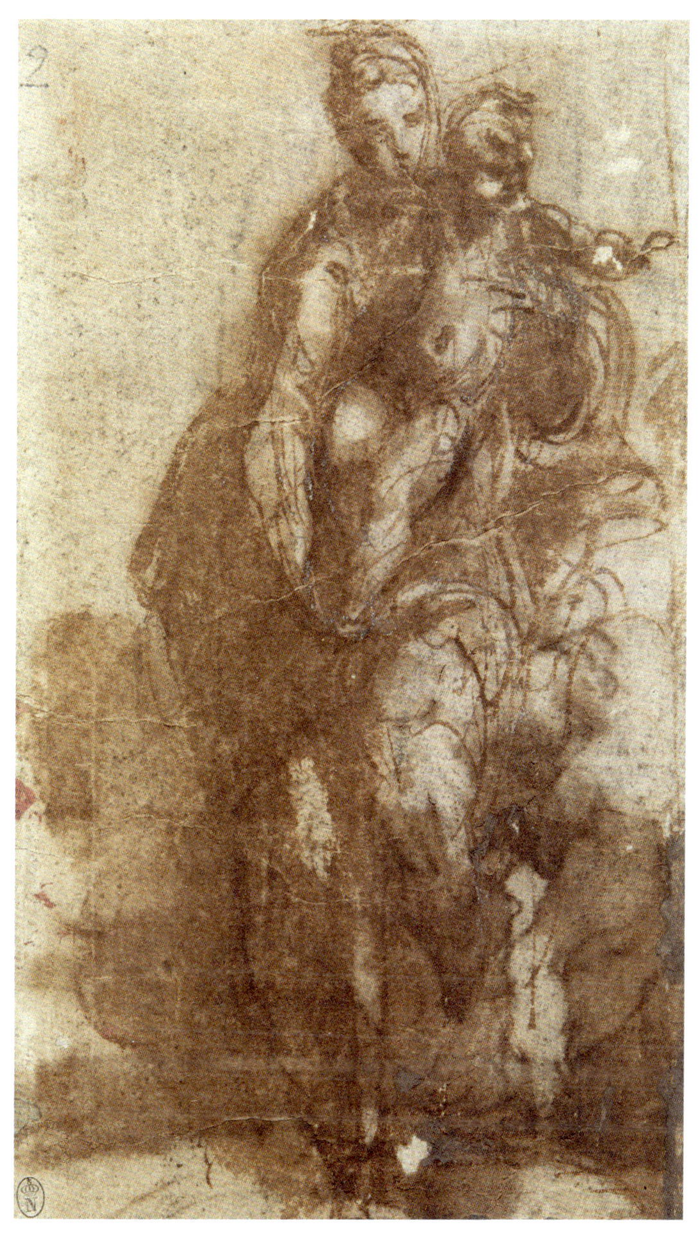

**3**

*The Virgin with the Christ Child,
standing*, 1526–7

Pen and brown ink, brown wash on
paper, 15.9 × 9.2 cm (actual size)
Département des Arts graphiques,
Musée du Louvre, Paris (INV 6379 recto)

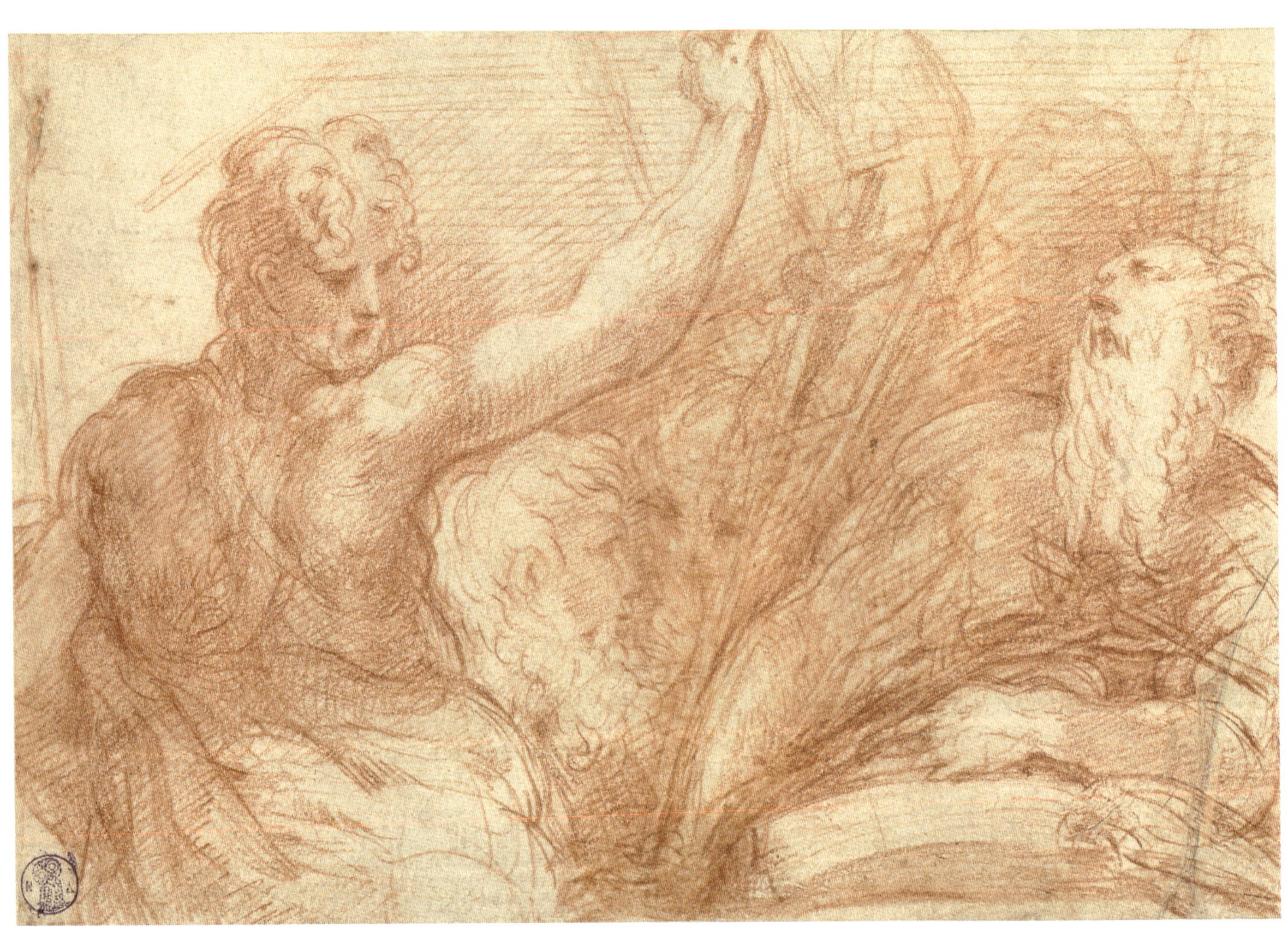



*Studies of Saints John the Baptist and
Jerome, a Crucifix and Various Heads*
(recto), about 1526

Red chalk on paper, 13.5 × 22.1 cm
The J. Paul Getty Museum, Los Angeles
(87.GB.9)

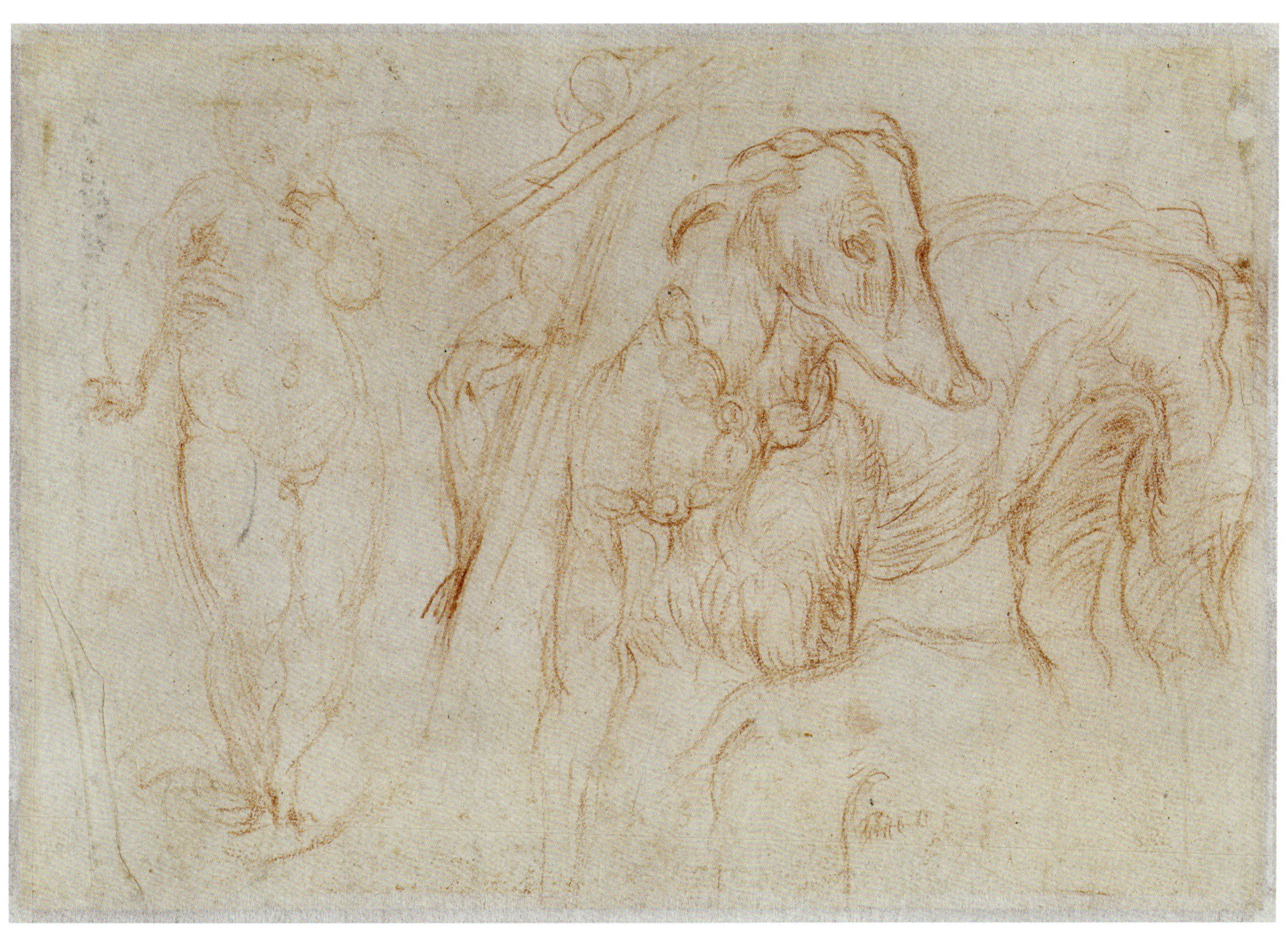

**4v**
*Studies of the Christ Child, a Crucifix
and Dogs* (verso), about 1526

Red chalk on paper, 13.5 × 22.1 cm
The J. Paul Getty Museum, Los Angeles
(87.GB.9)

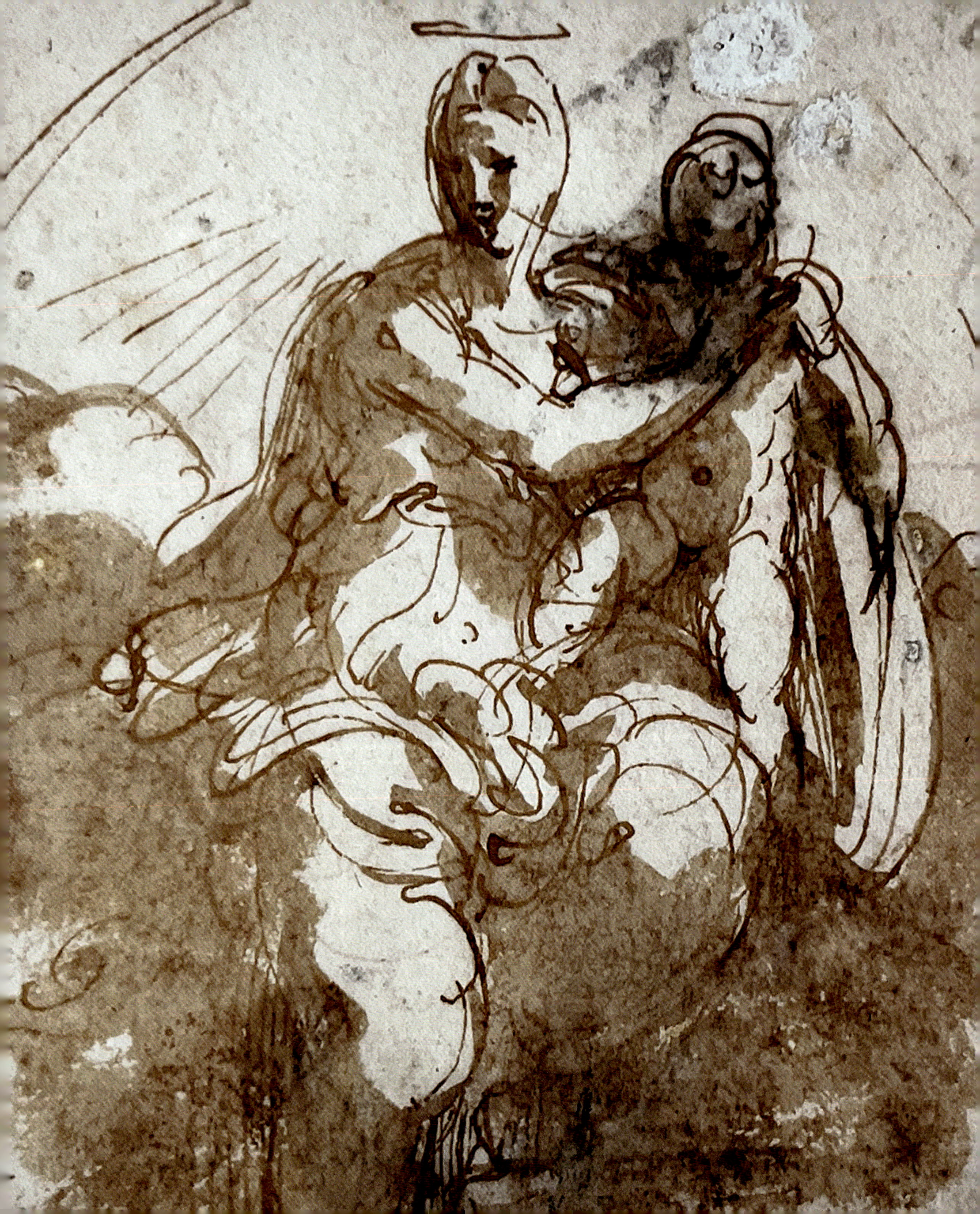

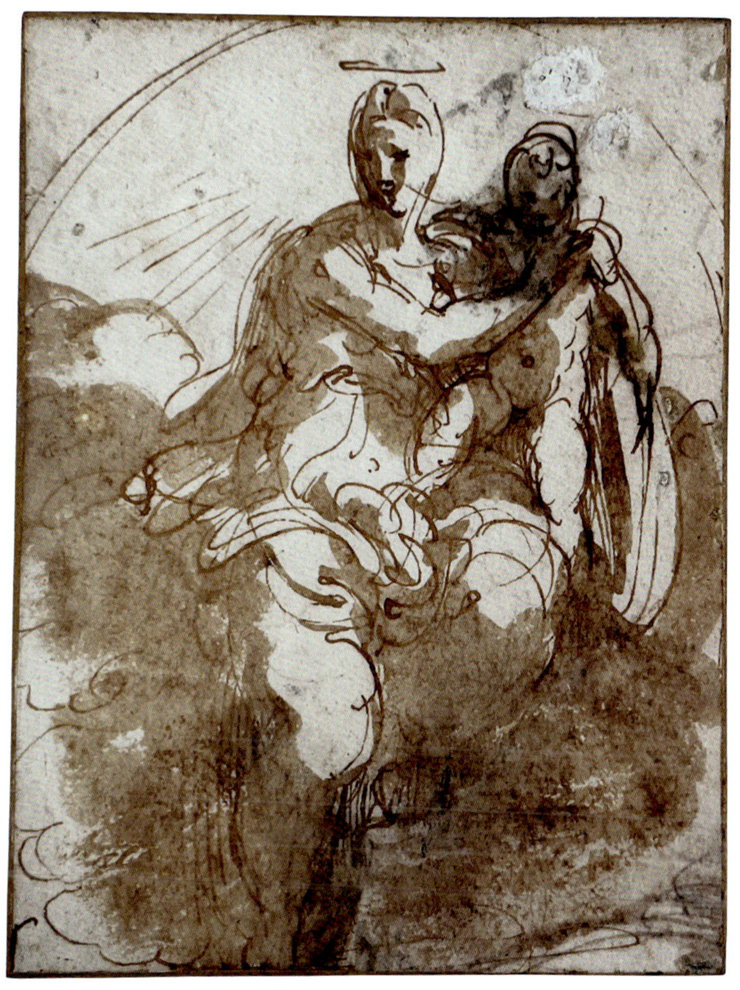

**5**

*The Virgin and Child*, 1526

Pen and brown ink with brown wash
on paper, 13 × 10 cm (actual size)
The Ashmolean Museum, University of Oxford.
Presented by Mr F. E. Maitland in memory of his
wife, Margaret Maitland, 1949 (WA1949.212)

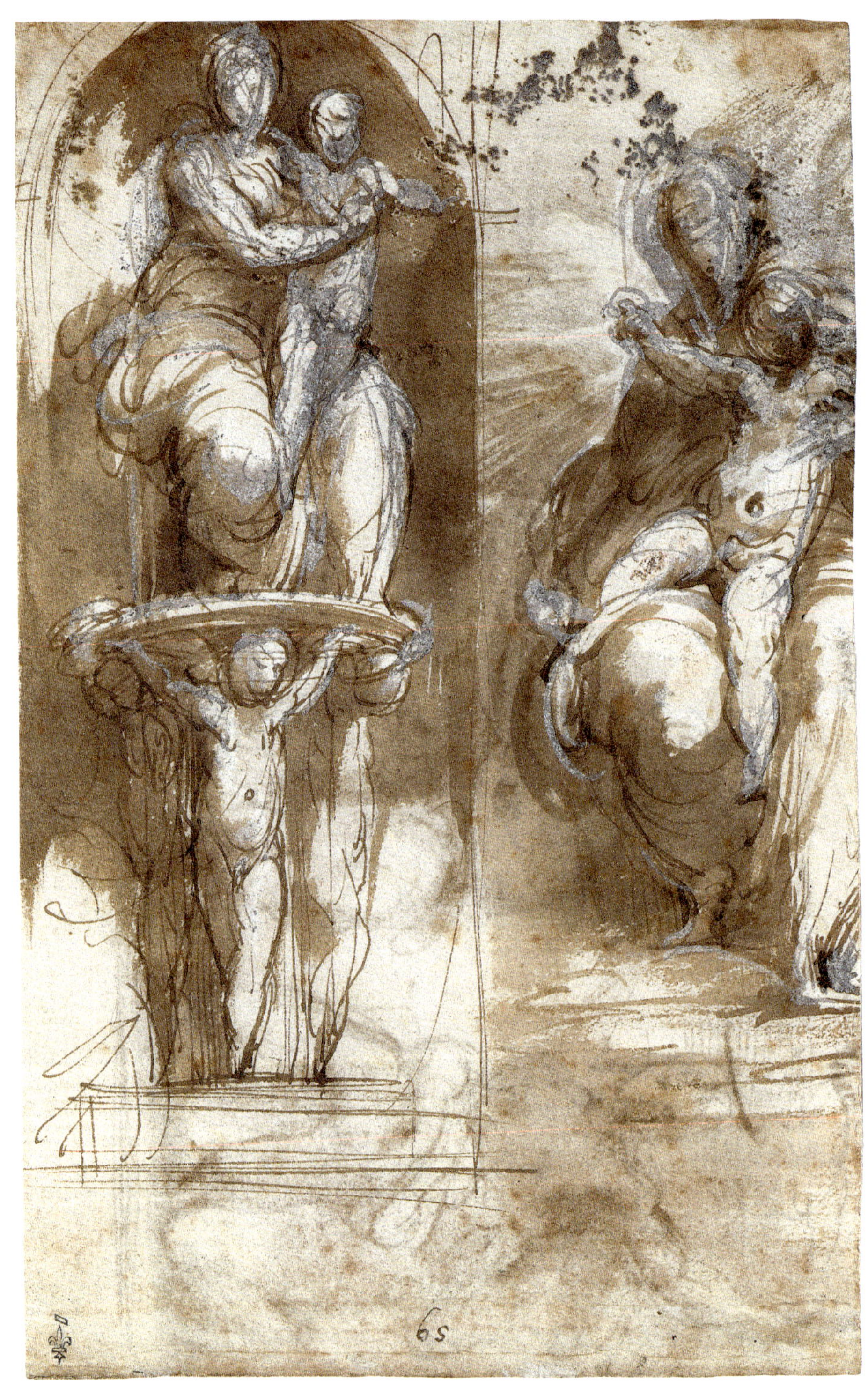

**6r**

*Two Studies of the Virgin and Child*
(recto), 1526

Pen and brown ink, brown wash, white
heightening on paper, 20.3 × 13 cm
(actual size)
Musée Condé, Chantilly (inv. 142)

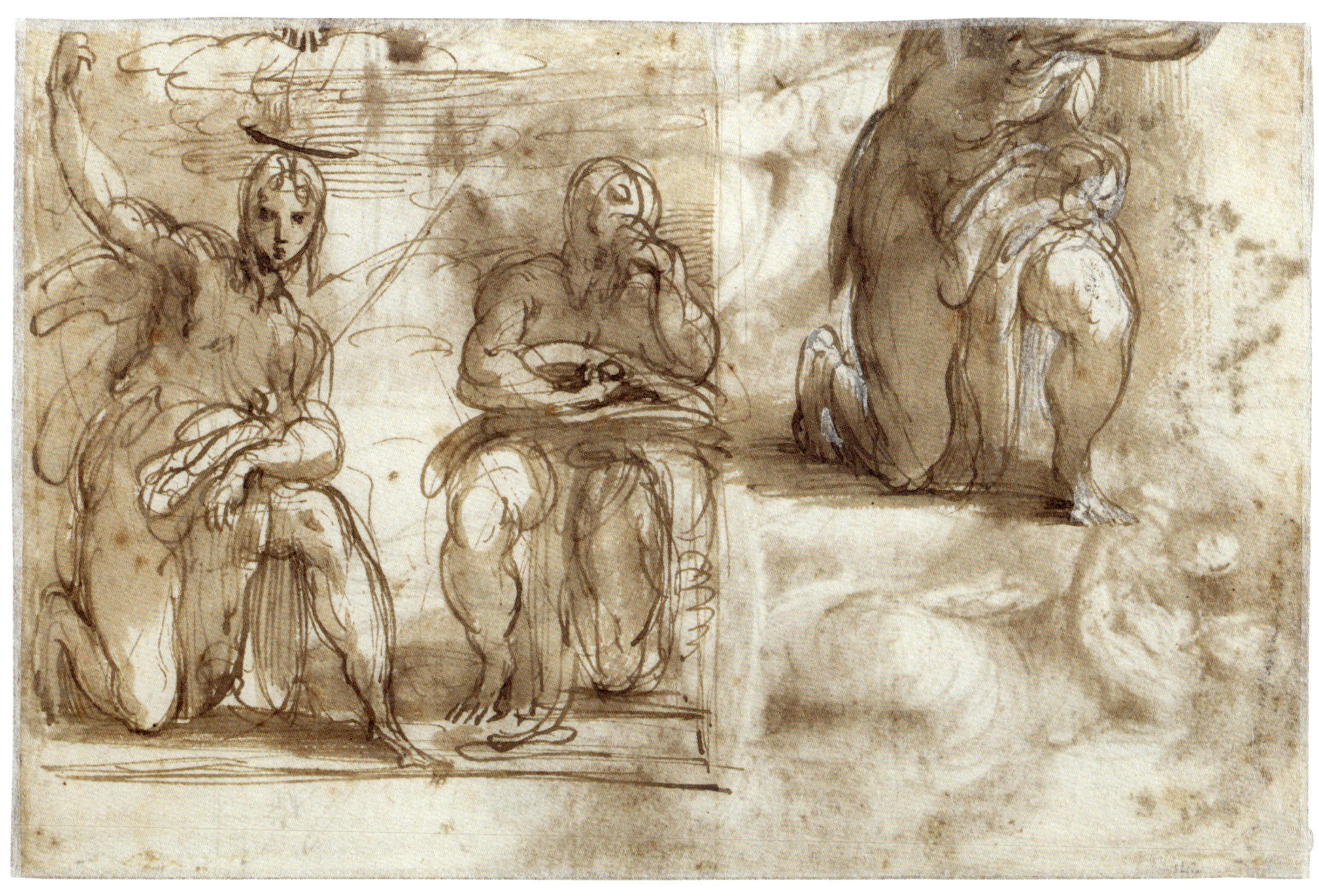

**6v**
*Three Studies of Saints* (verso), 1526

Pen and brown ink, brown wash, white
heightening on paper, 13 × 20.3 cm
(actual size)
Musée Condé, Chantilly (inv. 142)

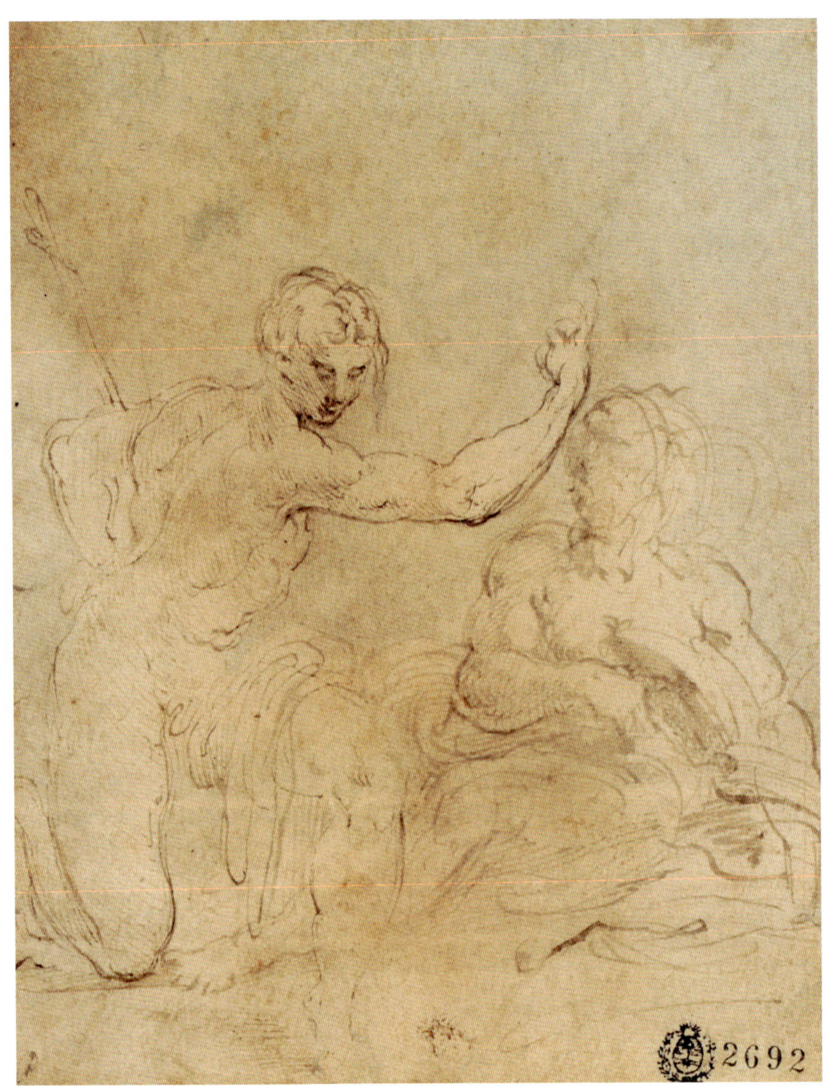

**7**

*Studies of Saint John the Baptist
and Saint Jerome*, 1526

Pen and brown ink, brown wash on paper,
14 × 11 cm (actual size)
Museo Nacional de Bellas Artes, Buenos Aires
(inv. 173)

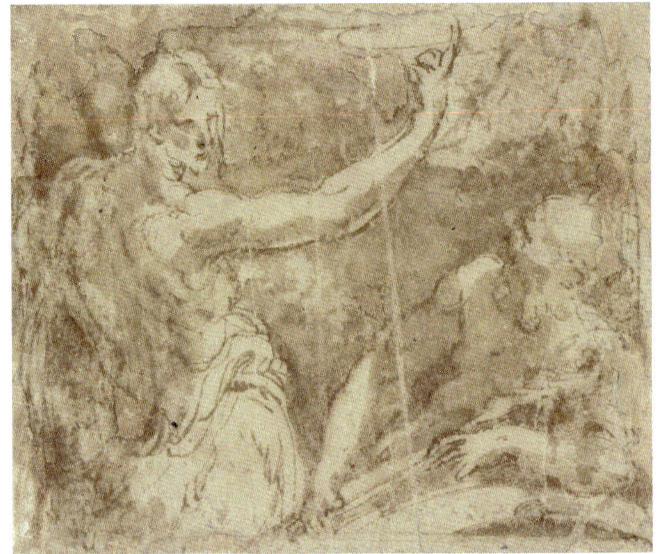

**8**

*Saints John the Baptist and Jerome*, 1526

Pen and brown ink, brown wash on paper,
7.3 × 8.6 cm (actual size)
Städel Museum, Frankfurt am Main (inv. 13772)

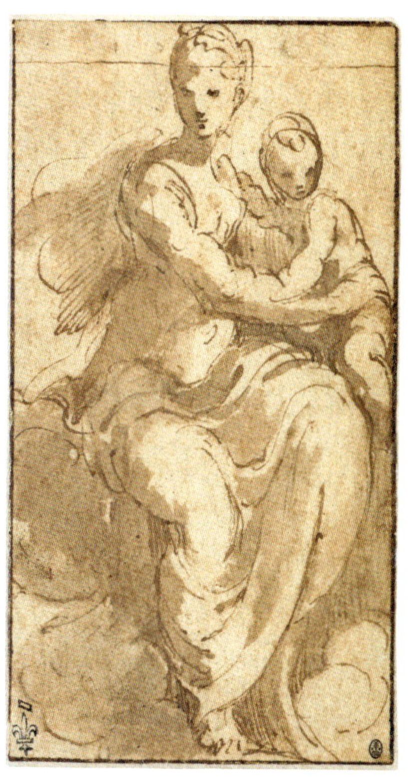

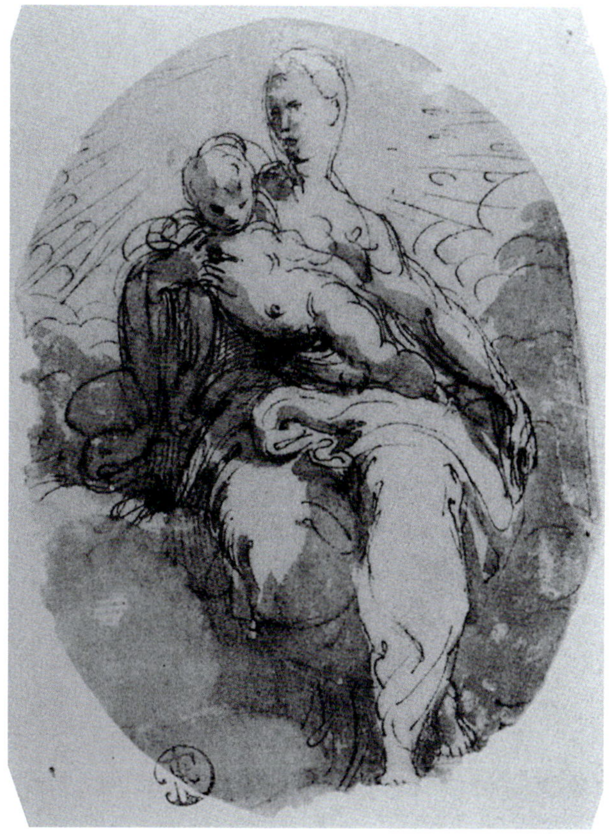

**9**

*Virgin and Child on a Cloud*, 1526

Pen and ink, brown wash on paper,
9.9 × 5.3 cm (actual size)
Musée Condé, Chantilly (inv. 144)

**10**

*Virgin and Child in the Clouds*, 1526

Pen and brown wash on paper,
10.9 × 8.2 cm (actual size)
Private collection

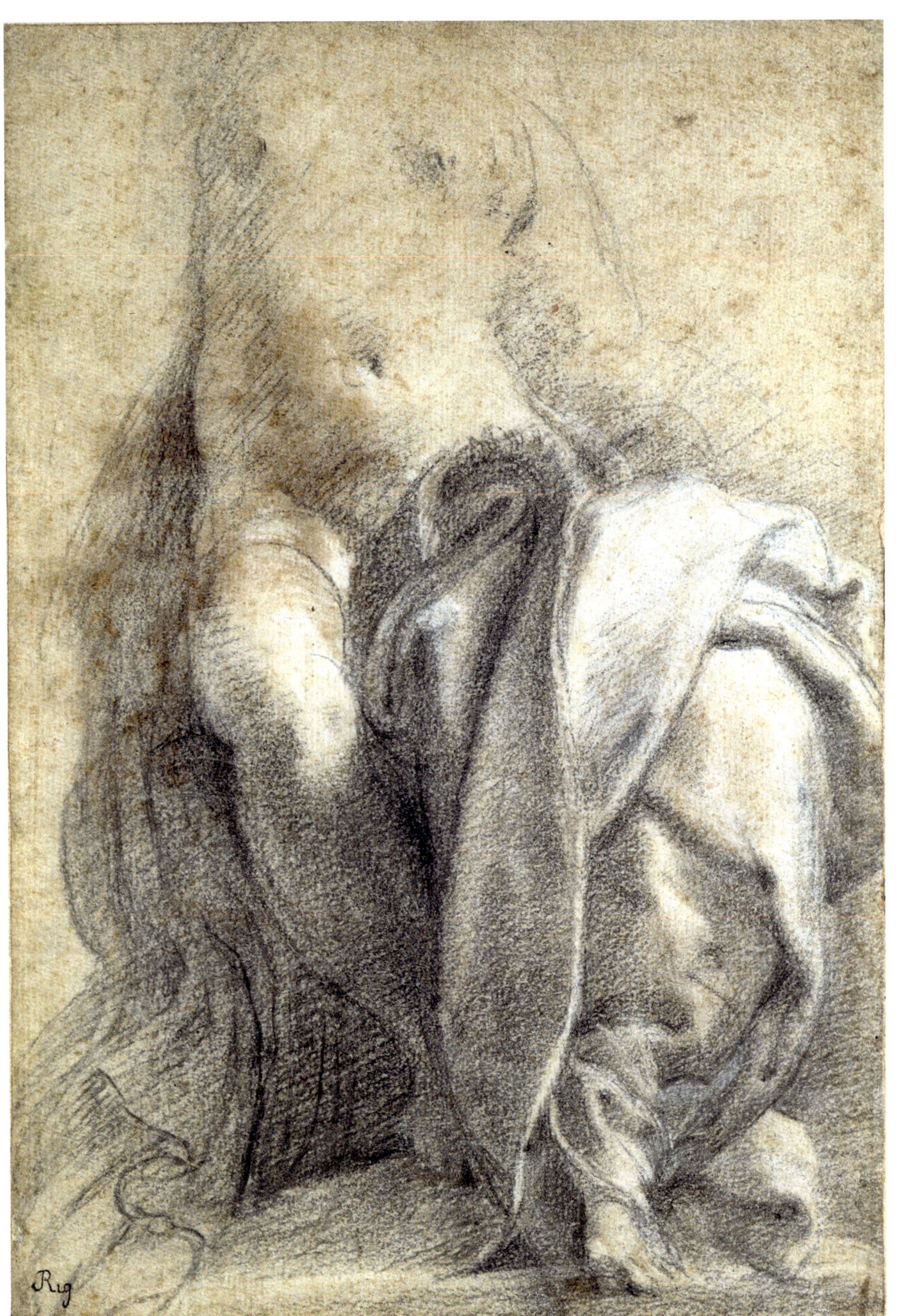



**11r**
*Seated Semi-nude Female
wearing Drapery* (recto),
1526–7

Black and white chalk on paper,
23.2 × 16.1 cm
The Ashmolean Museum,
University of Oxford. Purchased,
1939 (WA1939.76)

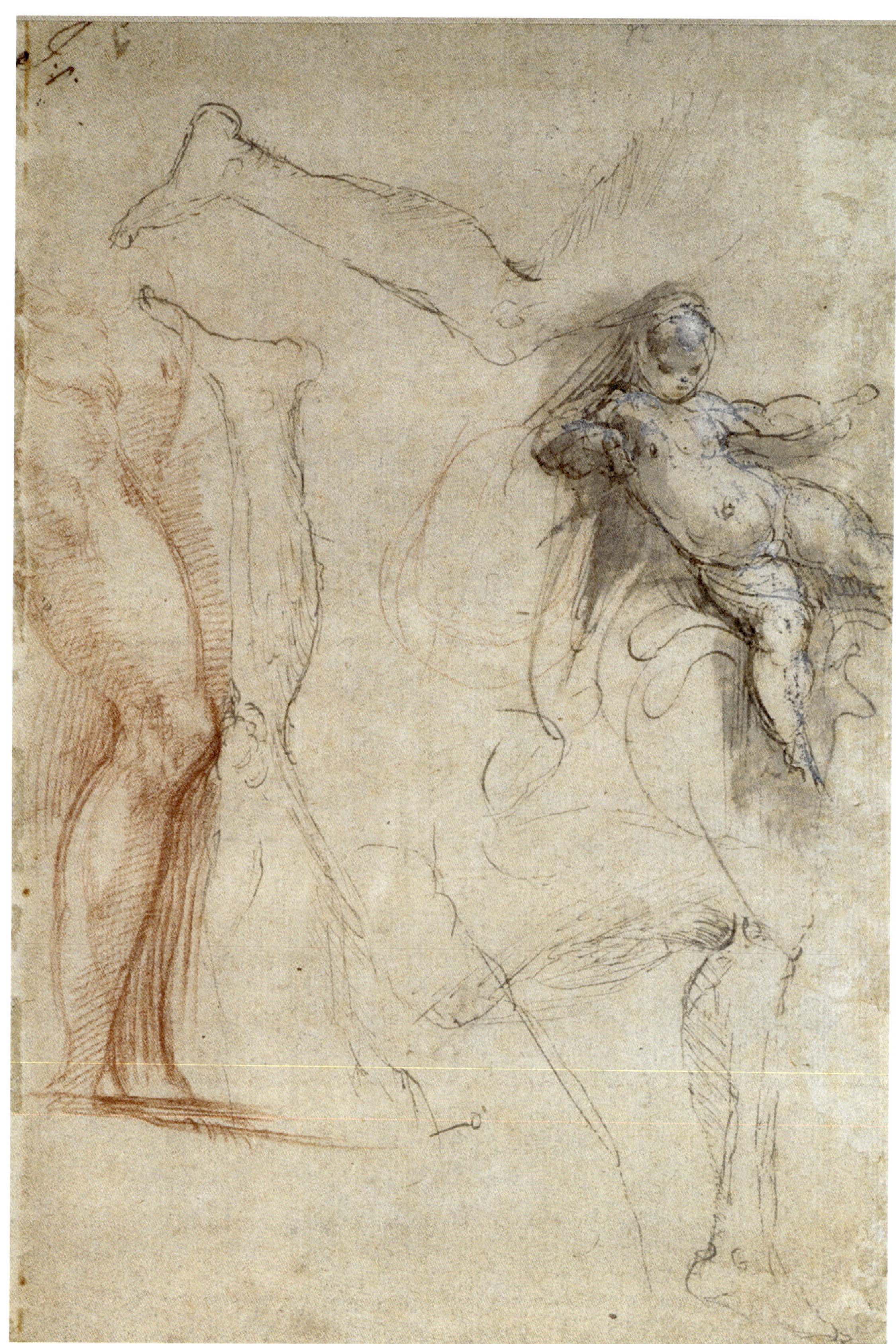

**11v**

*Study of a Child on his Mother's Lap; Studies of Legs* (verso), 1526–7

Pen and brown ink with grey wash, heightened with white bodycolour (oxidised) and separate studies in red chalk on paper, 23.2 × 16.1 cm
The Ashmolean Museum, University of Oxford. Purchased, 1939 (WA1939.76)

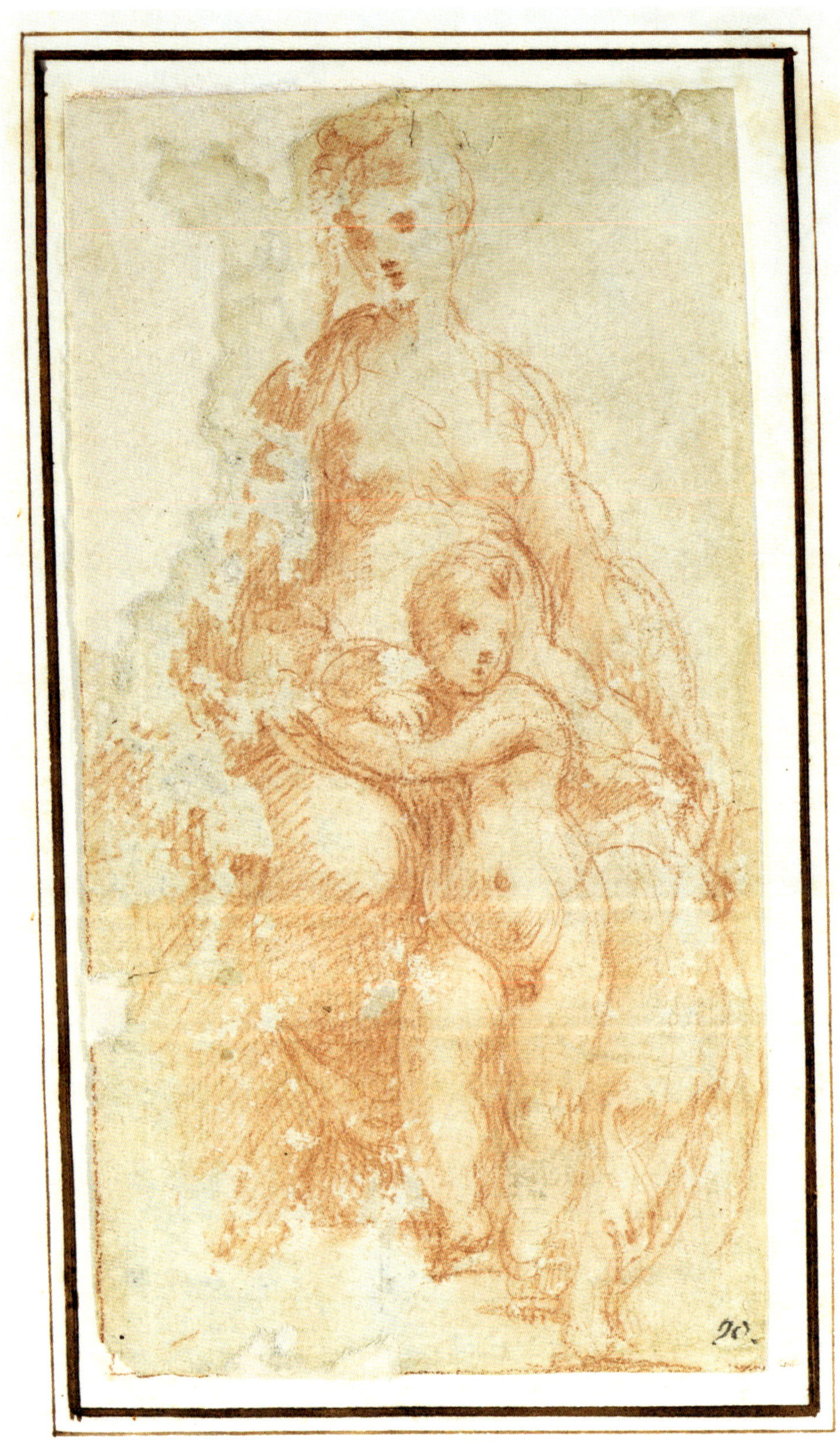



**12**
*Virgin and Child* (recto), 1526–7
Red chalk on paper,
20.8 × 11.2 cm
Museo Nazionale di Capodimonte,
Naples (inv. GDS 1023)

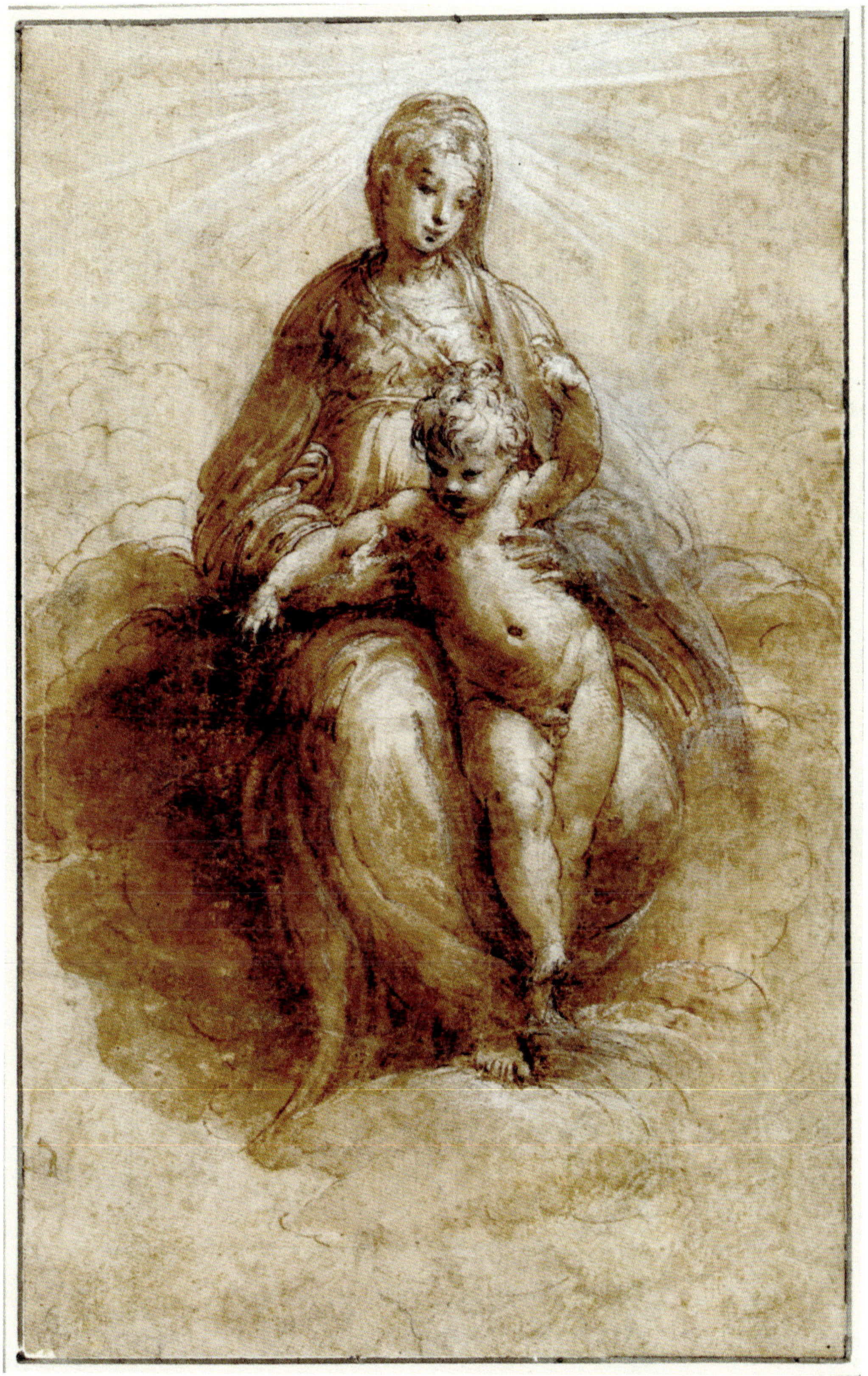

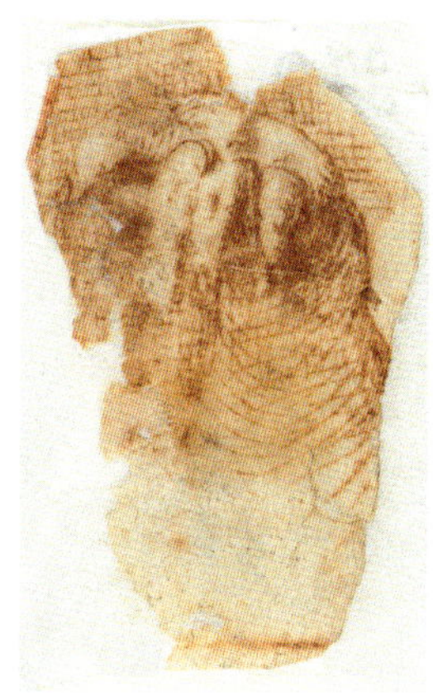

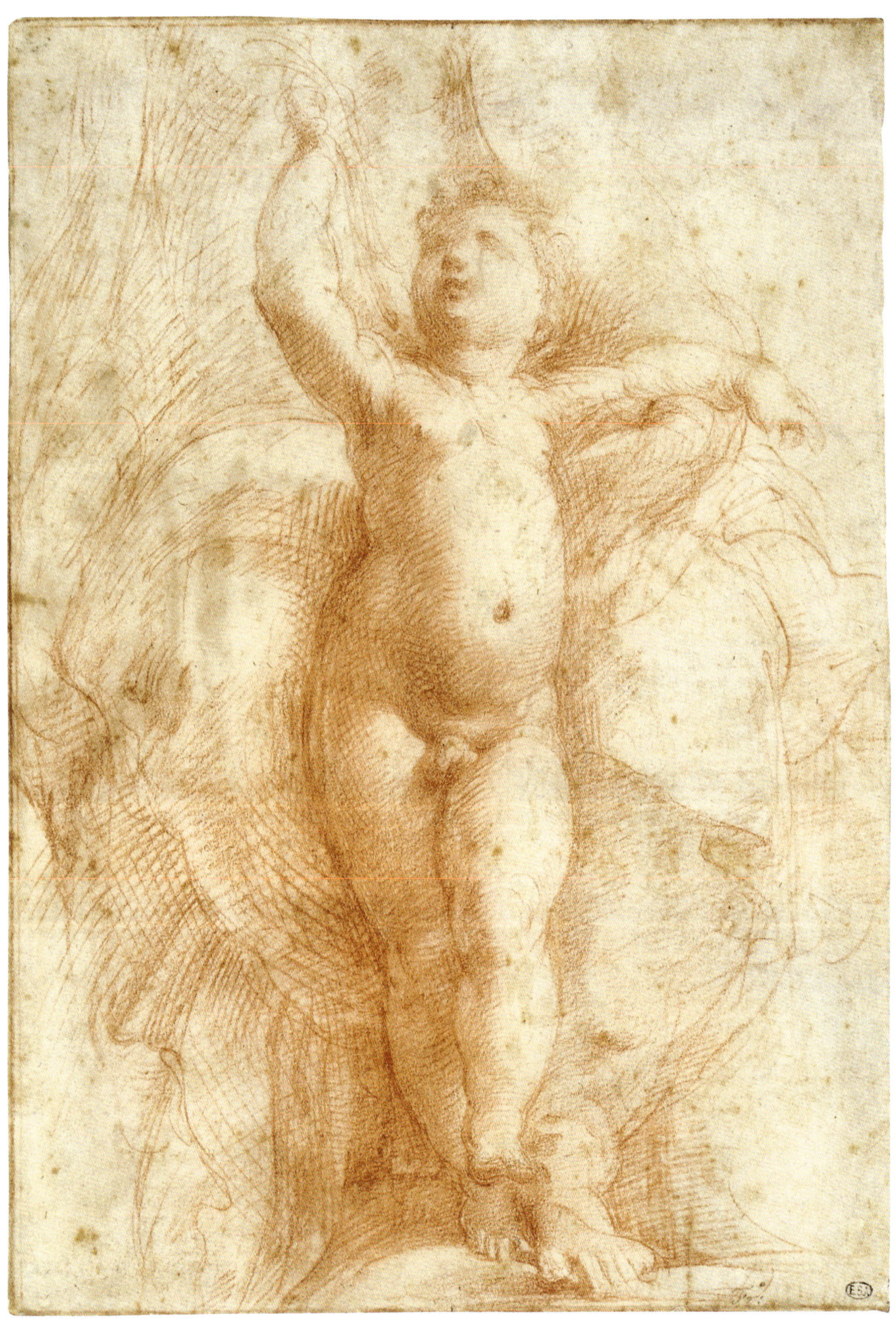



*The Infant Christ standing
between his Mother's Knees*,
about 1527

Red chalk on paper, 23.8 × 16.7 cm
Ecole nationale supérieure des
beaux-arts, Paris (inv. 221)

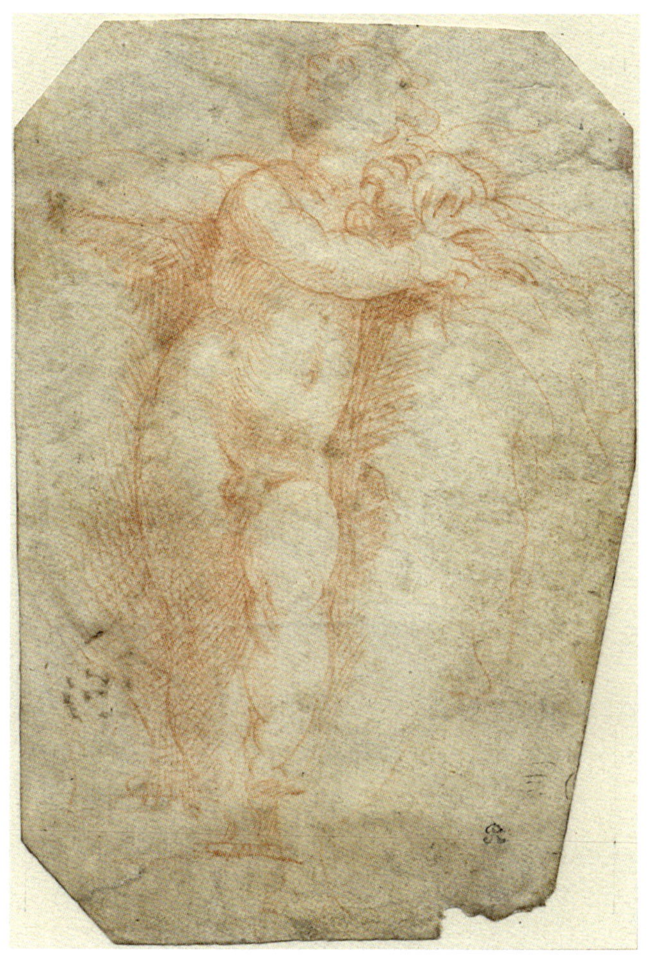

**16**
*The Infant Christ*, 1526–7
Red chalk on paper, 14.3 × 10 cm
Private collection

**17**
*The Infant Christ*, 1526–7
Red chalk on paper, 24.5 × 11.4 cm
Ecole nationale supérieure des
beaux-arts, Paris (inv. MAS 2368)

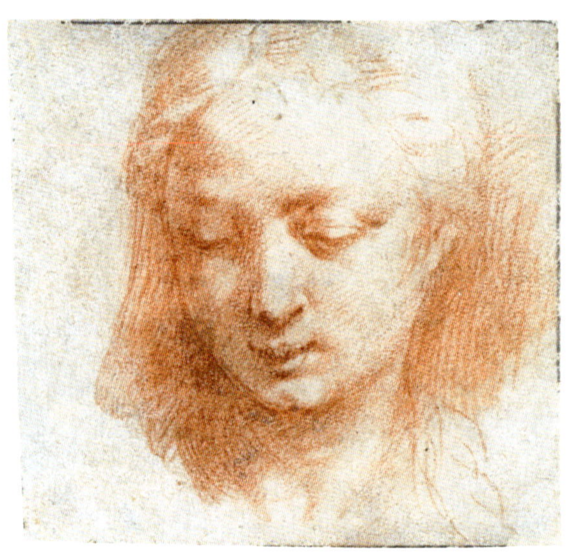

**18**

*Head of a Woman, looking down to the Left*, 1526–7

Red chalk on paper, 7 × 8 cm (actual size)
Private collection

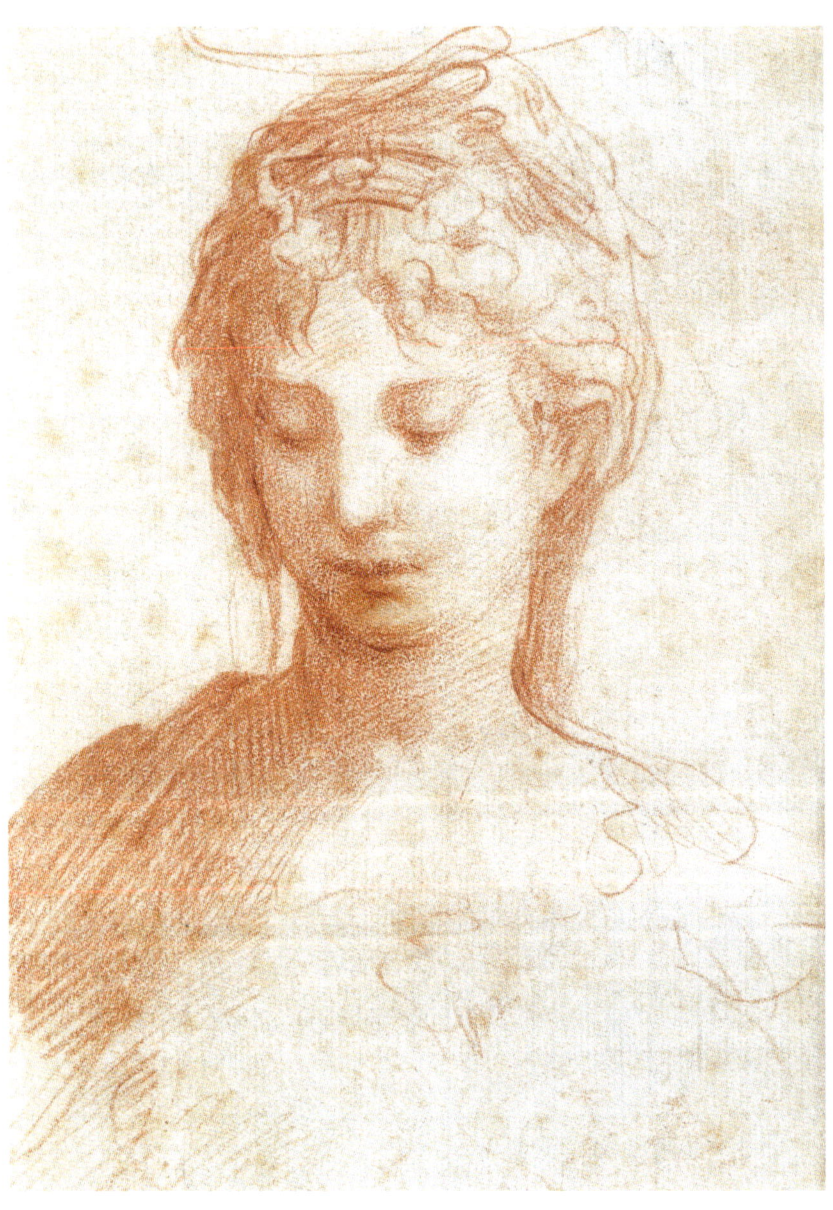

**19**

*Bust of the Virgin*, 1526–7

Red chalk on paper, 16.3 × 11.8 cm
Private collection

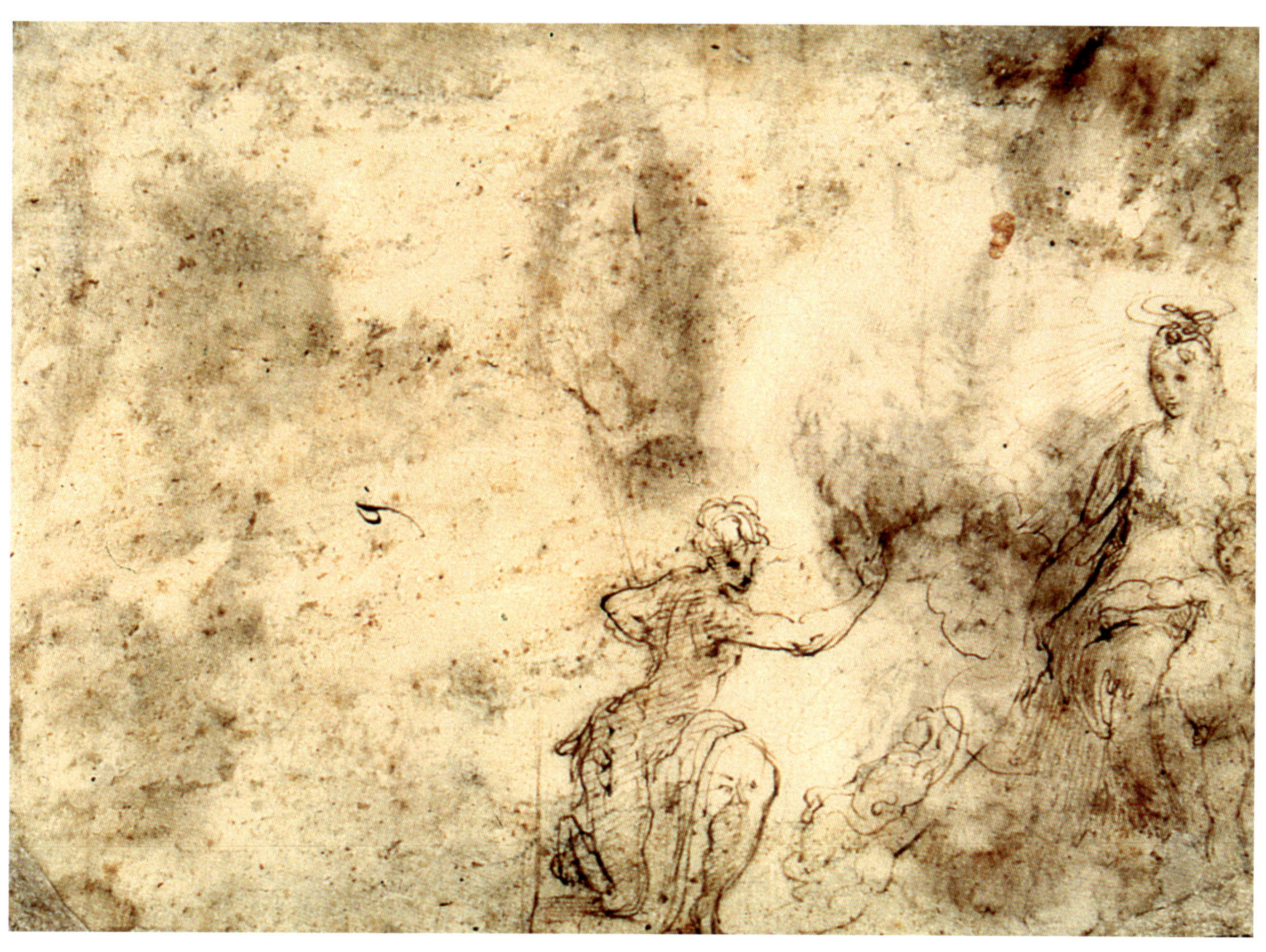

**20**

*Virgin and Child with Saint John the Baptist,*
1526–7

Pen and brown ink on paper,
13.7 × 19.2 cm
Galleria Nazionale di Parma
(inv. 510/16)

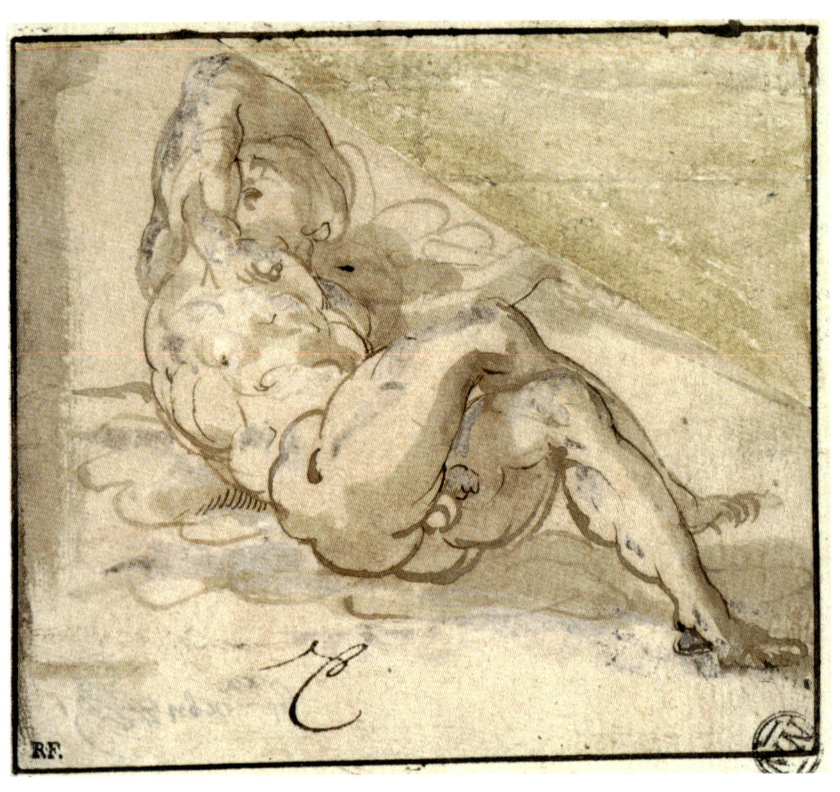



**21**

*Nude Man lying on the Ground with his
Legs crossed* (recto), about 1526

Pen and brown ink, brown wash
with white heightening (partly oxidised)
on paper, 10 × 11.1 cm (actual size)
Département des Arts graphiques,
Musée du Louvre, Paris (INV 6447)

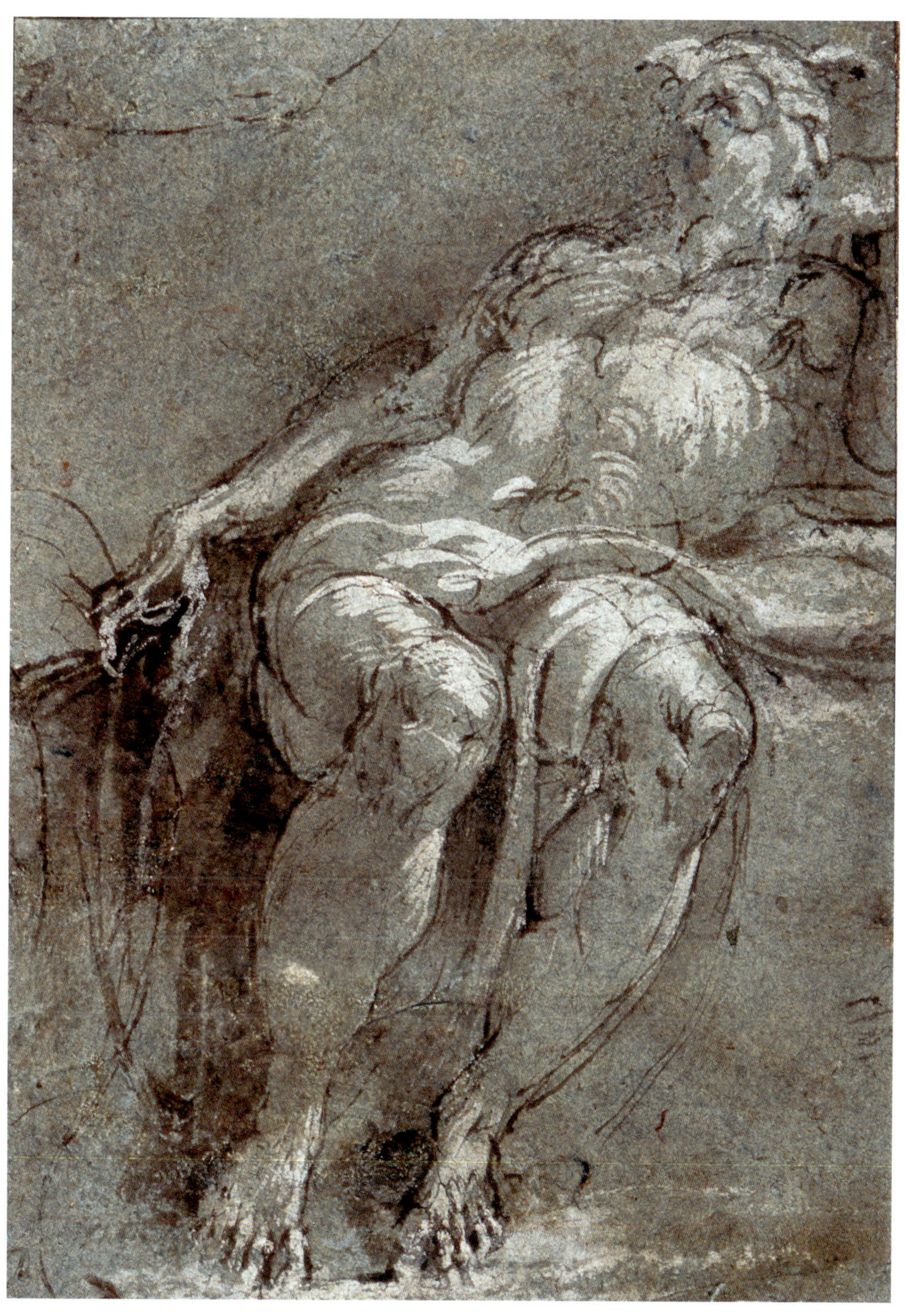



**22**

*Study for Saint Jerome*, 1526

Pen and brown wash, white
heightening on light-blue paper,
17.3 × 12.4 cm (actual size)
Stephen Kohl Art Foundation

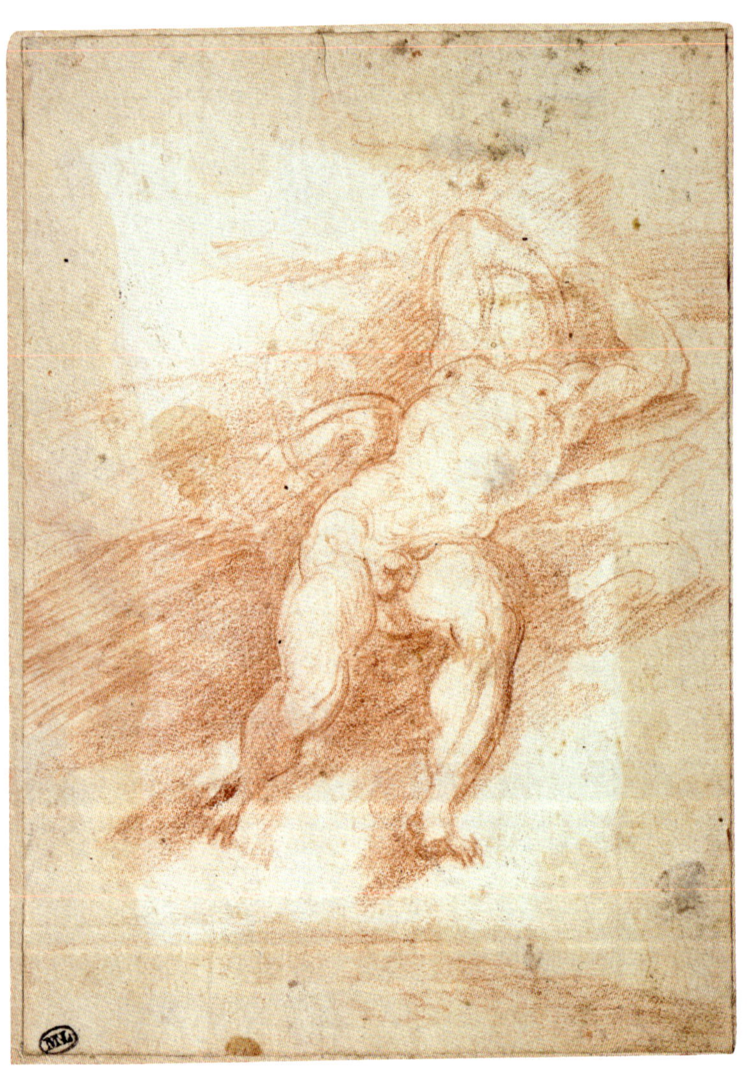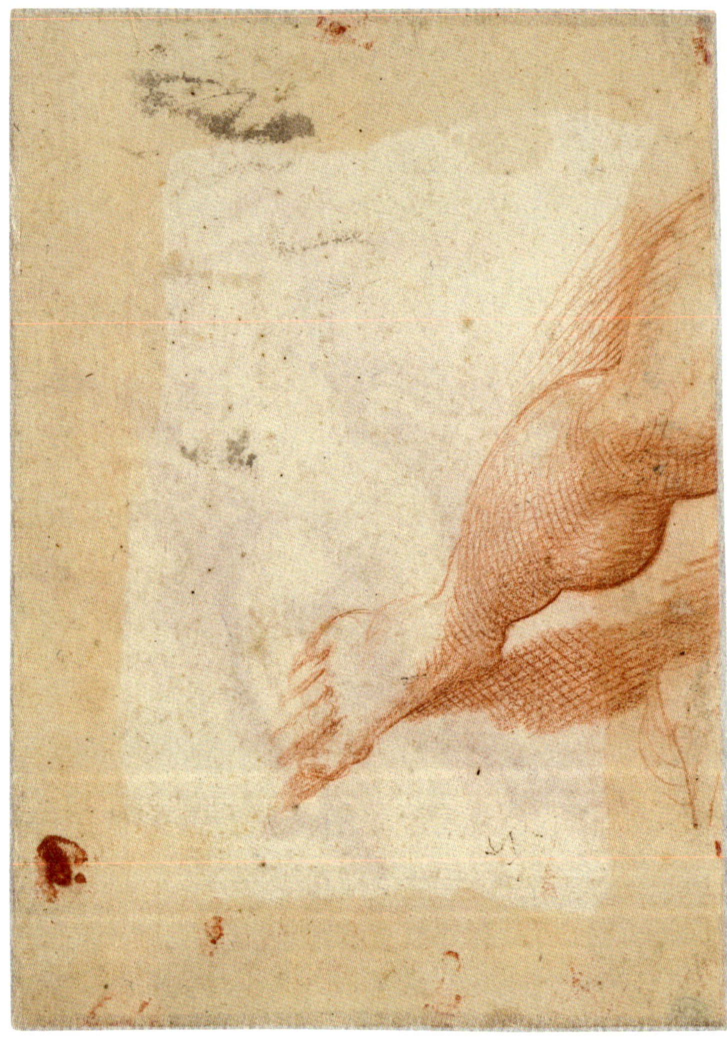


*Nude Man lying on his Back* (recto);
*Study of Right Leg* (verso), 1526–7

Red chalk on paper, 13.7 × 9.8 cm (actual size)
Département des Arts graphiques, Musée du
Louvre, Paris (INV 6423)

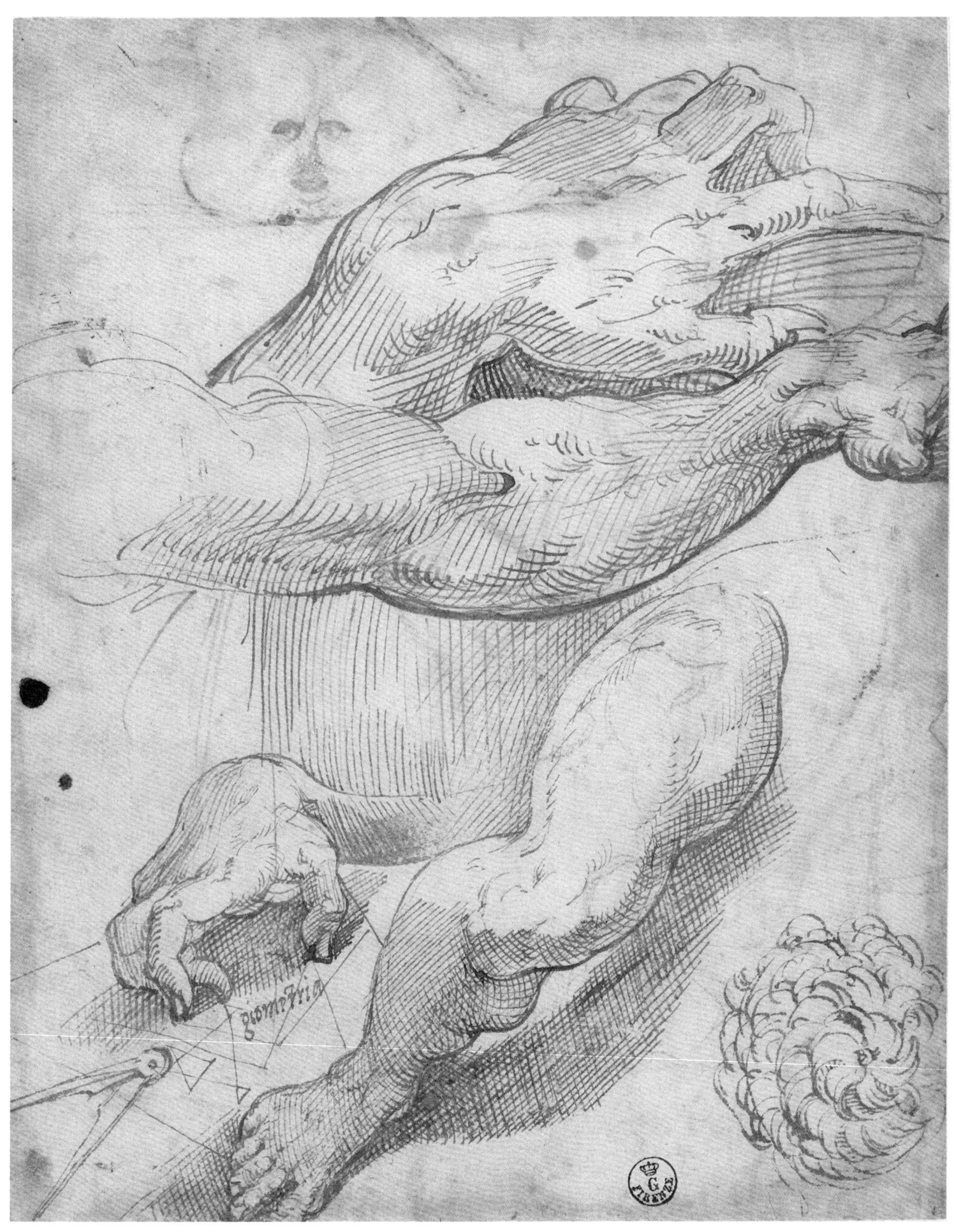

**24**

*Studies of Arm, Hands and Leg* (recto), about 1526–7

Pen and ink, black chalk on paper, 20.7 × 16.6 cm (actual size)
Gabinetto dei Disegni e delle Stampe, Gallerie degli Uffizi,
Florence (inv. 13611 F)

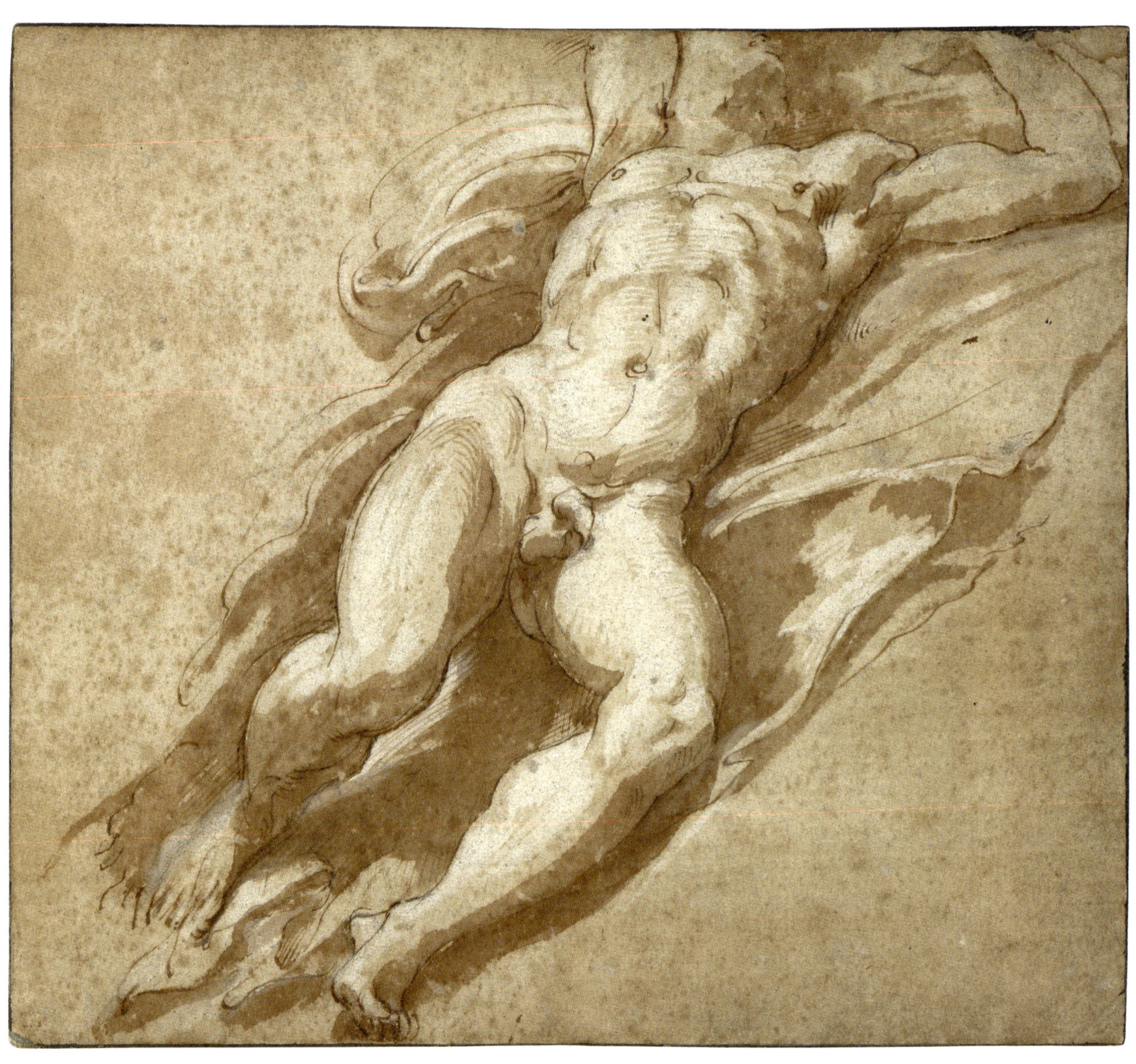



**25**

*Figure Study*, 1526

Pen and brown ink, brown wash,
with white heightening on paper,
21.6 × 24.3 cm
The J. Paul Getty Museum,
Los Angeles (84.GA.9)

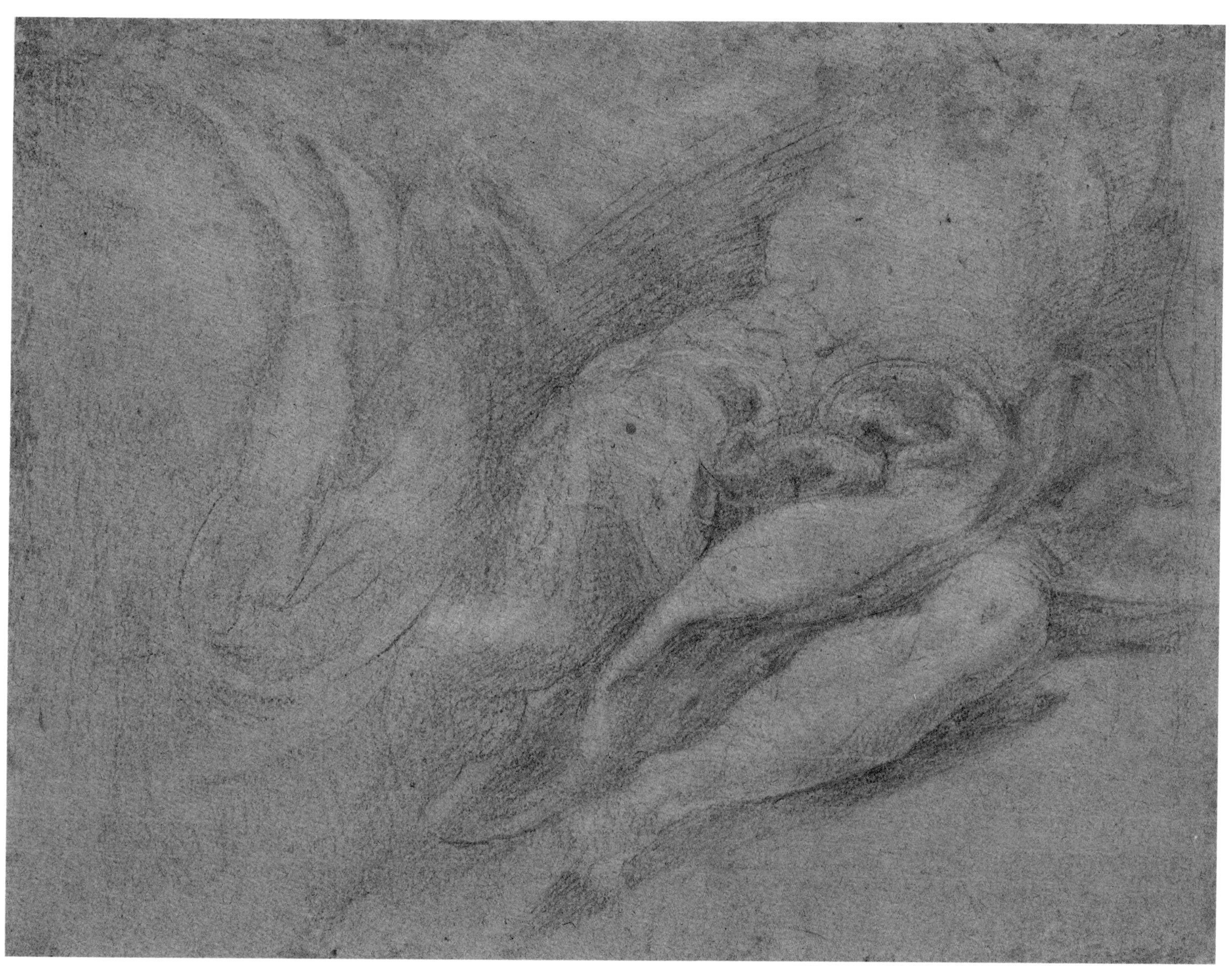

**26**
*The Legs and Drapery of a reclining
Figure*, about 1526–7
Black and white chalk on grey-blue paper,
19.3 × 25 cm
The Royal Collection / HM King Charles III
(RCIN 900883)

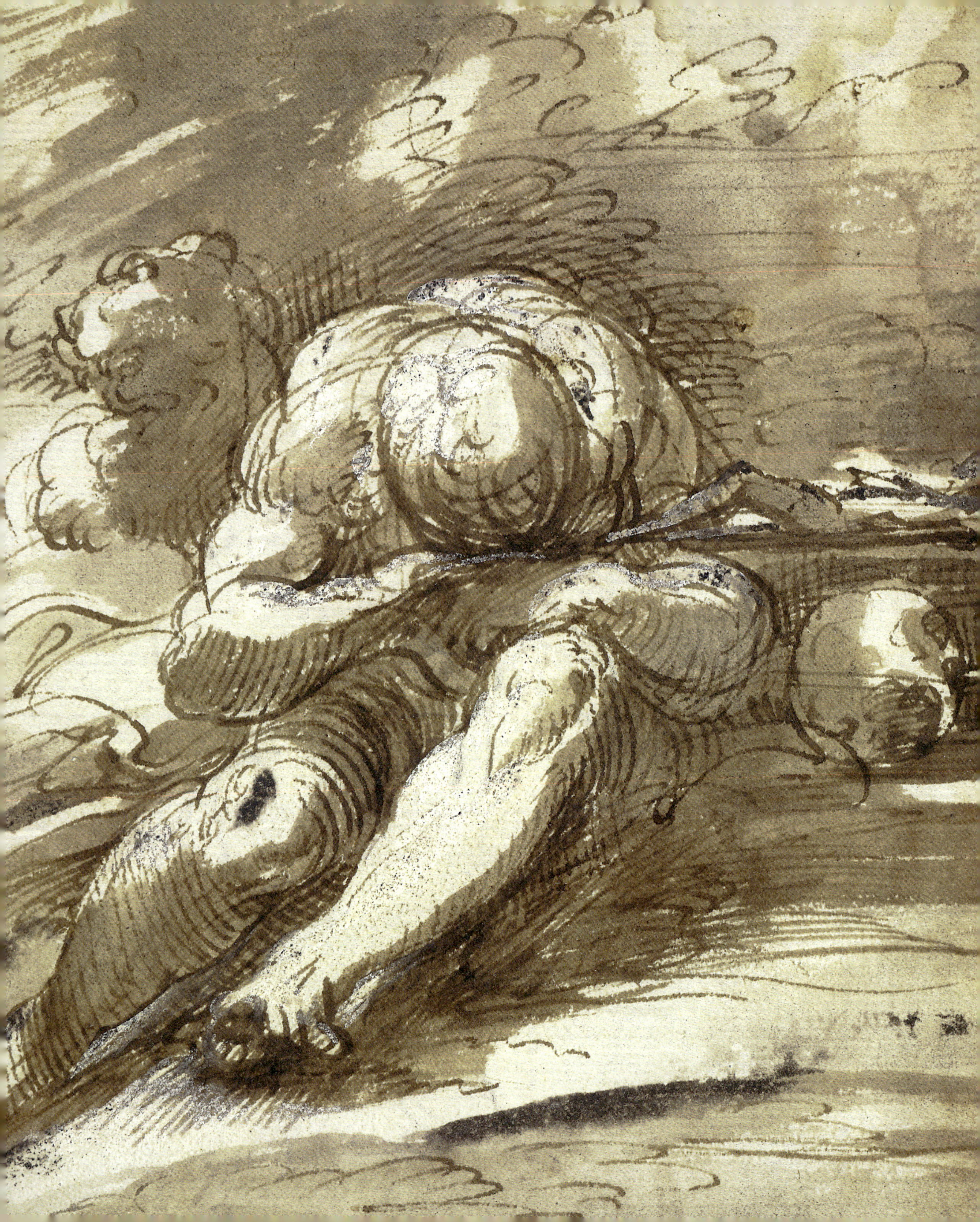

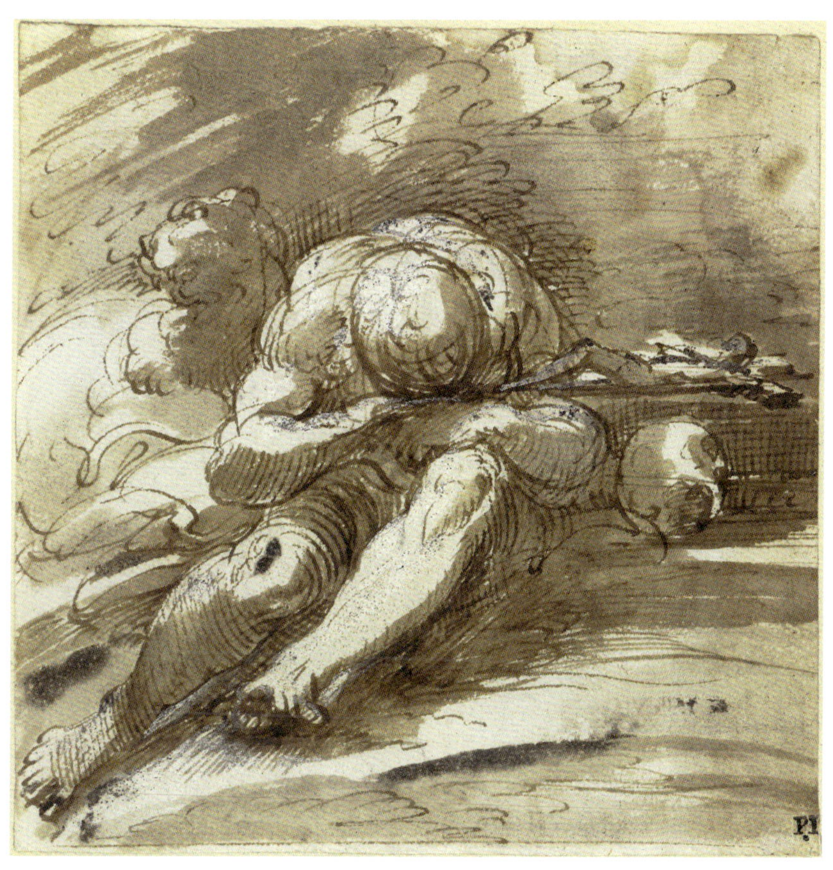

**27**

*Saint Jerome in Penitence, his Head on his
Lap, seated on the Ground*, about 1526–7

Pen and brown ink with brown-grey wash
with white heightening (partly discoloured)
on paper, 11.1 × 11.1 cm (actual size)
British Museum, London (1905, 1110.32)

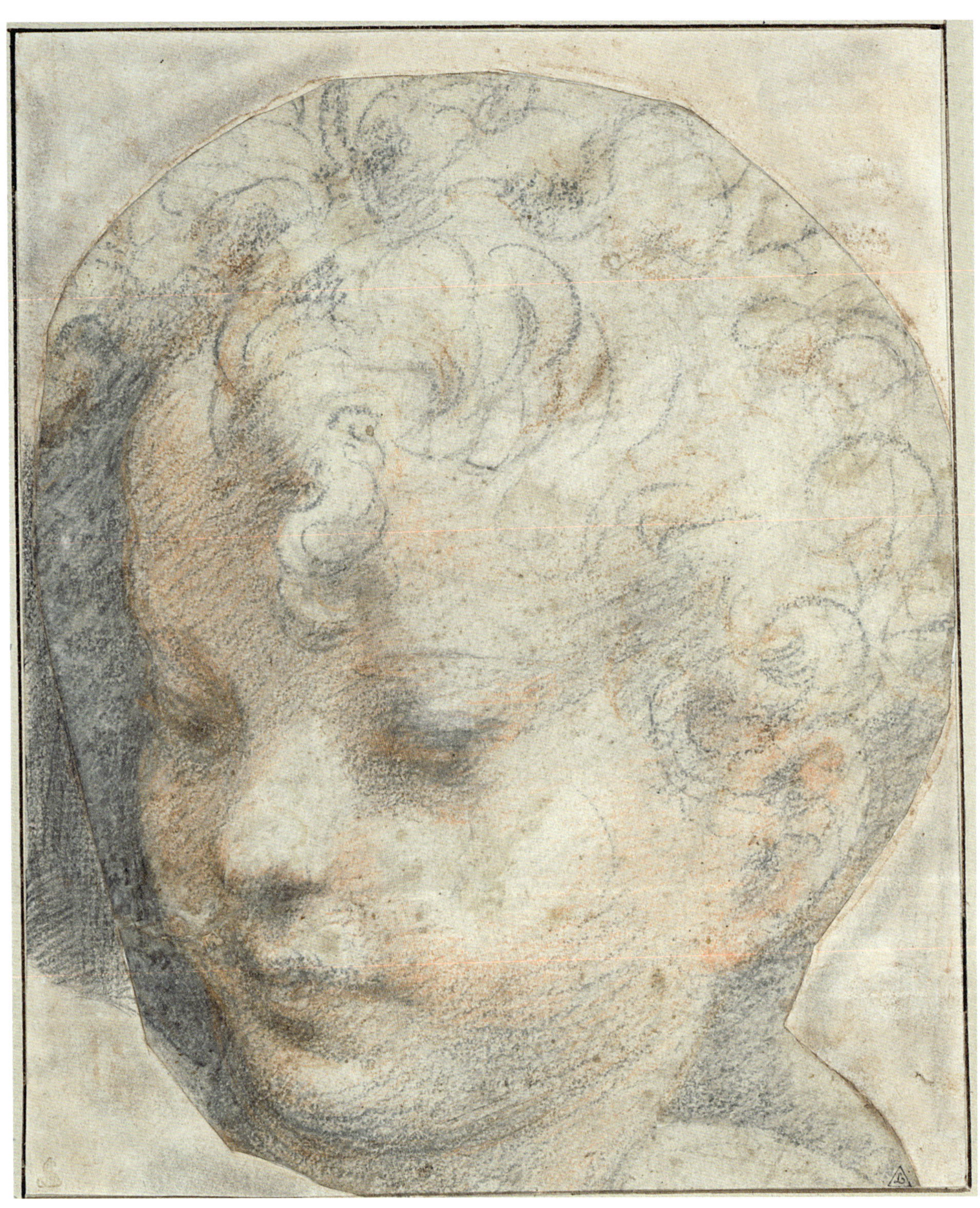

**28**

*Head of the Christ Child*, probably 1527

Black chalk or charcoal and red chalks on
paper, 23.6 × 19.8 cm
Albertina Museum, Vienna (inv. 2615)

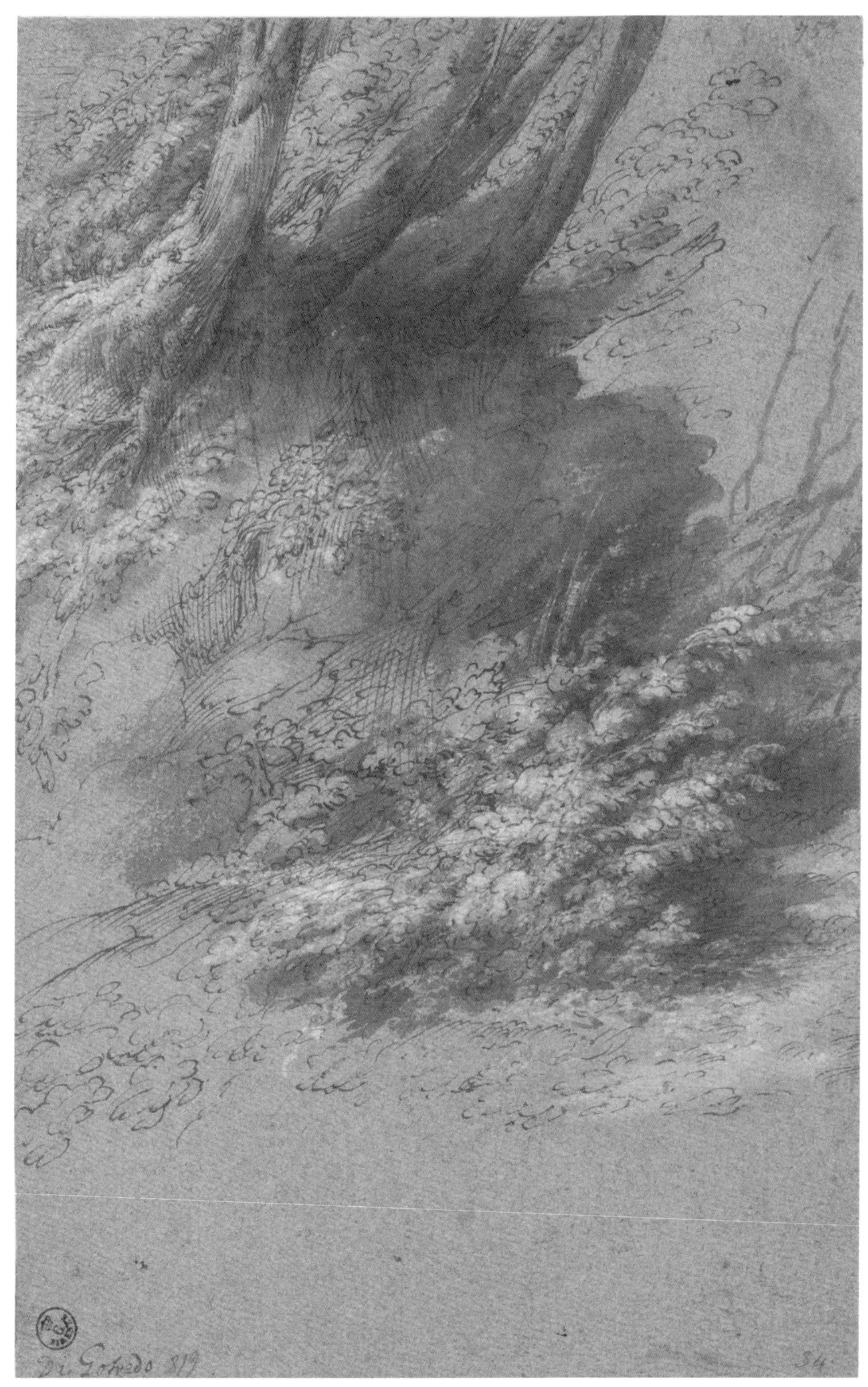

**29**

*Woodland Study*, 1524–7

Pen, ink and wash with white heightening
on blue paper, 27.8 × 17.7 cm
Gabinetto dei Disegni e delle Stampe,
Gallerie degli Uffizi, Florence (inv. GDS n. 753 P)

# APPENDIX: CONTRACT FOR THE CACCIALUPI ALTARPIECE AND EXCERPT FROM MARIA BUFALINI'S WILL

## TRANSLATED BY LIVIA LUPI, WITH EMMA FIRESTONE AND MATTHIAS WIVEL

Contract for the Caccialupi Altarpiece, dated 3 January 1526.
Manuscript. Archivio di Stato, Collegio Notai Capitolini, Rome,
vol. 14, Antonius de Alexis, fol 296r.

*With regard to the painting in the chapel of the Lady Maria Bufalini. On the 3rd of January 1526 Indiction[1] 14*

*The appointed masters Pietro* [Pier Ilario Mazzola] *and Francesco Mazzola of Parma, painters in the City* [of Rome], *willingly promise Lady Maria Bufalini Caccialupi, present here, a single panel with an image of the seated Holy Virgin Mary with the Child in her arms; and an image of Saint Jerome, Doctor of the Church, and Saint John the Baptist at the feet of the Virgin, between the above-mentioned images of Saint Jerome and Saint John the Baptist.[2] Likewise,* [Pier Ilario and Francesco agree to paint] *an image of the Conception of the Holy Virgin on one side* [of the main panel] *and an image of Saint Joachim and Saint Anne on the other within the chapel's architectural framing,[3] with the colours fully executed and as much gilding on the frame of the panel as is needed, within the next six months, for the price of 65 gold scudi, with 30 scudi to be paid up front by the aforementioned Lady Maria, in the presence of my notary and witnesses, to the same masters Pietro* [Pier Ilario] *and*

*Francesco, both present, and* [the remaining] *35 scudi to be paid on completion of the work.*

*In addition, this official arrangement includes that, should it be deemed that the work is not worth 65 scudi, and should the work be declared to be not resolved in either the figures or the colours and thereby insufficient, the same masters Pietro and Francesco are required to keep the panel for themselves and return the said 30 scudi to the same Lady Maria, present.*

*For this, they* [Pier Ilario and Francesco] *hereby place themselves under cameral obligation[4] and swear precisely to observe what is here stated.*

*Deed* [signed] *in Rome in the house of Lady Maria with Niccolò Bufalini and Guidone Alepergi as present witnesses.*

---

Excerpt from Maria Bufalini's will, dated 15 July 1528.
Manuscript. Archivio di Stato, Collegio Notai Capitolini, Rome,
vol. 14, Antonius de Alexis, fols 353r–354v, 382, at fol. 354.

*The said testator* [Maria Bufalini] *stated that, to honour his wages, she gave 16 golden ducats to the painter of the chapel of the said Sir Antonio her husband, located in the church of San Salvatore in Lauro in the City. She entrusts the heirs mentioned here to pay the remainder of the aforementioned painter's fee and to ensure that the painted panel is placed by the said painter in its dedicated place in that chapel and is appropriately ornamented by the painter according to the agreement she stipulated with him – which, she asserts, can be ascertained at the hands of the notary.*

**WHEN IN ROME: PARMIGIANINO IN THE ETERNAL CITY, 1524–7**

1 Aurenhammer 2016 offers a recent reflection on the term and its historiography. See Vasari 1966–87, vol. 4, pp. 3–13.

2 On interpretations of the long neck, see Vaccaro 2002, pp. 25–8.

3 On Parmigianino's family, see Chiusa 2001, p. 18, and Vaccaro 2002, pp. 11–12.

4 Vasari 1966–87, vol. 4, p. 533.

5 On Parmigianino and Correggio, see Rome 2016. See also p. 18 in this volume.

6 Vasari 1966–87, vol. 4, p. 533.

7 See, for example, Barkan 1999.

8 Dacos 1969, p. 146.

9 Ibid., p. 155.

10 Vasari 1966–87, vol. 4, pp. 534, 536.

11 On the air of Rome overwhelming the painter Rosso Fiorentino, see Vasari 1966–87, vol. 4, p. 480. On Vasari and the primacy of Rome, see especially Vaccaro 2009, pp. 115–24, and Pelta 2005, pp. 155–67.

12 Vasari 1966–87, vol. 4, p. 536. All translations are by the author unless otherwise noted.

13 Vasari 1966–87, vol. 4, p. 535. The first edition of Vasari's *Lives* states that Parmigianino sent the *Self Portrait* from Parma to Pope Clement, who subsequently beckoned the artist to Rome; this was altered in the second edition.

14 Vaccaro 2002, p. 194, notes that the date '1524' on the reverse of Parmigianino's *Gian Galeazzo Sanvitale* (Museo di Capodimonte, Naples, inv. 111) 'accords with the style of the portrait'. It thus may indicate that he left Fontanellato, outside Parma, for Rome in that year.

15 On Parmigianino and Florence, see Ekserdjian 2006, pp. 29–30.

16 On Zaccaria Mazzola intending to leave Parma in 1517, see Dall'Acqua 1984, p. 102. On Zaccaria and Parmigianino in Rome, see Fornari Schianchi 2002, p. 51. On patrons of Zaccaria in Foligno with connections to Rome, see Felicetti 2002, p. 35.

17 Felicetti 2001, pp. 294–5.

18 Though Benvenuto Cellini's (1500–1571) colourful accounts are not always dependable, there is no reason to doubt his description (Cellini 2002, p. 48 ff.) of the reunion of the artistic community in Rome after the dissipation of plague in 1524 and its dispersal after Giulio Romano (1499?–1546) left for Mantua later that year.

19 On the Flemish Pope Adrian VI's short reign (January 1522–September 1523) and limited interest in art, see for example Gnann in Mantua and Vienna 1999, p. 40.

20 On Clement's artistic patronage, see Reiss 1999.

21 Vasari 1966–87, vol. 4, p. 535; Vaccaro 2002, p. 14, note 29. The austere Giberti ordered the imprisonment of the printmaker Marcantonio Raimondi for his role in creating erotic prints for the series known as *I Modi* (1524); he also commissioned works from Giulio Romano and Baldassare Peruzzi (1481–1536), through whom he may have met Parmigianino.

22 Vasari 1966–87, vol. 4, p. 535.

23 Vasari (1966–87, vol. 4, pp. 534–6) records having seen the *Self Portrait* as a young man in Aretino's home in Arezzo, from which it passed to the goldsmith Valerio Belli (1468–1546) and then to the sculptor Alessandro Vittoria (1525–1608). On the identifications of the other paintings presented to Clement as the *Holy Family* (about 1524, Museo Nacional del Prado, Madrid, inv. P000283), possibly a lost *Virgin and Child with the Young Saint John the Baptist and a Lamb* (recorded in a drawing in the Willumsen's Museum, Frederikssund, Denmark) and – according to Vasari one of the first works Parmigianino painted in Rome and that which Clement kept for himself – possibly the *Circumcision* (about 1523, Detroit Institute of Art, inv. 30.295), see Franklin 2003–4, p. 11, and Vaccaro 2002, p. 14, note 29.

24 On Parmigianino and printmaking, see, among others, Ekserdjian 2006, pp. 213–38.

25 Parmigianino's drawing was first linked with Ugo's painting by Harprath in Vatican City 1984, pp. 324–5.

26 Ugo's altarpiece remained installed until about 1606; see Ballardini 2022, p. 41. On the site of St Peter's in this period and Heemskerck's drawings, see Thoenes 2006.

27 On the *Saint Veronica* altarpiece and its relationship to the relic, see Blackwood 2013.

28 See Ballardini 2022, p. 45.

29 On the inscription, 'By Ugo da Carpi, woodcutter, made without a brush' (*Per Ugo / da Carpi Intaiatore / fata senza / penello*), see Blackwood 2013, p. 172. In Vasari's *Life* of Marcantonio, he describes Ugo's altarpiece as having been painted with Ugo's hands and other 'capricious instruments' (*instrumenti capricciosi*): Vasari 1966–87, vol. 5, p. 15.

30 Hook 2004 remains the authoritative history of the events of the Sack.

31 Chastel 1983, p. 18.

32 Hook 2004, p. 177.

33 Ibid., p. 220.

34 The story has long been recognised as echoing Pliny the Elder's account of the artist Protogenes during the siege of Rhodes in 305–304 BC. See Chastel 1983, pp. 171–2. Amanzio Cattaneo's (1828–1897) imaginative portrayal of the episode, which pictures Parmigianino painting a different composition, was published for the first time in Vaccaro 1993.

35 Vasari 1966–87, vol. 4, p. 541, listing works Parmigianino made in Bologna, including a portrait of Charles V, notes that he also '[a]bbozzò anco un quadro d'una Madonna, il quale fu poi venduto in Bologna a Giorgio Vasari aretino' ('sketched in a painting of a Madonna, which was then sold in Bologna to Giorgio Vasari the Aretine').

36 Vasari 1966–87, vol. 4, p. 538.

37 Hook 2004, pp. 93–102.

38 Ibid., p. 98. On Raphael's tapestries, which were stolen again during the Sack, see Shearman 1972, pp. 140–1, and Rodolfo 2020, pp. 54–6.

39 Vasari 1966–87, vol. 4, p. 538.

40 A document dated 8 May 1527 (transcribed in Bonaparte 1830, pp. 81–91) lists among the men, women and children in the palace names that may be identified with artists: Rosso Fiorentino ('Rossus de Rossis pictor'), Jacopo Sansovino and his wife ('Jacobus de S. Savino' and 'Simona uxor Jacobi de S. Savino') and Parmigianino ('Franciscus Maria Parmensis'). The wife of Giovanni Antonio Lappoli is listed ('Cherubina uxor Joannis Antonij pictoris') though Lappoli himself is not.

41 On artists' experiences of the Sack of Rome, see Ng 2012, Appendix.

42 Letter of 24 February 1531. *Carteggio* 1965, p. 299 (no. DCCCXI).

43 Vasari 1966–87, vol. 4, p. 265.

44 Chastel 1983, p. 174. Parmigianino, *Madonna of the Rose* (1529/30, Gemäldegalerie, Dresden, inv. 161).

45 Vasari 1966–87, vol. 4, p. 539. In the 1550 edition, Vasari does not mention Pier Ilario's depositing of the painting at the Pace; in the 1568 edition, he includes this detail as well as its relocation after 'molti anni' ('many years') to Città di Castello by 'messer Giulio Bufolini'. This information may have been recounted to Vasari by Parmigianino's relative Girolamo Mazzola Bedoli, when Vasari visited Parma in 1567. Vaccaro 1993, p. 27 includes documents regarding the painting at the Pace and its move to Città di Castello in 1558.

46 Vasari 1966–87, vol. 4, pp. 537–8: 'La quale opera quasi a fine ridusse di tal profezzione, che, se la fortuna non lo impediva … [m]a venne la ruina del sacco di Roma' (1550 edition); 'Ma quest'opera non gli lasciò condurre a perfezzione la rovina et il sacco di Roma' (1568 edition).

47 Vaccaro (1993, p. 26, note 37) notes that the patron did not appear to have connections to the church, whose archive no longer survives. On the Pace, its history and its place in the city, see recently Benedetti, Carlevaris and Ercolino 2022.

48 The painting, with original battens, weighs 92.5 kilograms. Thanks to Larry Keith for this information and for many helpful discussions.

49 Sanuto 1969–70, vol. 42, p. 237 ff.

50 Corradini 1993, p. 28.

51 Ekserdjian (2006, p. 48) calls Saint Roch a 'virtual *Doppelgänger* of his own Saint John the Baptist in the National Gallery altarpiece'.

52 On references to Rome in Bologna after the Sack, see Ng 2012, p. 79 ff.

53 See Bosman 2008, pp. 73–88.

## A VISION OF SALVATION

1 Vasari 1966–87, vol. 4, pp. 532–3. All translations are by the author unless otherwise noted.
2 Wolk-Simon 2017.
3 Mercati 1997, p. 6.
4 *Dizionario biografico degli italiani* 1972, pp. 790–1.
5 Vaccaro 2001, p. 178. On Maria Bufalini as patron, see also King 1998, pp. 110–12.
6 Corradini 2000, pp. 124, 127.
7 Vaccaro 1993, p. 22.
8 Franzini 1588, p. 44. Vasari notes that Polidoro and Maturino Fiorentino collaborated to fresco one of their chiaroscuro *grotteschi* (an antique-style ornamental decoration) designs around the side door of the church. Vasari 1966–87, vol. 4, p. 457.
9 Corradini 2000, pp. 127–9.
10 Vasari 1966–87, vol. 4, p. 537.
11 Ekserdjian 2006, p. 7.
12 See p. 84 in this volume for full translation. The contract was first published in Corradini 1993.
13 Vaccaro 2001, pp. 178–9.
14 King 1998, p. 110 (and see p. 11 in this volume). Ekserdjian (2006, p. 7) comments that Pier Ilario is included in the contract here in an administrative rather than artistic capacity.
15 Vasari repeats this sentiment twice. Vasari 1966–87, vol. 4, pp. 534, 536.
16 Vaccaro 2002, p. 155.
17 Mercati 1997, p. 7. Nicolò also worked as a prestigious Vatican lawyer under the pontificate of Sixtus IV.
18 Vaccaro 2001, p. 179; Vaccaro 2002, p. 155.
19 *Madonna of Saint Sebastian* (about 1524, Gemäldegalerie, Dresden, inv. 151) and *Venus, Cupid and Satyr* (about 1524–7, Musée du Louvre, Paris, inv. 42). Faietti 2013, p. 263; Vaccaro 2002, p. 155.
20 Ekserdjian 2006, p. 29.
21 Freedberg 1975, pp. 219–20; Gould 1995, pp. 70–3; Hall 1999, p. 82.
22 Hartt 1975, p. 516; Krüger 2000, pp. 106–7.
23 Muzzi 2003, pp. 104–13.
24 Lora 2017.
25 Cracco 1959, p. 73.
26 Corradini 2000, p. 124.
27 Neher 1999, p. 119.
28 Nolin 2011, pp. 8–10.
29 Humfrey 1993, pp. 94–5; Douglas-Scott 1997.
30 Nolin 2011, p. 92.
31 Revelation 12: 1.
32 Doménech García 2023.
33 Stefaniak 1995, pp. 105–7 and note 11.
34 Levi D'Ancona 1957, p. 18; Vaccaro 1993, p. 26. As Levi D'Ancona notes, the National Gallery's Dalmatian/Venetian *Altarpiece of the Virgin Mary* (about 1400; NG4250.1–8) is one notable early example of this type of imagery.
35 Vuong 2013, p. 3.
36 Levi D'Ancona 1957, pp. 45–6.
37 Francia 2004, pp. 60–2.
38 Galizzi Kroegel 2005, pp. 216–17.
39 Stefaniak 1995, p. 106.
40 Zuccari 2005, p. 67.
41 Francia 2004, pp. 229–30; Zuccari 2005, p. 65.
42 Parma 1986, pp. 55–65; Brugnoli 1962. Completed by Federico and Taddeo Zuccari: Markou 2020. Perino's patron, Lorenzo Pucci, would later commission his portrait from Parmigianino.
43 Shearman 1967, pp. 19–160; Barbieri 2012, pp. 246–50.
44 Zuccari 2005, p. 67.
45 Levi D'Ancona 1957, p. 55.
46 Ekserdjian 2003, pp. 61–64; Acidini Luchinat 2006, p. 98. Now in the Onze-Lieve-Vrouwekerk, Bruges.

47 Galizzi Kroegel 2004, p. 84.
48 Ibid., pp. 85–7. For an alternative interpretation of Genga's altarpiece, see Ekserdjian 2018.
49 Another symbol of Christ's future Passion and sacrifice is suggested in the pentimento of the red coral beads around his right wrist.
50 Kleinbub 2011, p. 58.
51 Nagel 2017, pp. 393–6.
52 Morel 2011, pp. 49–65.
53 See esp. 'The Era of Collecting 1480–1527' in Christian 2010.
54 Nova 1998, pp. 161–4.
55 Gaston 1995, pp. 260–1.
56 Ekserdjian 1993, p. 392; Serra in Paris 2015–16, cat. 22, pp. 92–3. The collection was sold to Ottavio Farnese in 1546 and the majority of it eventually deposited in what is now the Museo Archeologico, Naples.
57 Ferino-Pagden 2003, p. 42; Hirst 2001; Ekserdjian 2001; Ekserdjian 2003, p. 64; Ekserdjian 2006, p. 19.
58 Mendelsohn 2002, pp. 108, 131. Vasari here draws on the classical topos from Cicerone's *De inventione*, where the painter Zeuxis borrows from the features of the five most beautiful virgins of Croton in order to paint Helen, deemed the most beautiful woman of all. Vasari 1966–87, vol. 1, p. 186.
59 Garrard 1975, p. 49, note 28; Bober and Rubinstein, 2010, p. 85, no. 36. Garrard notes that the elision between the seated Casa Sassi sculpture and Sansovino's Madonna may well have been apparent at the time, given the apocryphal legend that the latter was in fact an original antique work transformed into the holy Christian mother and child.
60 Raphael's *Madonna dell'Impannata* (1513–14, Gallerie degli Uffizi, Galleria Palatina, Florence, inv. Palatina (1912) n.94) was commissioned by the Florentine banker Bindo Altoviti and sent to Florence. Perino's composition in turn is indebted to the *Madonna of the Book* (after 1518, Gallerie degli Uffizi, Galleria Palatina, Florence, inv. 247) attributed to the school of Raphael by Linda Wolk-Simon. See Meyer zur Capellen 2001–9, vol. 2, pp. 239–41, no. A5. I am grateful to David Ekserdjian for this connection.
61 Wolk-Simon in Frankfurt 2016, cat. 40, pp. 120–1.
62 Rice 1985, pp. 7, 24–5.
63 McNally 1985, p. 153.
64 Lora 2017, p. 302.
65 Florence 2013, p. 82.
66 Published in Venice by Francisci Bindoni and Maphei Pasini. Florence 2013, cat. 47, pp. 160–1.
67 Lauster 2002, pp. 64–5.
68 Confirmed by examination of IRR imagery, undertaken by Rachel Billinge at the National Gallery, 2023. Other attributes – the book, the palm, the Baptist's reed cross, Jerome's crucifix and Christ's red coral bracelet – do not appear consistently, if at all, in the drawings and also seem to be late-stage decisions elaborating on the liturgical and iconographical meaning of the work.
69 Di Resta 2020, pp. 203–4.
70 Thimann 1999, pp. 143–5.

## DRAWING *THE VISION*

1 Vasari 1966–87, vol. 4, pp. 533.
2 Ibid., p. 536.
3 See Wivel 2022a, p. 43.
4 See Faietti 2015–16, pp. 21–42.
5 For stimulating analyses of Parmigianino's style, see Freedberg 1950, pp. 3–27; Oberhuber 2003, pp. 71–81; and Gnann 2007, vol. 1, pp. 12–25.
6 See Cropper 1976 for an analysis of how this became

constituent of Parmigianino's depiction of feminine beauty, in step with contemporaneous Petrarchist poetics that likened feminine forms to classical pottery.
7 Vasari 1966–87, vol. 4, p. 8; for discussion, see Wittkower 1961, pp. 291–302; Kemp 1977 and 1989; Koerner 1993, esp. chapters 1–2; Ames-Lewis 2000, esp. chapters 8–10; Wittkower and Wittkower 2007, esp. chapter 5; Rosand 2000; Wivel 2022b.
8 Lomazzo 1584, pp. 74–5; see Faietti 2015–16, pp. 30–1.
9 See for example Dolce 1557, p. 50; Sohm 1995, pp. 764–7 provides further context.
10 See Thomas 2017.
11 See Wivel 2022a, p. 43.
12 Friedländer 1957, p. 36 proposed it as a creative choice.
13 Ekserdjian 2006, p. 7. This eliminates for example a black chalk over metalpoint drawing in the Pushkin Museum, Moscow (about 1522–3, inv. 6190; Maiskaja 1986, cat. 7; Béguin, Di Giampaolo and Vaccaro 2000, pp. 208–9, cat. 108; Gnann 2007, vol. 1, p. 439, cat. 562). For an overview of Parmigianino's Roman drawings, see Gnann 2000.
14 British Museum, London, inv. Ff,1.94; Popham 1971, vol. 1, p. 91, cat. 182; Gnann 2007, vol. 1, pp. 437–8, cat. 553.
15 Devonshire Collection, Chatsworth, inv. 1072; Popham 1971, vol. 1, p. 213, cat. 741. See also Chapman in London and New York 2000–1, p. 138, cat. 90.
16 Musée Condé, Chantilly, inv. 142; Popham 1971, vol. 1, p. 59, cat. 54; Villard in Chantilly 1998–9, pp. 103–7, cat. 27. David Ekserdjian suggests a connection with Jacopo and Damiano da Gonzate's bronze *Saint Matthew* (1508) at Parma Cathedral, which employs a similar motif: Ekserdjian 2006, pp. 45, 269, note 15; for more, see Planiscig 1929. The motif recurs in Michelangelo Anselmi's (about 1492–about 1554) altarpiece of the *Virgin and Child with Angels and Saints Sebastian and Roch* originally in the cathedral (about 1536, Galleria Nazionale di Parma, inv. GN35); see Siveri in Fornari Schianchi 1998, pp. 90–1. My thanks to Maria Alambritis.
17 Musée du Louvre, Paris, inv. 6379; Popham 1971, vol. 1, pp. 134–5, cat. 360.
18 In drawings and the Bardi altarpiece (1521, Santa Maria Addolorata, Bardi, Parma); Vaccaro 2002, pp. 125–6, cat. 2.
19 British Museum, London, inv. 1882,0812.488; Popham 1971, vol. 1, p. 90, cat. 181; see also Chapman in London and New York 2000–1, pp. 134–6, cat. 88.
20 There is no indication that he traced the figure, as has been suggested in the past.
21 The J. Paul Getty Museum, Los Angeles, inv. 87.GB.9, and Städel Museum, Frankfurt am Main, inv. 13772; Béguin, Di Giampaolo and Vaccaro 2000, p. 206, cat. 95, and Popham 1971, vol. 1, p. 81, cat. 145.
22 Compelling as it is, I find it hard to confirm George Goldner's suggestion that the sheet contains two separate drawing campaigns; London and New York 2000–1, p. 141, cat. 92. My thanks to Julian Brooks for his close scrutiny and helpful comments.
23 See Ekserdjian 2006, pp. 45–7.
24 This kind of juxtaposition of heads was a mainstay of Parmigianino's career. It occurs in his *Nativity* (1525, Galleria Doria Pamphilj, Rome, inv. FC 292; Vaccaro 2002, pp. 151–2, cat. 16), as well as in two studies for the *Madonna and Child with Three Saints* (Gallerie degli Uffizi, Florence, inv. 1517 E and Musée du Louvre, Paris, inv. 6550; Popham 1971, vol. 1, p. 68, cat. 79 and p. 248, cat. OR 22; Gnann 2007, vol. 1, p. 457, cat. 663 and p. 514, Kopie 2). This composition

is also preserved in prints, see Gnann 2007, vol. 1, pp. 219–22. One by Francesco Rosaspina (1762–1841) locates the lost drawing in the collection of the 'Brothers Malaguti', presumably in Bologna (Gini 1788, print 16; Weigel 1865, p. 463, cat. 5493; Parma 2003, pp. 190–1, cat. 389). My thanks to Maria Alambritis and Mary Vaccaro.

25 British Museum, London, inv. Ff, 1.87 verso; Popham 1971, vol. 1, p. 91, cat. 183; Gnann 2007, vol. 1, p. 441, cat. 577.

26 Museo Nacional de Bellas Artes, Buenos Aires, inv. 173; Navarro 2001, pp. 46–7.

27 Drawings that are probably free variations rather than directly preparatory include a sheet in a private collection showing the *Virgin nursing the Child* (Ekserdjian 1999, pp. 21–2, cat. 34; Béguin, Di Giampaolo and Vaccaro 2000, p. 208, cat. 107) and one in the Städel Museum, Frankfurt (inv. 4255; Popham 1971, vol. 1, p. 80, cat. 142; Gnann 2007, vol. 1, p. 438, cat. 559), which may be connected to a later project recorded in a print (see Popham 1971, vol. 1, p. 155, cat. 464; Gnann 2007, vol. 1, p. 453, cat. 639; Francesco Rosaspina made a print after a variation, see Weigel 1865, p. 462, cat. 5483; Parma 2003, p. 192, cat. 392). A 1788 print by Roasapina referring to a lost drawing in the collection of Marcello Oretti may also be related (Gini 1788, Print 14; Weigel 1865, p. 458, cat. 5443; Ekserdjian 2008, p. 448).

28 The Metropolitan Museum of Art, New York, inv. 1970.238, and Musée du Louvre, Paris, inv. 6398; Popham 1971, vol. 1, p. 227, cat. 794, and p. 138, cat. 378; the former is also in Paris 2015–16, pp. 112–13, cat. 32; see also Gnann 2007, vol. 1, pp. 128–30, and Ekserdjian 1994, p. 203.

29 Musée Condé, Chantilly, inv. 134; Popham 1971, vol. 1, pp. 59–60, cat. 56; Gnann 2007, vol. 1, p. 438, cat. 557; Chantilly 1998–9, p. 108, cat. 28. Copies in the Hermitage, St Petersburg (inv. OP-4917) and the Albertina, Vienna (inv. 2709), preserve its arrangement before it was cropped on all sides; see Fröhlich-Bum 1921, pp. 20–1, fig. 10. A reversed version in red chalk in the Uffizi (inv. 9212) is probably a counterproof from a lost copy. A print after the Chantilly drawing by Antonio Maria Zanetti indicates that he owned it and thus a possible Arundel provenance (see p. 41 in this volume). Conrad Metz's (1749–1827) *Imitation of Ancient and Modern Drawings* (1789) includes a print after a drawing that is similar in arrangement, then in the London collection of Henry Reveley (1737–1798), formerly in those of Peter Lely (1618–1680), Jonathan Richardson (1667–1745) and Thomas Hudson (1701–1779), and untraced today; see British Museum, London, inv. 1981,U.12.

30 Milan, Finarte 21–2 April 1975, lot 21, and 22 March 1999, lot 49; Ekserdjian 1999, p. 21, cat. 33; Béguin, Di Giampaolo and Vaccaro 2000, p. 207, cat. 99. Parmigianino, *Madonna of the Rose* (1529/30, Gemäldegalerie, Dresden, inv. 161).

31 A drawing of the *Virgin and Child* seated on a pedestal and lit from the left may relate to this putative niche composition; Uffizi, Florence, inv. 1521E; Popham 1971, vol. 1, p. 68, cat. 83; Gnann 2007, vol. 1, p. 438, cat. 556.

32 Ashmolean Museum, Oxford, inv. P.II 442; Popham 1971, vol. 1, pp. 129–30, cat. 336; Gnann 2007, vol. 1, p. 439, cat. 561; see also Chapman in London and New York 2000–1, pp. 139–40, cat. 91. Michelangelo, *The Virgin and Child with the Infant Saint John* (about 1504–5, Royal Academy of Arts, London, inv. 03/1774).

33 Parmigianino seems to have picked up this

34 arrangement in the later 1520s in a drawing now in Parma (inv. 510/10; Popham 1971, vol. 1, p. 170, cat. 539; Gnann 2007, vol. 1, pp. 458–9, cat. 673); see Ekserdjian 2006, p. 171.

34 Ecole Nationale Supérieure des Beaux-Arts, Paris, inv. 221; Popham 1971, vol. 1, p. 166, cat. 519; Gnann 2007, vol. 1, p. 440, cat. 567; and private collection, United Kingdom, Gnann 2007, vol. 1, p. 440, cat. 569.

35 A black chalk drawing of the Child's lower body in The Metropolitan Museum of Art, New York (inv. 90.20.1) attributed to Pomerancio (1552–1626) seems to have been copied after a lost original by Parmigianino; Bolzoni 2013, p. 431, cat. R54. My thanks to Maria Alambritis.

36 Ecole Nationale Supérieure des Beaux-Arts, Paris, inv. M 2368; Popham 1971, vol. 1, p. 168, cat. 529; Gnann 2007, vol. 1, p. 440, cat. 568.

37 Ekserdjian 1993, p. 309.

38 Uffizi, Florence, inv. 233F, and British Museum, London, inv. 1859,0625.564. Tolnay 1975, vol. 1, pp. 52–3, no. 37, and pp. 56–7, no. 46. See Hirst 1963, pp. 166–7, note 2; Ekserdjian 1993, p. 390; Ekserdjian 2006, p. 30; and Popham 1971, vol. 1, p. 118.

39 Museo di Capodimonte, Naples, inv. GDS 1023; Popham 1971, vol. 1, pp. 117–18, cat. 291; Gnann 2007, vol. 1, pp. 439–40, cat. 565; Van Cleave 2024, cat. 26. On its verso is a drapery study which has unpersuasively been connected with Parmigianino's *Madonna di San Zaccaria* (1531–3, Gallerie degli Uffizi, Florence, inv. 1890, no.1328). See Funel 2011; the painting is Vaccaro 2002, pp. 177–8, cat. 32.

40 Albertina, Vienna, SL 59, B 359 inv. 2629; Popham 1971, vol. 1, p. 187, cat. 609; Gnann 2007, vol. 1, p. 440, cat. 566; see also Gnann in Parma and Vienna 2003, pp. 313–14, cat. II.3.50.

41 Museo di Capodimonte, Naples, inv. GDS 1390. A tiny *Child's Head*, also at Capodimonte (inv. GDS 1976, 1328), has been linked to the Caccialupi Altarpiece but is lit from the left and appears earlier in style; see Leone de Castris 2003, pp. 79–80; Gnann 2007, vol. 1, p. 440, cats 570–1; Van Cleave 2024, cats 37–8).

42 Winner in Berlin 1999, pp. 66–7; Ekserdjian 1999, pp. 20–1, cat. 32; Béguin, Di Giampaolo and Vaccaro 2000, p. 198, cat. 27; Gnann 2007, vol. 1, cats 573–4. The latter has a dynamically loose sketch of a putto on its verso.

43 Through large parts of his career Parmigianino would explore this motif in free drawings unrelated to specific works in paint. British Museum, London, inv. 1905,1110.32 (Popham 1971, vol. 1, p. 91, cat. 185; Gnann 2007, vol. 1, p. 442, cat. 580); Musée Atger, Montpellier, inv. 222; Uffizi, Florence, inv. 1520 E; British Museum, inv. Pp 2.131; Hermitage, St Petersburg, inv. OP-14147; Victoria and Albert Museum, London, inv. Dyce 277; and Museo di Capodimonte, Naples, inv. 1292 M119, have all been linked to the Caccialupi Altarpiece, but are too different for the association to be more than tentative. See Popham 1971, vol. 1, pp. 68, 83, 91, 111, 116, cats 82, 153, 184, 267, 285; Gnann 2007, vol. 1, pp. 442–4, cats 584–9; and Chapman in London and New York 2000–1, p. 143, cat. 94. See also Gnann 2007, vol. 1, p. 374, cats 152–3; p. 375, cat. 162; p. 415, cats 416–17; p. 418, cat. 434.

44 Galleria Nazionale, Parma, inv. 510/16; Popham 1971, vol. 1, pp. 171–2, cat. 544; Gnann 2007, vol. 1, p. 444, cat. 590. Popham proposes that the sketches were made after the painting for some other purpose, which seems unnecessarily complicated, and as mentioned, the Child is not arranged exactly as in the painting.

45 See Gnann 2007, vol. 1, p. 159.

46 See p. 18 in this volume.

47 Musée du Louvre, Paris, inv. 6447; Popham 1971, vol. 1, p. 148, cat. 427; Gnann 2007, vol. 1, pp. 441–2, cat. 578.

48 Ekserdjian 1999, pp. 21–2, cat. 35; Béguin, Di Giampaolo and Vaccaro 2000, p. 199, cat. 34; Gnann 2007, vol. 1, p. 442, cat. 582.

49 Musée du Louvre, Paris, inv. 6423; Popham 1971, vol. 1, p. 143, cat. 402; Gnann 2007, vol. 1, p. 442, cat. 579.

50 There are general, but not necessarily direct, parallels to one of Michelangelo's so-called *ignudi* on the Sistine ceiling; see e.g. Ekserdjian 2006, p. 29 and Serra in Paris 2015–16, pp. 116–17, cat. 35.

51 The verso was uncovered during restoration in preparation for the 2015 Parmigianino exhibition at the Louvre and is mentioned in neither Popham nor Gnann; see Roberta Serra in Paris 2015–16, pp. 116–17, cat. 35.

52 Uffizi, Florence, inv. 13611; Popham 1971, vol. 1, p. 74, cat. 107; Gnann 2007, vol. 1, p. 444, cat. 592.

53 Bartsch 1803–21, vol. 15, p. 94, cat. 61, and vol. 12, p. 100, cat. 10; for the most recent detailed treatments, see Gnann in Vienna 2013–14, pp. 138–43, cats 53–5, and Naoko Takahatake in Los Angeles 2018–19, pp. 100–3, cats 22–5.

54 The J. Paul Getty Museum, Los Angeles, inv. 84.GA.9; Béguin, Di Giampaolo and Vaccaro 2000, p. 206, cat. 92; Gnann 2007, vol. 1, p. 442, cat. 583. As pointed out by Popham 1971, vol. 1, p. 255, cat. OR 83, Rosaspina's print after it shows it before it was cropped.

55 For Parmigianino's synthesis of the spiritual and the erotic, see Nova 1998 and Morel 2011.

56 Royal Collection, Windsor, inv. RCIN 900883; Popham 1971, vol. 1, p. 74, cat. 107; Gnann 2007, vol. 1, pp. 53, 442, cat. 581. A pen-and-ink wash study based on the antique, so-called *Belvedere Torso* in the Vatican is on the verso and does not appear to be by Parmigianino.

57 Albertina, Vienna, inv. 2630; Popham 1971, vol. 1, pp. 188–9, cat. 616; Gnann 2007, vol. 1, p. 464, cat. 705.

58 Albertina, Vienna, inv. 2615; Popham 1971, vol. 1, p. 187, cat. 610; Gnann 2007, vol. 1, p. 441, cat. 572. See also Gnann in Parma and Vienna 2003, pp. 315–16, cat. II.3.53; and Ekserdjian in Rome 2015–16, p. 215, cat. 64. The only other surviving cartoon-like drawing by Parmigianino is the *Bishop Saint in Bust-Length* in The Metropolitan Museum of Art, made for the leftmost figure in his *Saint Margaret* altarpiece (1529, Pinacoteca Nazionale Bologna, inv. 588). While at scale, it too has no indentation marks along the contours and no pouncing holes, nor does it match in detail the head as painted; The Metropolitan Museum of Art, New York, inv.1995.306; Bambach in London and New York 2000–1, pp. 149–50; Gnann 2007, vol. 1, p. 457, cat. 664. The painting is Béguin, Giampaolo and Vaccaro 2000, pp. 166–8, cat. 24.

59 I am grateful to Rachel Billinge for her thoughts on this.

60 Uffizi, Florence, inv. 753 P; Popham 1971, vol. 1, p. 76, cat. 118; Florence 2003, pp. 39–42, cat. 24; Gnann 2007, vol. 1, p. 395, cat. 296. An instructive contrast to this atmospheric drawing is a linear, analytical study of a shrubbery and a landscape view, also in the Uffizi (inv. 501 P): Popham 1971, vol. 1, pp. 75–6, cat. 117; Gnann 2007, vol. 1, p. 451, cat. 631.

61 Uffizi, Florence, inv. 9253 S v; Popham 1971, vol. 1, p. 77, cat. 126; Gnann 2007, vol. 1, p. 373, cat. 149.

## A REUNITED STUDY FOR THE CACCIALUPI ALTARPIECE

1 Ashmolean Museum, Oxford, inv. P.II 442; Popham 1971, vol. 1, p. 129, cat. 335; Gnann 2007, vol. 1, p. 438, cat. 558; Musée Condé, Chantilly, inv. 142; Popham 1971, vol. 1, p. 59, cat. 54; Villard in Chantilly 1998–9, pp. 103–7, cat. 27.
2 Chapman in London and New York 2000–1, p. 137.
3 Chantilly 1998–9, p. 106.
4 Confirmed by Angelamaria Aceto and Lara Daniels of the Ashmolean Museum paper conservation studio, 20 October 2023.
5 As confirmed by Angelamaria Aceto and Lara Daniels, 20 October 2023.
6 Examination undertaken in person at the Ashmolean Museum paper conservation studio, 5 December 2023.
7 Parker 1972, pp. 221–2; Villard in Chantilly 1998–9, p. 104, cat. 27.
8 Preti-Hamard 2007, p. 311.
9 Rodinò 1992.
10 Bottari and Ticozzi 1822–5, vol. 2, no. 55, p. 132.
11 Preti-Hamard 2007, p. 311; p. 319.
12 Tormen 2009, p. 39.
13 An expanded version of this research will appear in a forthcoming publication.

## FROM ROME TO LONDON

1 Vaccaro 1993, p. 27.
2 On Parmigianino's activity in Bologna, see Ekserdjian 2006, pp. 7–10.
3 'Un quadro della Madonna, molto meraviglioso': Biondo 1549, cap. 19. All translations are by the author unless otherwise noted.
4 Vasari confuses details of the commission and erroneously names Lorenzo Cybo as the patron. This would be corrected in the second edition of the *Lives* published in 1568; see Vaccaro 1993, p. 22; Vasari 1966–87, vol. 4, pp. 537–9.
5 Mercati 1997, p. 17.
6 As described by the carpenter and frame-maker Berto Alberti, who was commissioned by Giulio to make a frame and install the painting in the family chapel. Entry of 20 August 1558, Diary A of Berto Alberti, Archivio di Biblioteca della Gallerie degli Uffizi, Florence, MS 267, fol. 10r, published in Azzi 1915, and Gualandi 1845, p. 57; transcribed in letter from Christopher L.C. Ewart Whitcombe to Allan Braham, 8 August 1983, NG33 object file, National Gallery Archives.
7 'A cornu Epistole eravi il Famoso Quadro di Gio. Batt[ist]a, opera del Celebre Franc[esco] Manzuoli Parmeggiano': Luigi Andreocci, *Memorie delle chiese … di Città di Castello*, 1775, Archivio Vescovile, Città di Castello, MS 66 (fol. 20r).
8 Alessandro Certini, 'Origine delle chiese e monasteri di Città di Castello', 1726–8, Archivio Vescovile, Città di Castello, MS 1, fols 84v–92, at fol. 94r; Mavilla 2023, p. 211. I am grateful to Francesca Mavilla for generously sharing with me her research on the history and decoration of the Bufalini chapel in relation to Parmigianino's altarpiece, to be published.
9 Massari 2024, pp. 44–8, 276; Pacetti, *Crucifixion with Saints* (17th century, Museo Diocesano, Città di Castello). Pacetti adapted the figure of the Virgin seated on clouds for his *Madonna of the Girdle* (about 1650) in the church of Santa Maria Maggiore, Spello. A sixteenth-century copy after the head of the Baptist was formerly attributed to Barocci (British Museum, London, inv. 1860,0616.23).
10 Mancini 1832, vol. 1, pp. 186, 269, 'una copia magistrale' in the Casa Mancini; Amicizia 1899, p. 68, notes that the Mancini copy is painted by Bernardino Gagliardi (1609–1660).
11 Conti 1627, pp. 159–60.
12 Signorelli's *Adoration* is now in the Musée du Louvre, Paris; the *Nativity* is in the Museo di Capodimonte, Naples. Mavilla 2021, p. 22, and see p. 25 (fig. 7) for Mavilla's hypothetical reconstruction of the church and its altars.
13 Sapori 2023, p. 324. As Sapori details, the Bufalini archive inventory of 1771 reveals that the painting was initially displayed in the 'Appartamento vecchio', and subsequently moved to the gallery (p. 324 and see note 8). I am grateful to Francesca Mavilla for drawing my attention to this article.
14 'Deliberarono poi i Signori Buffalinì dì ritirarlo nel loro Palazzo, in cui al giorno d'oggi alquanto guasto e scrostato conservali con gelosia, e fecero nella detta Cappella sostituire una copia di buona mano': Affò 1784, pp. 61–2.
15 'Lo ripreso il Card. Buffalini … l'anno 1772': Andreocci, *Memorie delle chiese*, fol. 20r; Muzi 1843, p. 240. 'Nel 5° Altare il quadro con Nostra Donna in aria, e col Signorino suo Figlio in piedi, et a basso un S. Giovanni Battista, e S. Girolamo, che dorme, è una copia del Parmigianino': Tommaso Francesco Bernardi, after 1774, Biblioteca Statale di Lucca, MS 1918, fol. 64v.
16 Possibly to help fund the rebuilding of Sant'Agostino, like the patrons of Raphael's *Coronation* altarpiece. Signorelli's *Adoration* and *Nativity* were sold as a consequence of the earthquake. See Henry 2002, p. 269.
17 Parmigianino's *Portrait of Cardinal Lorenzo Pucci* (probably 1529–30, private collection) also formed part of the Abercorn collection from 1837.
18 Letter of James Durno to Sir William Hamilton, Rome, 16 December 1791, Abercorn Papers, Public Record Office, Northern Ireland, D/623/A/227/35.
19 Sir Abraham Hume to Giovanni Maria Sasso, 30 July 1792, Seminario Patriarcale di Venezia, MS 768.1; 861.1; published in Borean 2004, Letter 65. Original text: 'Un cavaliere inglese ha fatto ultimamente l'acquisto di un bellissimo quadro di Parmigianino, il quale è stato pochi anni fa un pezzo d'altare in un convento di una città non molto lontano di Perugia.'
20 Zannoni 1817, p. 122: 'quel celebre quadro … acquistato da un Lord Inglese pel vistoso prezzo di 7700 piastre. A sentimento di persona assai intelligente, il Parmigianino non fece mai opera più bella.'
21 Now Kimbell Art Museum, Fort Worth, Texas, inv. AP 1995.09.
22 Now private collection.
23 Now J. Paul Getty Museum, Los Angeles, inv. 2017.22.
24 See Thomas (forthcoming). I am grateful to Sarah Thomas for kindly sharing her essay with me prior to publication.
25 Between 1809 and 1819 it exchanged hands several times, being sold to a collector known as Harris, and then to merchant and MP Richard Hart Davis (1766–1842).
26 British Institution 1819, no. 1.
27 National Gallery, London, NG35.
28 Wallace Collection, London, P63. Christie's, London, 14 June 1823, lot. 61. The Rubens was sold for £2,730.
29 Anon., 'Fine Arts', *Examiner*, 27 July 1823, p. 490.
30 See Mussini 2003, pp. 15–41; Di Giampaolo 2000, pp. 177–90.
31 Spagnolo 2016, pp. 61–2.
32 As for example in: Conti 1627; Andreocci, *Memorie delle chiese*; Mancini 1832, vol. 1; Muzi 1843; Amicizia 1899.
33 Magherini-Graziani 1897, pp. 181–2.
34 Ottley 1826, p. 45.

35 NG6411 and NG6427 respectively. See Vaccaro 2002, cats 17, 39.
36 Passavant 1836, p. 37.
37 Jameson 1845, vol. 1, p. 440.
38 Letter from John Constable to Maria Bicknell, 12 November 1814, in Constable 1954–8, vol. 3.
39 Fuseli 1831, vol. 2, p. 106.
40 Waters 1879, pp. 398–9.
41 Berenson 1907, p. 143.
42 Bellori 1976, p. 31.
43 The historiography of Mannerism has been discussed extensively elsewhere. See Bosch 2020, pp. 72–115; Cropper 2014, pp. 343–53; and Aurenhammer 2016, pp. 14–23.
44 Aurenhammer 2016, p. 17.
45 'Leichter Grazie, Vollkommenheit der Gliedmaßen und Durchgeistigung des Ausdruckes gemessen': Fröhlich-Bum 1921, p. 5.
46 Quoted in Cropper 2014, p. 347; Aurenhammer 2016, p. 17.
47 Vasari 1966–87, vol. 4, pp. 3–13.
48 Rebecchini 2022, p. 25.
49 Roskill 1968, p. 317; Dolce 1557, p. 199.
50 Bosch 2020, pp. 52–3.
51 'Una diligenza mirabile': Dolce 1557, p. 199.
52 'Lume di grazia': Vasari 1966–87, vol. 4, p. 532.

## RESTORATION, CONSTRUCTION AND PAINTING TECHNIQUE

1 More planks with narrower boards is the consequence of choosing not to use wider planks with end-to-end joins, as found for example in the Vasarian redecoration schemes in the Florentine churches of Santa Croce and Santa Maria Novella some decades later. For a published example of the latter see Keith 1984.
2 Bartsch 1803–21, vol. 15, p. 127, cat. 62.
3 *Bishop Saint in Bust-Length (Cartoon for an Altarpiece)*, The Metropolitan Museum of Art, New York, inv. 1995.306. Gnann 2007, vol. 1, p. 457, cat. 664. See also note 58 on p. 87 in this volume.

## APPENDIX

With thanks to Amanda Lillie.
1 A fiscal period of 15 years used to date events and transactions, first established by Roman emperor Constantine in the fourth century CE.
2 This repetitive sentence instructs the painters to place Saint Jerome and Saint John the Baptist below the Virgin at either side of her feet.
3 'In cornicibus cappellae' is an ambiguous expression, here interpreted as referring to the possible presence of decorative moulding on the chapel's walls. This could suggest that the *Birth of the Virgin* and *Joachim and Anna's Meeting at the Golden Gate* may have been frescoes, as surmised in Vaccaro 1993, p. 26.
4 The cameral obligation (in forma *Camerae*) is a juridical institution adopted in the Papal States during the early modern period. This paragraph consists of abbreviated legal formulae referring to this specific type of obligation. For a concise history of the cameral obligation and how it affected artistic production, see Antonia Fiori, 'The Cameral Obligation in the Documents of the Accademia di San Luca', https://www.nga.gov/accademia/en/essays/Fiori-cameral-obligation.html (accessed 7 September 2024).

# BIBLIOGRAPHY

ACIDINI LUCHINAT 2006
C. Acidini Luchinat, *Michelangelo scultore*, Milan 2006

AFFÒ 1784
I. Affò, *Vita del graziossissima pittore Francesco Mazzola detto il Parmigianino*, Parma 1784

AMES-LEWIS 2000
F. Ames-Lewis, *The Intellectual Life of the Early Renaissance Artist*, New Haven, CT and London 2000

AMICIZIA 1899
G. Amicizia, *Guida Artistico-Commerciale di Città di Castello*, Città di Castello 1899

AURENHAMMER 2016
H. Aurenhammer, 'Manner, Mannerism, *maniera*: On the History of a Controversial Term', in Frankfurt 2016, pp. 14–23

AZZI 1915
G. degli Azzi, 'Archivio Alberti', *Gli Archivi della storia d'Italia*, ser. 2, vol. 4, Rocca S. Casciano 1915

BALLARDINI 2022
A. Ballardini, 'L'altare del Volto Santo nell'antico San Pietro', in S. Turiziani and P. Zander (eds), *Da San Pietro in Vaticano la tavola di Ugo da Carpi per l'altare del Volto santo*, exh. cat., Corte Medievale di Palazzo Madama, Turin 2022, pp. 20–49

BARBIERI 2012
C. Barbieri, 'La Pala della Concezione e Natività della Vergine di Sebastiano per la cappella Chigi e un disegno inedito', *Konsthistorisk tidskrift/Journal of Art History*, 81, no. 4 (2012), pp. 245–53

BARKAN 1999
L. Barkan, *Unearthing the Past: Archaeology and Aesthetics in the Making of Renaissance Culture*, New Haven, CT 1999

BARTSCH 1803–21
A. Bartsch, *Le peintre-graveur*, 21 vols, Vienna 1803–21

BÉGUIN 2000
S. Béguin, 'Mysterious Parmigianino', in Béguin, Di Giampaolo and Vaccaro 2000, pp. 9–27

BÉGUIN, DI GIAMPAOLO AND VACCARO 2000
S. Béguin, M. di Giampaolo and M. Vaccaro (eds), *Parmigianino: The Drawings*, Turin 2000

BELLORI 1976
G.P. Bellori, *Le vite de' pittori, scultori, e architettori moderni (1672)*, E. Borea (ed.), Turin 1976

BENEDETTI, CARLEVARIS AND ERCOLINO 2022
S. Benedetti, L. Carlevaris and M.G. Ercolino (eds), *Santa Maria della Pace in Roma. Storia urbana e vicende artistiche tra XV e XVII secolo: costruzione, trasformazioni, restauri, rilievi*, Rome 2022

BERENSON 1907
B. Berenson, *North Italian Painters of the Renaissance*, New York 1907 (second edn)

BERLIN 1999
A. Dückers (ed.), *Linie, Licht und Schatten: Meisterzeichnungen und Skulpturen der Sammlung Jan und Marie-Anne Krugier-Poniatowski*, exh. cat. Kupferstichkabinett, Berlin 1999

BIONDO 1549
M. Biondo, *Della nobilissima pittura*, Venice 1549

BLACKWOOD 2013
N. Blackwood, 'Printmaker as Painter: Looking Closely at Ugo da Carpi's *Saint Veronica Altarpiece*', *Oxford Art Journal*, 36, no. 2 (2013), pp. 167–84

BOBER AND RUBINSTEIN 2010
P.P. Bober and R. Rubinstein, *Renaissance Artists and Antique Sculpture: A Handbook of Sources*, London and Turnhout 2010 (second edn)

BOLZONI 2013
M.S. Bolzoni, *Il Cavalier Giusepe Cesari d'Arpino: Maestro del disegno. Catalogo ragionato dell'opera grafica*, Rome 2013

BONAPARTE 1830
J. Bonaparte, *Le Sac de Rome écrit en 1527 par Jacques Bonaparte, témoin oculaire*, trans. N.L. Bonaparte, Florence 1830

BOREAN 2004
L. Borean, 'I disegni della collezione Zanetti', in *Lettere artistiche del Settecento veneziano. Il carteggio Giovanni Maria Sasso–Abraham Hume*, vol. 2, Verona 2004, pp. 76–81

BOSCH 2020
L. Bosch, *Mannerism, Spirituality and Cognition: The Art of Enargeia*, London and New York 2020

BOSMAN 2008
S. Bosman, *The National Gallery in Wartime*, London 2008

BOTTARI AND TICOZZI 1822–5
G. Bottari and S. Ticozzi, *Raccolta di lettere sulla pittura*, Milan 1822–5

BRITISH INSTITUTION 1819
*British Institution: Catalogue of Pictures*, London 1819

BRUGNOLI 1962
M.V. Brugnoli, 'Gli affreschi di Perin del Vaga nella Cappella Pucci. Note sulla prima attività romana del pittore', in *Bolletino d'Arte*, XLVII, 1962, IV, pp. 327–50

CARTEGGIO 1965
M. Buonarroti, *Il carteggio di Michelangelo*, vol. 3, G. Poggi, P. Barocchi and R. Ristori (eds), Florence 1965

CELLINI 2002
B. Cellini, *My Life*, J. Conaway Bondanella and P. Bondanella (eds), Oxford 2002

CHANTILLY 1998–9
O. Villard with D. Cordellier (eds), *Dessins italiens du Musée Condé à Chantilly*, vol. 3, *Vénétie, Lombardie, Piémont, Émilie, XVe –XVIe siècle*, exh. cat., Musée Condé, Chantilly, 1998–9, Paris 1998

CHASTEL 1983
A. Chastel, *The Sack of Rome 1527*, trans. B. Archer, Princeton, NJ 1983

CHIUSA 2001
M.C. Chiusa, *Parmigianino*, Milan 2001

CHRISTIAN 2010
K.W. Christian, *Empire without End: Antiquities Collections in Renaissance Rome, c.1350–1527*, New Haven, CT and London 2010

VAN CLEAVE 2024
C. van Cleave, *The Farnese Collection of Drawings*, Naples 2024

CONSTABLE 1954–8
*Correspondence and other memorials of John Constable: typescript*, R.B. Beckett (ed.), manuscript, 20 vols

CONTI 1627
A. Conti, *Fiori Vaghi: Delle vite dei Santi e Beati, delle chiese e delle reliquie di Città di Castello*, Città di Castello 1627

CORRADINI 1993
S. Corradini, 'Parmigianino's Contract for the Caccialupi Chapel in San Salvatore in Lauro', *Burlington Magazine*, 135, no. 1078 (1993), pp. 27–9

CORRADINI 2000
S. Corradini, 'Note sul Cardinale Latino Orsini fondatore di S. Salvatore in Lauro ed il suo elogio funebre', in F. Benzi (ed.), *Sisto IV: Le Arti a Roma nel Primo Rinascimento*, Rome 2000, pp. 123–41

CRACCO 1959
G. Cracco, 'La fondazione dei Canonici secolari di S. Giorgio in Alga', *Rivista di storia della chiesa in Italia*, 23 (1959), pp. 70–88

CROPPER 1976
E. Cropper, 'On Beautiful Women, Parmigianino, *Petrarchismo*, and the Vernacular Style', *Art Bulletin*, 58 (1976), pp. 374–94

CROPPER 2014
E. Cropper, 'The Decline and Rise of Pontormo and Rosso Fiorentino: Mannerism and Modernity', in C. Falciani and A. Natali (eds), *Pontormo and Rosso Fiorentino: Diverging Paths of Mannerism*, exh. cat., Palazzo Strozzi, Florence 2014, pp. 343–53

DACOS 1969
N. Dacos, *La Découverte de la Domus Aurea et la formation des grotesques à la Renaissance*, London 1969

DALL'ACQUA 1984
M. Dall'Acqua, *Correggio e il suo tempo*, Parma 1984

DI GIAMPAOLO 2000
M. di Giampaolo, 'Parmigianino, Draughtsman in the Literature of Art: From Vasari to the Age of Neoclassicism', in Béguin, Di Giampaolo and Vaccaro 2000, pp. 177–90

DI RESTA 2020
J. di Resta, 'Negotiating the Numinous: Pordenone and the Miraculous Madonna di Campagna of Piacenza', *Mitteilungen des Kunsthistorischen Institutes in Florenz*, 62, no. 2/3 (2020), pp. 181–287

*DIZIONARIO BIOGRAFICO DEGLI ITALIANI* 1972
A.M. Ghisalberti (ed.), *Dizionario biografico degli italiani*, vol. 15, Rome 1972

DOLCE 1557
L. Dolce, *Dialogo della Pittura*, Venice 1557

DOMÉNECH GARCÍA 2023
S. Doménech García, 'The Woman and the Dragon: The Formation of the Image of the *Mulier Amicta Sole* in the Revelation of St John in Western Medieval Art', *Religions*, 14, no. 1 (2023), n.p.

DOUGLAS-SCOTT 1997
M. Douglas-Scott, 'Jacopo Tintoretto's Altarpiece of St Agnes at the Madonna dell'Orto in Venice and the Memorialisation of Cardinal Contarini', *Journal of the Warburg and Courtauld Institutes*, 60 (1997), pp. 130–63

EKSERDJIAN 1993
D. Ekserdjian, 'Parmigianino and Michelangelo', *Master Drawings*, 31, no. 4 (1993), pp. 390–4

EKSERDJIAN 1994
D. Ekserdjian, 'Sixteenth-Century Italian Drawings. New York, Metropolitan Museum' (review), *Burlington Magazine*, 136, no. 1092 (1994), pp. 202–3

EKSERDJIAN 1999
D. Ekserdjian, 'Unpublished Drawings by Parmigianino: Towards a Supplement to Popham's "Catalogue Raisonné"', *Apollo*, 150, no. 450 (1999), pp. 3–41

EKSERDJIAN 2001
D. Ekserdjian, 'Parmigianino and the Antique', *Apollo*, no. 473 (July 2001), pp. 42–50

EKSERDJIAN 2003
D. Ekserdjian, 'Parmigianino and Michelangelo', in F. Ames-Lewis and P. Joannides (eds), *Reactions to the Master: Michelangelo's Effect on Art and Artists in the Sixteenth Century*, Aldershot 2003, pp. 53–67

EKSERDJIAN 2006
D. Ekserdjian, *Parmigianino*, New Haven, CT and London 2006

EKSERDJIAN 2008
D. Ekserdjian, '*Parmigianino tradotto: La fortuna di Francesco Mazzola nelle stampe di riproduzione fra il Cinquecento e l'Ottocento* by Massimo Mussini and Grazia Maria de Rubeis; *Parmigianino und sein Kreis: Druckgraphik aus der Sammlung Baselitz* by Achim Gnann; *Parmigianino: Die Madonna in der Alten Pinakothek* by Achim Gnann, Veronika Poll-Frommel, Andreas Schumacher and Cornelia Syre' (review), *Print Quarterly*, 25, no. 4 (2008), pp. 446–50

EKSERDJIAN 2018
D. Ekserdjian, 'La pala di Genga per Cesena: committenza e iconografia', in Barbara Agosti et al. (eds), *Girolamo Genga: una via obliqua alla maniera moderna*, Bologna 2018, pp. 167–77

FADDA 2016
E. Fadda, 'Parmigianino in Rome', in Rome 2016, pp. 49–59

FAIETTI 2013
M. Faietti, 'Betrayals of the Gods and Metamorphoses of Artists: Parmigianino, Caraglio and Agostino Carracci', *Artibus et Historiae*, 34, no. 68 (2013), pp. 257–75

FAIETTI 2015–16
M. Faietti, 'Raphael redivivus', in Rome 2015–16, pp. 21–42

FELICETTI 2001
S. Felicetti, '*Locatio ad pingendum:* Nuovi spogli archivistici sui pittori in Umbria fra Trecento e Cinqueccento', *Studio di Storia del Arte*, 12 (2001), pp. 253–329

FELICETTI 2002
S. Felicetti, 'Maestro Zaccaria di Filippo da Parma pittore in Umbria nel 1525', in L. Fornari Schianchi (ed.), *Parmigianino e il manierismo europeo: atti del convegno internazionale di studi*, Milan 2002, pp. 33–44

FERINO-PAGDEN 2003
S. Ferino-Pagden, 'In Urbe: Parmigianino tra antico e moderno', in Parma and Vienna 2003, pp. 37–47

FLORENCE 2003
M. Di Giampaolo and A. Muzzi (eds), *Il Parmigianino e il fascino di Parma*, exh. cat., Gabinetto disegni e stampe Uffizi, Florence 2003

FLORENCE 2013
C. Rabbi-Bernard, A. Cecchi and Y. Hersant (eds), *Il sogno del Rinascimento*, exh. cat., Galleria Palatina, Palazzo Pitti, Florence, published Livorno 2013

FORNARI SCHIANCHI 1998
L. Fornari Schianchi (ed.), *Galleria Nazionale di Parma: Catalogo delle opere del cinquecento e iconografia farnesiana*, Milan 1998

FORNARI SCHIANCHI 2002
L. Fornari Schianchi, 'Zaccaria di Filippo Mazzola: La prima opera nota e il suo ruolo nella bottega', in L. Fornari Schianchi (ed.), *Parmigianino e il manierismo europeo: atti del convegno internazionale di studi*, Milan 2002, pp. 50–7

FORNARI SCHIANCHI 2003
L. Fornari Schianchi (ed.), *Il rinascimento a Parma e dintorni: Guida storico-artistica*, Milan 2003

FRANCIA 2004
V. Francia, *Splendore di Bellezza: L'iconographia dell'Immacolata Concezione nella pittura rinascimentale Italiana*, Vatican City 2004

FRANKFURT 2016
B. Eclercy (ed.), *Maniera: Pontormo, Bronzino, and Medici Florence*, exh. cat., Städel Museum, Frankfurt 2016

FRANKLIN 2003–4
D. Franklin, 'The Paintings of Parmigianino', in D. Franklin (ed.), *A Beautiful and Gracious Manner: The Art of Parmigianino*, exh. cat., National Gallery of Canada, Ottawa, 2003–4; Frick Collection, New York 2004, pp. 1-29

FRANZINI 1588
G. Franzini, *Le cose maravigliose dell'alma città di Roma*, Venice 1588

FREEDBERG 1950
S.J. Freedberg, *Parmigianino: His Works in Painting*, Cambridge, MA 1950

FREEDBERG 1975
S.J. Freedberg, *Painting in Italy 1500–1600*, Harmondsworth 1975 (first rev. edn)

FRIEDLÄNDER 1957
W. Friedländer, *Mannerism and Anti-Mannerism in Italian Painting*, New York 1957

FRÖHLICH-BUM 1921
L. Fröhlich-Bum, *Parmigianino und der Manierismus*, Vienna 1921

FUNEL 2011
S. Funel, 'Un disegno sconosciuto del Parmigianino', in C. Vargas, A. Migliaccio and S. Causa (eds), *Scritti in onore di Maria Causa Picone*, Naples 2011, pp. 189–200

FUSELI 1831
*The Life and Writings of Henry Fuseli*, John Knowles (ed.), 3 vols, London 1831

GALIZZI KROEGEL 2004
A. Galizzi Kroegel, 'A misunderstood iconography: Girolamo Genga's altarpiece for S. Agostino in Cesena' in G. Periti (ed.), *Drawing Relationships in Northern Italian Renaissance Art: Patronage and Theories of Invention*, Aldershot 2004, pp. 77–100

GALIZZI KROEGEL 2005
A. Galizzi Kroegel, 'Quando il centro usa prudenza e la periferia osa: L'iconografia dell'Immacolata Concezione in Emilia Romagna e nelle Marche (con una postilla sulla *Vergine delle rocce* di Leonardo)', in G. Periti (ed.), *Emilia e Marche nel Rinascimento: L'identità visiva della 'periferia'*, Bergamo 2005, pp. 215–51

GARRARD 1975
M.D. Garrard, 'Jacopo Sansovino's Madonna in Sant'Agostino: An Antique Source Rediscovered', *Journal of the Warburg and Courtauld Institutes*, 38 (1975), pp. 333–8

GASTON 1995
R.W. Gaston, 'Sacred Erotica: The Classical "Figura" in Religious Painting of the Early Cinquecento', *International Journal of the Classical Tradition*, 2, no. 2 (1995), pp. 238–64

GINI 1788
C.M. Gini, *Celleberrimi Francisci Mazzola Parmensis graphides per Ludovicum Inig Bononiæ collectæ*, Bologna 1788

GNANN 2000
A. Gnann, 'Per una cronologia dei disegni romani di Parmigianino', *Quaderni di Palazzo Te*, no. 7 (2000), pp. 49–73

GNANN 2007
A. Gnann *Parmigianino: Die Zeichnungen*, 2 vols, Munich 2007

GOULD 1995
C. Gould, *Parmigianino*, New York 1995

GUALANDI 1845
M. Gualandi, 'Memorie intorno la celebre famiglia degli Alberti di Borgo S. Sepolcro', in *Memorie Originale Italiane Risguardanti le Belle Arti*, serie 6, vol. 2, Bologna 1845, pp. 50–91

HALL 1999
M. Hall, *After Raphael: Painting in Central Italy in the Sixteenth Century*, Cambridge 1999

HARTT 1975
F. Hartt, *History of Italian Renaissance Art*, Englewood Cliffs, NJ 1975 (third edn)

HENRY 2002
T. Henry, 'Raphael's Altar-Piece Patrons in Città di Castello', *Burlington Magazine*, 144, no. 1190 (2002), pp. 268–78

HIRST 1963
M. Hirst, 'Michelangelo Drawings in Florence', *Burlington Magazine*, 105, no. 721 (1963), pp. 166–71

HIRST 2001
M. Hirst, 'Parmigianino and the Antique: a Supplement', *Apollo*, September 2001, p. 53

HOOK 2004
J. Hook, *The Sack of Rome, 1527*, London 1972

HUMFREY 1993
P. Humfrey, *The Altarpiece in Renaissance Venice*, New Haven, CT and London 1993

JAMESON 1845
A. Jameson, *Memoirs of the Early Italian Painters*, 2 vols, London 1845

KEITH 1984
L. Keith, 'The Structural Conservation of Maso da San Friano's "Visitation Altarpiece"', *Hamilton Kerr Institute Bulletin*, no. 2 (1984), pp. 78–83

KEMP 1977
M. Kemp, 'From "Mimesis" to "Fantasia": The Quattrocento Vocabulary of Creation, Inspiration and Genius in the Visual Arts', *Viator*, 8 (1977), pp. 347–98

KEMP 1989
M. Kemp, 'The "Super-Artist" as Genius: The Sixteenth-Century View', in P. Murray (ed.), *Genius: The History of an Idea*, Oxford 1989, pp. 32–53

KING 1998
C. King, *Renaissance Women Patrons: Wives and Widows in Italy, c.1300–1550*, Manchester and New York 1998

KLEINBUB 2011
C. Kleinbub, *Vision and the Visionary in Raphael*, University Park, PA 2011

KOERNER 1993
J.I. Koerner, *The Moment of Self-Portraiture in German Renaissance Art*, Chicago and London 1993

KRÜGER 2000
K. Krüger, 'Malerei als Poesie der Ferne im Cinquecento', in K. Krüger and A. Nova (eds), *Imagination und Wirklichkeit: Zum Verhältnis von mentalen und realen Bildern in der Kunst der frühen Neuzeit*, Mainz 2000, pp. 99–121

LAUSTER 2002
J. Lauster, 'Marsilio Ficino as a Christian Thinker', in M.J.B. Allen and V. Rees with M. Davies (eds), *Marsilio Ficino: His Theology, his Philosophy, his Legacy*, Leiden 2002, pp. 45–69

LEONE DE CASTRIS 2003
P. Leone de Castris, 'Nuovi disegni farnesiani del Parmigianino', *Confronto*, 2 (2003), pp. 78–82

LEVI D'ANCONA 1957
M. Levi D'Ancona, *The Iconography of the Immaculate Conception in the Middle Ages and Early Renaissance*, New York 1957

LOMAZZO 1584
G.P. Lomazzo, *Trattato dell'arte della pittura, scoltura, et architettura*, Milan 1584

LONDON AND NEW YORK 2000–1
C.C. Bambach et al., *Correggio and Parmigianino: Master Draughtsmen of the Renaissance*, exh. cat., British Museum, London 2000–1; The Metropolitan Museum of Art, New York 2001

LONDON 2022
K. Gottardo and G. Rebecchini, *The Art of Experiment: Parmigianino at the Courtauld*, exh. cat., Courtauld Gallery, London 2022

LORA 2017
M. Lora, 'Comment voir l'au-delà: La *Vision d'après saint Jérôme* de Parmigianino', in P. Morel, A. Beyer and A. Nova (eds), *Voir l'au-delà: L'Expérience visionnaire et sa représentation dans l'art italien de la Renaissance*, Turnhout 2017, pp. 219–312

LOS ANGELES 2018–19
N. Takahatake et. al., *The Chiaroscuro Woodcut on Renaissance Italy*, exh. cat., Los Angeles Country Museum of Art 2018–19, published Munich, London and New York 2018

MAGHERINI-GRAZIANI 1897
G. Magherini-Graziani, *L'arte a Città di Castello*, Città di Castello 1897

MAISKAJA 1986
M. Maiskaja, *I grandi disegni italiani del Museo Puškin*, Milan 1986

MANCINI 1832
G. Mancini, *Istruzione storico-pittorica per visitare le chiese e palazzi di Città di Castello, colle Memorie di alcuni artefici del disegno che in detta città fiorirono*, 2 vols, Perugia 1832

MANTUA AND VIENNA 1999
K. Oberhuber and A. Gnann, *Roma e lo stile classico di Raffaello, 1515–1527*, exh. cat., Palazzo Te, Mantua; Graphische Sammlung Albertina, Vienna 1999

MARKOU 2020
G.E. Markou, 'Taddeo Zuccaro and the Pucci Chapel in Santissima Trinità dei Monti, Rome', *Notes in the History of Art*, 39, no. 4 (2020), pp. 241–51

MASSARI 2024
A.M.A. Massari, 'Federico Barocci 1533–1612: storia di un canone inverso', in L. Gallo and A.M.A. Massari (eds), *Federico Barocci Urbino: L'emozione della pittura moderna*, exh. cat., Galleria Nazionale delle Marche, Urbino, published Milan 2024, pp. 36–49

MAVILLA 2021
F. Mavilla, 'La chiesa di Sant'Agostino a Citta di Castello al tempo di Luca Signorelli e Raffaello: Nuove opere e nuovi committenti', in M. Mercalli and L. Terza (eds), *Raffaello Giovane a Città di Castello e il suo sguardo*, Milan 2021, pp. 17–27

MAVILLA 2023
F. Mavilla, 'Vicende artistiche tra Città di Castello e Sansepolcro nei secoli XV–XVI: Rosso Fiorentino, Raffaellino del Colle, gli Alberti e le famiglie Vitelli e Bufalini', in A. Czortek and M. Martelli (eds), *Politica, economia, società nell'Alta Valle del Tevere: Sansepolcro, Città di Castello, Sestino (secoli XV–XVI)*, Florence 2023, pp. 189–212

MCNALLY 1985
S. McNally, 'Ariadne and Others: Images of Sleep in Greek and Early Roman Art', *Classical Antiquity*, vol. 4, no. 2 (1985), pp. 152–92

MENDELSOHN 2002
L. Mendelsohn, 'The Sum of the Parts: Recycling Antiquities in the *Maniera* Workshops of Salviati and his Colleagues', in C. Monbeig Goguel, P. Costamagna and M. Hochmann (eds), *Francesco Salviati et la bella maniera: Actes des colloques de Rome et de Paris*, Paris and Milan 1998, pp. 107–48

MERCATI 1997
E. Mercati, 'Cenni storici sulla famiglia Bufalini', *Bollettino della Deputazione di Storia Patria per l'Umbria*, 94 (1997), pp. 5–27

MEYER ZUR CAPELLEN 2001–9
J. Meyer zur Capellen, *Raphael: The Paintings*, 3 vols, Landshut 2001–9

MOREL 2011
P. Morel, 'L'Érotisme de la grâce dans la peinture religieuse de Parmigianino', in E. de Halleux and M. Lora (eds), *Nudité sacrée: Le nu dans l'art religieux de la renaissance entre érotisme, dévotion et censure*, Paris 2011, pp. 49–65

MUSSINI 2003
M. Mussini, 'Parmigianino e l'incisione', in Parma 2003, pp. 15–41

MUZI 1843
G. Muzi, *Memorie Ecclesiastiche a Città di Castello*, vol. 4, Città di Castello 1843

MUZZI 2003
A. Muzzi, 'Metodo di lavoro e riflessioni religiosi del Parmigianino dalla *Visione di san Girolamo* alla *Steccata*', in Parma and Vienna 2003, pp. 104–13

NAGEL 2017
A. Nagel, 'Experiments in Art and Reform in Italy in the Early Sixteenth Century', in K. Gouwens and S. Reiss (eds), *The Pontificate of Clement VII: History, Politics, Culture*, Aldershot, 2017, pp. 385–409

NAVARRO 2001
A.M. Navarro, 'Italian Drawings in Buenos Aires', *Master Drawings*, 39, no. 1 (2001), pp. 47–57

NEHER 1999
G. Neher, 'Moretto and Romanino: Religious Painting in Brescia, 1510–1550', PhD thesis, University of Warwick, 1999

NEW YORK 2008
C. Neilson, *Parmigianino's Antea: A Beautiful Artifice*, exh. cat., Frick Collection, New York 2008

NEW YORK AND SAN FRANCISCO 2014
A. Ng, *The Poetry of Parmigianino's 'Schiava Turca'*, exh. cat., Frick Collection, New York; Fine Arts Museums of San Francisco, published New York 2014

NG 2012
A. Ng, 'Ruptures in Painting after the Sack of Rome: Parmigianino, Rosso, Sebastiano', PhD thesis, Columbia University, New York 2012

NOLIN 2011
H. Nolin, 'Uniting Faith and Image: The Collective Visual Identity of the Congregation of Secular Canons and its Expression in the Artistic Commissions at San Giorgio in Braida, Verona (1441–1668)', PhD thesis, Rutgers, State University of New Jersey, 2011

NOVA 1998
A. Nova, 'Erotismo e spiritualità nella pittura romana del Cinquecento', in C. Monbeig Goguel, P. Costamagna and M. Hochmann (eds), *Francesco Salviati et la bella maniera: Actes des colloques de Rome et de Paris*, Paris and Milan 1998, pp. 149–69

OBERHUBER 2003
K. Oberhuber, 'Parmigianino disegnatore', in Parma and Vienna 2003, pp. 71–81

OTTLEY 1826
W.Y. Ottley, *A Descriptive Catalogue of the Pictures in the National Gallery: with Critical Remarks on their Merits*, London 1826

PARIS 2015–16
D. Cordellier, *Parmigianino: Dessins du Louvre*, exh. cat., Musée du Louvre, Paris 2015–16

PARKER 1972
K.T. Parker, *Catalogue of the Collection of Drawings in the Ashmolean Museum*, vol. 2, *Italian Schools*, Oxford 1972

PARMA 1986
E. Parma, *Perino del Vaga: L'anello mancante*, Genoa 1986

PARMA 2003
M. Mussini and G.M. De Rubeis (eds), *Parmigianino tradotto: La fortuna di Francesco Mazzola nelle stampe di riproduzione fra il Cinquecento e l'Ottocento*, exh. cat., Biblioteca Palatina di Parma, published Cinisello Balsamo 2003

PARMA AND VIENNA 2003
L. Fornari Schianchi and S. Ferino-Pagden (eds), *Parmigianino e il manierismo europeo*, exh. cat., Galleria Nazionale, Parma; Kunsthistorisches Museum, Vienna, published Milan 2003

PASSAVANT 1836
J.D. Passavant, *Tour of a German Artist in England*, London 1836

PELTA 2005
M. Pelta, '"If He, with His Genius, Had Lived in Rome": Vasari and the Transformative Myth of Rome', in A.B. Barrriault et al. (eds), *Reading Vasari*, London 2005, pp. 155–67

PLANISCIG 1929
L. Planiscig, 'Bronzeplastiken der Gonzate', *Pantheon* (1929), pp. 43–7

POPHAM 1971
A.E. Popham, *The Drawings of Parmigianino*, 3 vols, Cambridge 1971

PRETI-HAMARD 2007
M. Preti-Hamard, '"Celleberrimi Francisci Mazzola Parmensis graphides": Les Collections de dessins du Parmesan à Venise et à Bologne – collectionneurs, marché, edition', in M.T. Caracciolo and G. Toscano (eds), *Jean-Baptiste Wicar et son temps 1762–1834*, Calais 2007, pp. 311–38

REBECCHINI 2022
G. Rebecchini, 'Parmigianino and the Grace of Art', in London 2022, pp. 25–30

REISS 1999
S. Reiss, 'Clemens VII', in P. Kruse and G. Alteri (eds), *Hoch Renaissance im Vatikan (1503–1534): Kunst und Kultur in Rome der Papiste*, Ostfildern 1999, pp. 55–69

RICE 1985
E. Rice, *Saint Jerome in the Renaissance*, Baltimore, MD and London 1985

RODINÒ 1992
S.P.V. Rodinò, 'Anton Maria Zanetti', in G. Fusconi et al., *Il Disegno: I grandi collezionisti*, Cinisello Balsamo 1992, pp. 116–19

RODOLFO 2020
A. Rodolfo, 'Raphael's Tapestries: Past and Present',
in Ana Debenedetti (ed.), *The Raphael Cartoons*,
London 2020, pp. 46–61

ROME 2015–16
M. Faietti (ed.), *Raffaello, Parmigianino, Barocci: Metafore
dello sguardo*, exh. cat., Musei Capitolini, Rome 2015–16

ROME 2016
D. Ekserdjian (ed.), *Correggio and Parmigianino: Art in
Parma during the Sixteenth Century*, exh. cat., Scuderie
del Quirinale, Rome, published Milan 2016

ROSAND 2000
D. Rosand, 'Raphael's *School of Athens* and the Artist of
the Modern Manner', in S. Fletcher and C. Shaw (eds),
*The World of Savonarola: Italian Élites and the Perceptions
of Crisis*, Aldershot 2000, pp. 213–32

ROSKILL 1968
M. Roskill, *Dolce's Aretino and Venetian Art Theory of the
Cinquecento*, New York 1968

SANUTO 1969–70
M. Sanuto, *I diarii di Marino Sanuto, 1466–1536*, 58 vols,
Bologna 1969–70

SAPORI 2023
G. Sapori, 'Masucci, Conca, Labruzzi, Pozzi, Angeletti
e Bertuzzi nella collezione del Cardinale Giovanni
Ottavio Bufalini (1709–1782)', *Rivista dell'Istituto
Nazionale d'Archaeologica e Storia dell'Arte*, 78 (2023),
pp. 323–40

SHEARMAN 1967
J. Shearman, *Mannerism*, London 1967

SHEARMAN 1972
J. Shearman, *Raphael's Cartoons in the Collection of
Her Majesty the Queen and the Tapestries for the Sistine
Chapel*, London 1972

SOHM 1995
P. Sohm, 'Gendered Style in Italian Art Criticism from
Michelangelo to Malvasia', *Renaissance Quarterly*, 48,
no. 4 (1995), pp. 759–808

SPAGNOLO 2016
M. Spagnolo, 'A City of "Excellent Artists and Ingenious
Men": Sixteenth-Century Painters in Parma between
Literature and the Geography of Art', in Rome 2016,
pp. 61–71

STEFANIAK 1995
R. Stefaniak, 'Amazing Grace: Parmigianino's *Vision of
Saint Jerome*', *Zeitschrift für Kunstgeschichte*, 58, no. 1
(1995), pp. 105–15

THIMANN 1999
M. Thimann, '"Un lume di grazia tanto piacevole":
Parmigianinos Londoner Madonna im Lichte einer
Künstleranekdote Vasaris', *Marburger Jahrbuch für
Kunstwissenschaft*, 1999, pp. 139–55

THOENES 2006
C. Thoenes, 'St Peter's as Ruins: On Some *vedute* by
Heemskerck', in Michael W. Cole (ed.), *Sixteenth-Century
Italian Art*, Malden, MA 2006, pp. 25–39

THOMAS 2017
B. Thomas, 'Raphael and the Idea of Drawing', in
C. Whistler and B. Thomas with A. Gnann and
Angelamaria Aceto, *Raphael: The Drawings*, exh. cat.
Ashmolean Museum, Oxford 2017, pp. 42–55

THOMAS (forthcoming)
S. Thomas, 'Long Shadows in the Gallery: George
Watson Taylor as Collector, Connoisseur and Slave-
Owner', in A. Faucquez, R. Gosson and A. Michael (eds),
*Narrativizing Slavery in European Museums: Arts and
Representations*, Liverpool (forthcoming)

TOLNAY 1975
C. de Tolnay, *Corpus dei disegni di Michelangelo*, 4 vols,
Novara 1975

TORMEN 2009
G. Tormen (ed.), *Lettere artistiche del Settecento veneziano
3: L'epistolario Giovanni Antonio Armano–Giovanni Maria
Sasso*, Vicenza 2009

VACCARO 1993
M. Vaccaro, 'Documents for Parmigianino's *Vision of
St Jerome*', *Burlington Magazine*, 135, no. 1078 (1993),
pp. 22–7

VACCARO 2001
M. Vaccaro, 'Dutiful Widows: Female Patronage and
Two Marian Altarpieces', in D. Wilkins and S. Reiss (eds),
*Beyond Isabella: Secular Women Patrons of Art in
Renaissance Italy*, Kirksville, MO 2001, pp. 177–92

VACCARO 2002
M. Vaccaro, *Parmigianino: The Paintings*, Turin 2002

VACCARO 2009
M. Vaccaro, 'Correggio and Parmigianino: On the Place
of Rome in the Historiography of Sixteenth-Century
Parmese Drawing', *Artibus et Historiae*, 30, no. 59 (2009),
pp. 115–24

VASARI 1966–87
G. Vasari, *Le Vite de' più eccellenti pittori scultori e
architettori: nelle redazioni del 1550 e 1568*,
R. Bettarini and P. Barocchi (eds), 5 vols, Florence
1966–87

VASARI 2008
*Giorgio Vasari: The Lives of the Artists*, trans. J. Conaway
Bondanella and P. Bondanella, Oxford University Press
2008

VATICAN CITY 1984
G. Muratore, *Raffaello in Vaticano*, exh. cat., Monumenti,
Musei e Gallerie Pontificie, Vatican City 1984

VIENNA 2013–14
A. Gnann, *In Farbe! Clair-obscur-Holzschnitte der
Renaissance*, exh. cat., Albertina, Vienna 2013–14

VUONG 2013
L.C. Vuong, *Gender and Purity in the Protevangelium of
James*, Tübingen, 2013

WATERS 1879
C.E. Waters, *Painters, Sculptors, Architects, Engravers, and
their Work: A Handbook*, Boston 1879

WEIGEL 1865
R. Weigel, *Die Werke der Maler in ihren Handzeichnungen:
Beschreibendes Verzeichniss der in Kupfer gestochenen,
lithographirten und photographirten: Facsimiles von
Originalzeichnungen grosser Meister*, Leipzig 1865

WITTKOWER 1961
R. Wittkower, 'Individualism in Art and Artists:
A Renaissance Problem', *Journal of the History of Ideas*,
22, no. 3 (1961), pp. 291–302

WITTKOWER AND WITTKOWER 2007
M. and R. Wittkower, *Born under Saturn*, New York
2007

WIVEL 2022A
M. Wivel, 'The Death and Life of Raphael', in T. Henry
and D. Ekserdjian with M. Wivel (eds), *Raphael*, exh. cat.
National Gallery, London 2022, pp. 36–55

WIVEL 2022B
M. Wivel, 'The Venetian Modern: Leonardo, Giorgione,
Titian', *Artibus et Historiae*, 84 (2022), pp. 114–47

WOLK-SIMON 2017
L. Wolk-Simon, 'Competition, Collaboration and
Specialization in the Roman Art World, 1520–27',
in K. Gouwens and S. Reiss (eds), *The Pontificate of
Clement VII: History, Politics, Culture,* Aldershot 2017,
pp. 253–92

ZANNONI 1817
G.B. Zannoni et al., *Reale Galleria di Firenze Illustrata:
Ritratta di Pittori*, vol. 1, Florence 1817

ZUCCARI 2005
A. Zuccari, 'L'Immacolata a Roma: istanze
immacolistiche e cautela pontificia in un complesso
percorso iconografico', in G. Morello, V. Francia and
R. Fusco (eds), *Una donna vestita di sole: l'Immacolata
Concezione nelle opere dei grandi maestri*, exh. cat.,
Braccio di Carlo Magno, Vatican City, published Milan
2005, pp. 64–77

# ACKNOWLEDGEMENTS

Almost 500 years since Parmigianino painted his Roman masterpiece, *The Madonna and Child with Saints John the Baptist and Jerome* (*'The Vision of Saint Jerome'*) continues to fascinate and intrigue its audiences. Its bequest to the National Gallery by the British Institution in 1826 affirmed its status as a pivotal work in the history of sixteenth-century central Italian painting. This exhibition and catalogue celebrate its timely return to public view for the first time in 10 years as part of the National Gallery's Bicentenary celebrations and would not have been possible without the invaluable support of numerous lenders, colleagues and friends.

The first debt of gratitude is due to Larry Keith for his meticulous conservation treatment. The time and attention he dedicated to the painting are second only to those of Parmigianino himself and we are immensely grateful for his knowledge and insight, which have informed this project throughout. We also wish to thank Britta New, who undertook the structural treatment of the panel, Paul Ackroyd and Olivia Stoddart, who contributed to the conservation. Rachel Billinge recorded and analysed the painting using infrared reflectography and we have benefited greatly from her expertise in helping us understand the resultant images. Peter Schade created the beautiful and befitting new frame.

Deepest thanks are due to our lenders for their enthusiasm in support of this project and to the numerous colleagues who have facilitated our loan requests. Especial thanks to the Stephen Kohl Art Foundation and to National Gallery trustee Katrin Henkel for her invaluable guidance. We gratefully acknowledge the support of the Ashmolean Museum, the British Museum, the Gallerie degli Uffizi, the J. Paul Getty Museum and the Royal Collection Trust. We have benefited significantly from the expertise of Angelamaria Aceto, Julian Brooks, Hugo Chapman, Martin Clayton, Laura Donati, Davide Gasparotto, Achim Gnann, George Goldner, Ketty Gottardo, Tom Henry, Guido Rebecchini, Cristiana Romalli, Mary Vaccaro and Sarah Vowles.

Larry Keith and Aimee Ng contributed their fluent scholarship as co-authors of the catalogue. We are privileged that David Ekserdjian provided his expertise to the catalogue overall. Livia Lupi carefully translated – for the first time – the related documents into English, while Emma Firestone and Amanda Lillie both offered insightful comments.

The research and development of this project would not have been possible without the kindness of numerous colleagues who facilitated access to – and stimulating discussion of – Parmigianino drawings and archival material: Paola Aveta, Dominique Cordellier, Maria Elena De Luca, Mathieu Deldicque, Hélène Gasnault, Victor Hundsbuckler, Grant Lewis, Francesca Mavilla, Antonella Parisi, Alice de Quidt, Ilaria Rizzitelli, Caterina Maria Rizzuto, Baptiste Roelly and Claire Van Cleave.

Sunnifa Hope and Giulia Segreto expertly managed the project. Our thanks also to Sonia D'Orsi and Aaron Jones for the beautiful exhibition design, and Lydia Cooper for her detailed attention to the interpretation. This publication is the result of the immense work and indefatigable energy of Diana Adell, the support of Laura Lappin, and the attentive care of Suzanne Bosman, Robert Davies, Jane Hyne and Raymonde Watkins.

A special thanks to Pat O'Sullivan and the Art Handling team for installing the exhibition flawlessly during an exceptionally busy year. We are grateful to other colleagues across the Gallery: Flora Allen, Rickie Burke, Alice Cox, Margherita Di Ceglie, Jeanne Kenyon, Maria Vittoria Pellini, Lizzie Phillips, Harry Rosehill and Esmee Wright.

Our sincere thanks to the generosity of our funders and supporters: the Capricorn Foundation, the Rick Mather David Scrase Foundation, Katrin Henkel, Marco Voena and Wolfgang Ratjen Stiftung.

**Maria Alambritis and Matthias Wivel**

I am indebted to my co-curator Matthias Wivel for his continual support and guidance throughout my time at the Gallery and for generously entrusting me with the reins to steer this exhibition. Emma Capron has unfailingly championed my work and her mentorship and example have been formative. To Emma, Nicholas Flory and Imogen Tedbury I am indebted for their generous reading of draft texts and their perceptive feedback. I owe heartfelt thanks to colleagues in the Gallery's curatorial department and externally for their support: Susanna Avery-Quash, Caroline Campbell, Chiara Di Stefano, Tom Henry, Amanda Hilliam, Peter Humfrey, Siobhan Jolley, Laura Llewellyn, Mary McMahon, Aimee Ng, Daniel Sobrino Ralston, Christine Riding, Per Rumberg, Christine Seidel, Sarah Thomas, Letizia Treves, Francesca Whitlum-Cooper and Charlotte Wytema.

I wish to extend my sincerest gratitude to Dr Simone Verde, who supported the project when I first presented it to him at the Palazzo della Pilotta, Parma, and the help of Ilaria Azzoni, Carla Campanini, Elisa Montali and Maria Quagliotti there. In Città di Castello, I am very grateful to Patrizia Montani, Silvia Palazzi and Diva Santucci at the Biblioteca Carducci, and Giuseppe Sterparelli for his kindness as an erudite guide.

I am immensely grateful to the following colleagues who so generously shared their expertise and advice in the development of my research on the reunited Ashmolean–Chantilly composition: Angelamaria Aceto, Lara Daniels, David Ekserdjian, Baptiste Roelly, Cristiana Romalli and Mary Vaccaro.

The invaluable support of the Rick Mather David Scrase Foundation ensured my continued work and research on this exhibition.

Finally, my deepest thanks to my parents, Athy and Stephen Alambritis, for their unconditional support, and to Argyris Machairas for his loving care, grounding humour and abounding encouragement.

**Maria Alambritis**

# LIST OF LENDERS

**FLORENCE**
Gallerie degli Uffizi

**GLENCOE, IL**
Stephen Kohl Art Foundation

**LONDON**
British Museum
His Majesty the King

**LOS ANGELES, CA**
The J. Paul Getty Museum

**OXFORD**
The Ashmolean Museum,
University of Oxford

# LIST OF EXHIBITED WORKS

*The Madonna and Child with Saints John the Baptist and Jerome ('The Vision of Saint Jerome')*, 1526–7
Oil on poplar, 342.9 × 148.6 cm
The National Gallery, London. Presented by the Directors of the British Institution, 1826 (NG33)
fig. 9

*Study for a Composition of the Virgin and Christ Child with Saint John the Baptist and Saint Jerome below* (recto); *the same subject* (verso), 1526
Recto: Pen and brown ink, with brown wash, with white heightening (oxidised), over red chalk on paper; verso: red chalk on paper, 25.8 × 15.6 cm
British Museum, London (1882,0812.488)
pls 1r and 1v

*Studies of Saints John the Baptist and Jerome, a Crucifix and Various Heads* (recto); *Studies of the Christ Child, a Crucifix and Dogs* (verso), about 1526
Red chalk on paper, 13.5 × 22.1 cm
The J. Paul Getty Museum, Los Angeles (87.GB.9)
pls 4r and 4v

*The Virgin and Child*, 1526
Pen and brown ink with brown wash on paper, 13 × 10 cm
The Ashmolean Museum, University of Oxford. Presented by Mr F. E. Maitland in memory of his wife, Margaret Maitland, 1949 (WA1949.212)
pl. 5

*Seated Semi-nude Female wearing Drapery* (recto); *Study of a Child on his Mother's Lap; Studies of Legs* (verso), 1526–7
Recto: black and white chalk on paper; verso: pen and brown ink with grey wash, heightened with white bodycolour (oxidised) and separate studies in red chalk on paper, 23.2 × 16.1 cm
The Ashmolean Museum, University of Oxford. Purchased, 1939 (WA1939.76)
pls 11r and 11v

*Study for Saint Jerome*, 1526
Pen and brown wash, white heightening on light-blue paper, 17.3 × 12.4 cm
Stephen Kohl Art Foundation
pl. 22

*Figure Study*, 1526
Pen and brown ink, brown wash, with white heightening on paper, 21.6 × 24.3 cm
The J. Paul Getty Museum, Los Angeles (84.GA.9)
pl. 25

*The Legs and Drapery of a reclining Figure*, about 1526–7
Black and white chalk on grey-blue paper, 19.3 × 25 cm
The Royal Collection / HM King Charles III (RCIN 900883)
pl. 26

*Woodland Study*, 1524–7
Pen, ink and wash with white heightening on blue paper, 27.8 × 17.7 cm
Gabinetto dei Disegni e delle Stampe, Gallerie degli Uffizi, Florence (inv. GDS n. 753 P)
pl. 29

# PHOTOGRAPHIC CREDITS

**Berlin**
Kupferstichkabinett, Staatliche Museen zu Berlin-Preussischer Kulturbesitz © Photo Scala, Florence/bpk, Bildagentur für Kunst, Kultur und Geschichte, Berlin Kulturbesitz / Jörg P. Anders: fig. 16.

**Bologna**
Church of San Petronio, Bologna © Mario Bonotto / Photo Scala, Florence: fig. 7.

**Buenos Aires**
© Colección del Museo Nacional de Bellas Artes, Buenos Aires, Argentina: pl. 7.

**Chantilly**
© Musée Condé, Chantilly: fig. 27; © RMN-Grand Palais (domaine de Chantilly) / Gérard Blot: pl. 6; figs 24, 25; © RMN-Grand Palais (Domaine de Chantilly) / Michel Urtado: pl. 9.

**Chatsworth**
Devonshire Collection, Chatsworth © Devonshire Collection, Chatsworth. Reproduced by permission of the Chatsworth Settlement Trustees: fig. 20.

**Florence**
Gabinetto dei Disegni e delle Stampe, Gallerie degli Uffizi, Florence © Gabinetto Fotografico delle Gallerie degli Uffizi: pls 24, 29; figs 3, 22; © Photo Scala, Florence: fig. 1.

**Fontanellato**
Museo Rocca Sanvitale, Fontanellato © Photo Scala, Florence: fig. 21.

**Frankfurt am Main**
© Städel Museum, Frankfurt am Main: pl. 8.

**Geneva**
Krugier-Poniatowski Collection, Geneva © Photo courtesy of the owner: pl. 19.

**Glencoe, Illinois**
Stephen Kohl Art Foundation © Photo courtesy of the owner: pl. 22.

**London**
The British Library, London © By Permission of The British Library, London / Bridgeman Images: fig. 6.
The British Museum, London © The Trustees of the British Museum: pls 1, 2, 27; fig. 19.
The Samuel Courtauld Trust, The Courtauld Gallery, London © The Samuel Courtauld Trust, The Courtauld Gallery, London: fig. 38.
© Getty Images: fig. 8.
© The National Gallery, London: figs 9, 13, 29 to 36.
© The National Portrait Gallery, London: fig. 28.
The Royal Collection / HM King Charles III © Royal Collection Enterprises Limited 2024 | Royal Collection Trust: pl. 26.

**Los Angeles, California**
The J. Paul Getty Museum, Los Angeles, California. Digital image courtesy of the Getty's Open Content Program: pls 4, 25; fig. 10.

**Milan**
Pinacoteca di Brera, Milan © Photo Scala, Florence: fig. 14.

**Naples**
Museo Nazionale di Capodimonte, Naples © Soprintendenza Speciale per il Polo Museale di Napoli: pls 12, 14.

**New York**
© The Metropolitan Museum of Art, New York: fig. 17.

**Oxford**
© Ashmolean Museum, University of Oxford: pls 5, 11; figs 24, 25.

**Paris**
Ecole nationale supérieure des beaux-arts, Paris © Beaux-Arts de Paris, Dist. Grand Palais Rmn / image Beaux-arts de Paris: pls 15, 17.
Musée du Louvre, Paris, Département des Arts graphiques © RMN-Grand Palais (musée du Louvre) / Gérard Blot: pls 3, 21; © RMN-Grand Palais (musée du Louvre) / Michel Urtado: pl. 23.

**Parma**
Galleria Nazionale, Parma. Su concessione di Ministero per I Beni e le Attivita Culturali

© Soprintendenze per il Patrimonio Storico Artistico e Demoetnoantroplogico di Parma e Piacenza: pl. 20; fig 5.

**Private collections**
© Photo courtesy of the owners: pl. 10.
© courtesy of C.G. Boerner, Düsseldorf / New York: pl. 16.
© Photograph courtesy of Sotheby's / Bridgeman Images: pl. 18.

**Rome**
Chiesa di Sant'Agostino © Maria Alambritis: fig. 16.

**Saint Louis, Missouri**
© The Saint Louis Art Museum, Missouri: fig. 23.

**Vatican City, Rome**
Vatican Museums, Vatican City © Album / Alamy Stock Photo: fig. 4; © Artothek / Bridgeman Images: fig. 12; © Photo Scala, Florence: figs 11, 18, 26.

**Vienna**
© The Albertina Museum, Vienna: pls 13, 28. Kunsthistorisches Museum Vienna, Gemäldegalerie: © Photo Fine Art Images/ Heritage Images/Scala, Florence: fig. 2.

**Washington, DC**
National Gallery of Art, Washington, DC. Image courtesy National Gallery of Art, Washington: fig. 37

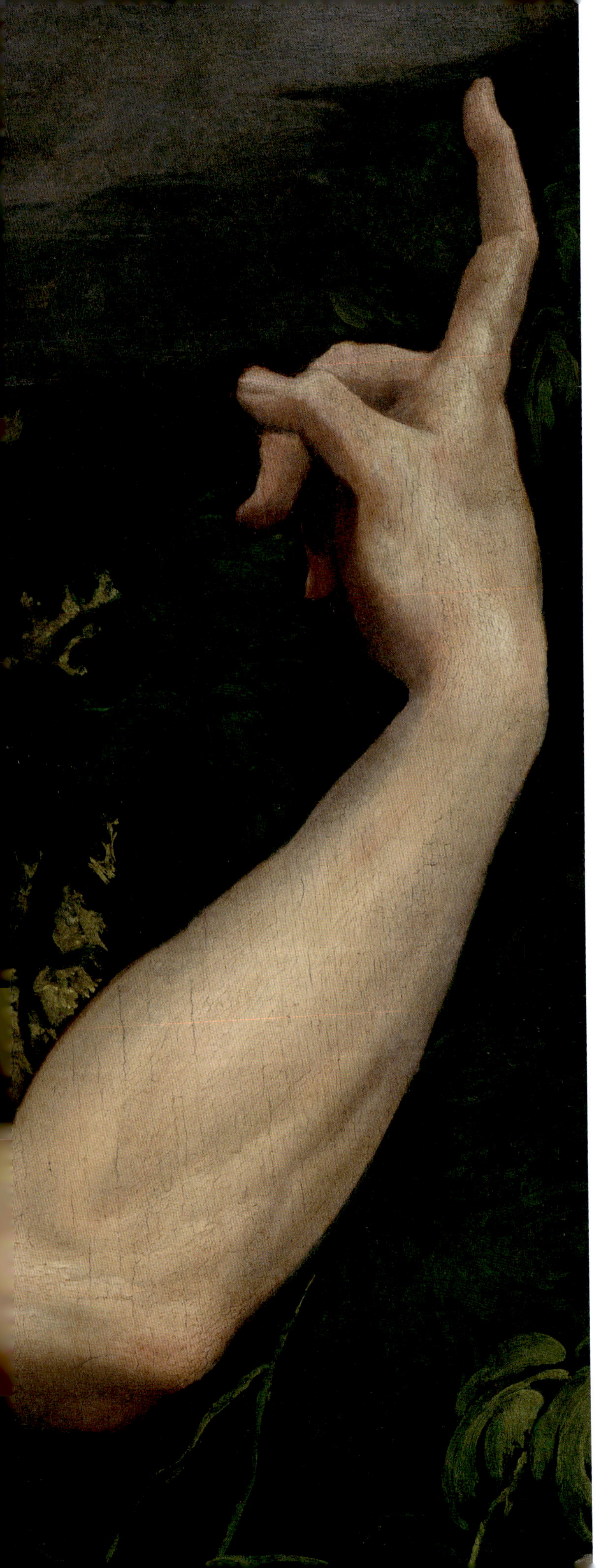

Published to accompany the exhibition

*Parmigianino: The Vision of Saint Jerome*

The National Gallery, London
5 December 2024 – 9 March 2025

Exhibition curated by
Maria Alambritis
Matthias Wivel

# NG**200**

The H J Hyams Exhibition Programme
Supported by The Capricorn Foundation

Exhibition supported by

The Rick Mather David Scrase Foundation
Katrin Henkel
Marco Voena

Publication supported by

WOLFGANG RATJEN STIFTUNG, Liechtenstein


This exhibition has been made possible by the provision of insurance through
the Government Indemnity Scheme. The National Gallery would like to thank
HM Government for providing Government Indemnity and the Department for
Culture, Media and Sport and Arts Council England for arranging the indemnity.



First published in 2024 by
National Gallery Global Limited
Trafalgar Square
London WC2N 5DN
www.shop.nationalgallery.org.uk

ISBN: 978 1 85709 724 5
1053896

British Library Cataloguing-in-Publication Data
A catalogue record is available from the British Library
Library of Congress Control Number: 2024943866

Publisher: Laura Lappin
Managing Editor: Diana Adell
Copy-editor: Robert Davies
Proofreader: Caroline Ellerby
Picture Researcher: Suzanne Bosman
Production: Jane Hyne

Designed by Raymonde Watkins
Origination by DL Imaging, London
Printed in Belgium by Graphius

All works are by Parmigianino (1503–1540) unless otherwise stated.
All measurements give height before width. Plates 2, 3, 5, 6r, 6v, 7, 8,
9, 10, 14, 18, 21, 22, 23r, 23v, 24 and 27 are reproduced at actual size.

Cover and pp. 2–3, 6, 96: details from fig. 9; p. 4: detail from pl. 29;
p. 8: detail from pl. 25; pp. 52–3: detail from pl. 4r.